MANIFESTO FOR THE HUMANITIES

DIGITAL HUMANITIES

The Digital Humanities series provides a forum for ground-breaking and benchmark work in digital humanities, lying at the intersections of computers and the disciplines of arts and humanities, library and information science, media and communications studies, and cultural studies.

Series Editors:
Julie Thompson Klein, Wayne State University
Tara McPherson, University of Southern California
Paul Conway, University of Michigan

———————————

Manifesto for the Humanities: Transforming Doctoral Education in Good Enough Times
Sidonie Smith

Teaching History in the Digital Age
T. Mills Kelly

Hacking the Academy: New Approaches to Scholarship and Teaching from Digital Humanities
Daniel J. Cohen and Tom Scheinfeldt, Editors

Writing History in the Digital Age
Jack Dougherty and Kristen Nawrotzki, Editors

Pastplay: Teaching and Learning History with Technology
Kevin Kee, Editor

Interdisciplining Digital Humanities: Boundary Work in an Emerging Field
Julie Thompson Klein

Digital Rhetoric: Theory, Method, Practice
Douglas Eyman

Ethical Programs: Hospitality and the Rhetorics of Software
James J. Brown Jr.

———————————

DIGITALCULTUREBOOKS, an imprint of the University of Michigan Press, is dedicated to publishing work in new media studies and the emerging field of digital humanities.

Manifesto for the Humanities

TRANSFORMING DOCTORAL EDUCATION
IN GOOD ENOUGH TIMES

Sidonie Smith

University of Michigan Press

ANN ARBOR

Published in the United States of America by the
University of Michigan Press
Manufactured in the United States of America
⊗ Printed on acid-free paper

2018   2017   2016   2015   4   3   2   1

A CIP catalog record for this book is available from the British Library.

DOI: http://dx.doi.org/10.3998/dcbooks.13607059.0001.001

Names: Smith, Sidonie, author.
Title: Manifesto for the humanities : transforming doctoral education in good enough times / Sidonie Smith.
Description: Ann Arbor : University of Michigan Press, 2015. | Includes bibliographical references and index.
Identifiers: LCCN 2015040301| ISBN 9780472073047 (hardcover : alk. paper) | ISBN 9780472053049 (pbk. : alk. paper) | ISBN 9780472121717 (ebook)
Subjects: LCSH: Doctor of philosophy degree. | Universities and colleges—Graduate work. | Humanities—Study and teaching. | Educational change.
Classification: LCC LB2386 .S648 2015 | DDC 378.2—dc23
   LC record available at http://lccn.loc.gov/2015040301

To Roger Salomon, my revered dissertation advisor

Acknowledgments

What ended up as this long manifesto (perhaps an oxymoronic phrase) began as two short newsletter columns written in 2010 when I served as president of the Modern Language Association. Having watched so many doctoral students struggle through writing a proto-monograph dissertation, I thought, why not reimagine this capstone to doctoral study. That task, of making a case for expanding the repertoire of forms the dissertation might take, became the impetus for understanding what a 21st-century doctoral education in the humanities might look like. Over five years, I've been consumed with this question. But it has not been a lonely task. In fact, it has been a densely peopled, sociable, interactive, collaborative experience for me. And so, there are many thanks to spread around.

Over the years, MLA staff have given me invaluable advice, information, and support as I pursued this project on doctoral education. Executive Director Rosemary Feal exercises her leadership role with unflagging energy and enthusiasm. I was the beneficiary of her advocacy skills and her ability to flow with the criticism and with the opportunities for collaboration. David Laurence, Nelly Furman, Doug Steward, and Kathleen Fitzpatrick have always been willing to share their prodigious knowledge in various areas of the profession of professing. Members of the 2010 MLA Working Group on the New Dissertation, David Damrosch, Kathleen Fitzpatrick, Richard Miller, and Kathleen Woodward, all brilliant around the table, helped me achieve a fuller understanding of the historical context, politics, and intellectual significance of proposing an alternative to the proto-monograph. Kathy Woodward, in particular, whom I came to know when she served on the MLA Executive Council, has been a friend and coconspirator in transformation for almost a decade now. I benefited from the passionate, yet disparate styles of leadership and lines of approach to the transformation of doctoral education that the MLA presidencies of Russell Berman and Michael Bérubé put on the agenda.

Through 2011 and 2012 I was fortunate to serve as a member of two task forces on doctoral education: one constituted by the MLA, under the leadership of Russell Berman, Professor of Comparative Literature and German at Stanford University, and the other constituted by the Canadian Social Science and Humanities Research Council, under the leadership of Paul Yachnin, Director of the Institute for the Public Life of Arts and Ideas at McGill University. I owe a debt of gratitude to members of the MLA task force: Chair Russell Berman and Carlos J. Alonso, Columbia University; Sylvie Debevec Henning, East Carolina University; Lanisa Kitchiner, Smithsonian National Museum of African Art; Bethany Nowviskie, University of Virginia; Elizabeth Schwartz Crane, San Joaquin Delta College, CA; Kathleen Woodward, University of Washington, Seattle; and staff liaisons Kathleen Fitzpatrick, director, MLA Office of Scholarly Communication, and David Laurence, director, MLA Office of Research and ADE. So too, my thanks to Paul Yachnin for inviting me to Canada and putting me in conversation with Robert Barsky and Jay Clayton, both of Vanderbilt University; Lesley Cormack, University of Alberta; Rebecca Duclos, School of the Art Institute of Chicago; Geoffrey Harpham, National Humanities Center (United States); and Michael Jemtrud, Martin Kreiswirth, Bronwen Low, Christopher Manfredi, Stéfan Sinclair, and Leigh Yetter, all of McGill University. These interlocutors, voluble, visionary, practical, and politically astute, will recognize in this manifesto their concerns, perspectives, and imaginings of transformation.

I've been the beneficiary of numerous discussions with humanities scholars, librarians, and administrators brought together through initiatives funded by the Andrew W. Mellon Foundation. The Open Review white paper project out of New York University brought me into conversation with Kathleen Fitzpatrick, Monica McCormick, Cathy Davidson, Dan Cohen, Nick Mirzoeff, Lisa Gitelman, Cheryl Ball, Avi Santo, and Eric Zinner. Activities organized by the Scholarly Communication Institute provided occasions to learn about and assess the important work of the Alliance for Networking Visual Culture led by Tara McPherson, PressForward, led by Dan Cohen, and the MLA Commons, led by Kathleen Fitzpatrick. SCI also cosponsored, along with the Consortium of Humanities Centers and Institutes and centerNet, a broad conversation on the future of graduate education hosted by Kathleen Woodward at the Simpson Center of the University of Washington. The 15-institution collaboration that is the Humanities Without Walls initiative, led by Dianne Harris out of the Illinois Program for Research in the Humanities, has enabled me to engage with and learn from directors of humanities centers across the Midwest through HWW pilot projects focused on collaborative scholarship in the humanities and expanded professional development opportunities for doctoral students. Through participation here at the University of Michigan in the Mellon-funded initiative on subvention models for supporting scholarly publication in the humanities and humanistic social sciences, I learned from Paul Courant and Meredith Kahn, both of them deeply knowledgeable about the economics of academic publishing and the new ecology of scholarly communication.

I owe an enormous debt of gratitude to my colleague Paul Conway of Michigan's School of Information. Ever patient and generous, he provided expertise about all things related to digital scholarship in the humanities. He read through parts of Part II with a granularity that was entirely supportive and inescapably demanding. I know I am an observer when it comes to digitally environed and born-digital humanities scholarship; Paul helped make that status less tenuous for me.

Graduate students have also been invaluable colleagues throughout this project. Elizabeth Rodrigues, Emily Johnston, Christina LaRose, and Katy Kidd provided research support through all the stages of researching and writing this manifesto. Katy offered a close reading of Part I, and also taught me how to use Zotero as my bibliographic tool. Cass Adair, Tiffany Ball, and Jina Kim workshopped an earlier version of the introduction and Part I as part of our course Writing for Publication. Their enthusiasm buoyed me at that moment when the stress of staying alert to the implications of my argument and rhetorical tone gnawed away at me. They were particularly incisive in their comments about the multiple audiences to which I wanted to speak; and they sharpened my understanding of what is at stake in the transformation I propose for students alienated from the environment of the academy. I owe thanks also to the graduate student fellows at the Institute for the Humanities at Michigan for their close readings of parts of the manuscript over the past three years; and to students in Peggy McCracken's 2015 Theories of Posthumanism course for their openness to my manifesto.

Two generous readers for the University of Michigan Press understood my project, supported it, and offered close commentary and astute critique. And three peer reviewers, Charles Watkinson, A. W. Strouse, and Carlos Alonso accepted the invitation to read the penultimate version of this book online at the University of Michigan Press Digital Culture Books website. They offered critique and commentary and encouragement for my ideas. I admit I was hesitant to expose the book to open peer-to-peer review; but I knew I had to practice what the book was preaching. Having done so, I would recommend the process to anyone anxious to receive as much excellent critique as possible. My dear friend and coauthor Julia Watson also responded to the call to review the book online. She read the introduction and Part I with her eagle eye and challenged me again and again to peel away material that did not drive to my main argument about change. I recognize the labor all of them put into someone else's project.

I thank Leonard Cassuto for giving me access to *The Graduate School Mess* as I was making final revisions. And I thank my colleagues here at Michigan, whose commitment to public scholarship and graduate education has changed the environment in which change takes place: Sara Blair, Julie Ellison, Jonathan Friedman, Margaret Hedstrom, Danny Herwitz, June Howard, Debbie Keller-Cohen, and Peggy McCracken. They have modeled for me the life of the engaged and visionary administrator. At the Institute for the Humanities, Patrick Tonks has kept me up-to-date on issues in digital pedagogies and scholarship; and Sheri Sytsema-Geiger and Doretha Coval have protected my time.

The people at the University of Michigan Press and the University Library have been there all along. Phil Pochoda and Tom Dwyer, formerly of the Press, and Shana Kimball, formerly of MPublishing, were there at the beginning. Aaron McCollough has been there for the concluding stages, as have Meredith Kahn, Allison Peters, and Marcia LaBrenz.

I thank all those, too many to name, who sent me items they read in newspapers, or received in e-mail messages, or noticed on websites. Shards of their messages found their way into the final version. I am inspired by their collaborative spirit. I am appreciative as well of all the audiences I've addressed in the last several years in the United States, Canada, and Australia. Participants in those venues expressed their eagerness for change and voiced their critiques of my vision, especially of my call for expanding forms of the dissertation. I trust all the critiques energized me to make arguments in favor of that change more convincing.

And finally, as ever, there is the appreciation I owe to my partner, Gregory Grieco. He may no longer remember what this book is about; but he has never forgotten to support me lovingly and lastingly.

Contents

Introduction

At this historical moment, the challenge facing faculty invested in educating future generations of academic humanists is the conceptualization of a 21st-century doctoral education. It must be an education adequate to the lived realities of the academy now; to the energies of students who make the choice to pursue a doctorate; and to the intellectual, affective, and social attachments that drive the pursuit of excellence in scholarly inquiry and teaching. The imperatives are multiple: to be purposeful in sustaining passionate conviction about the value of advanced study in the disciplines of the humanities; to be flexible in adapting to the shifting environment in which that study will take place; to be strategic in addressing concerns about the high level of attrition, the continuing lack of diversity in the humanities professoriate, and the exploitative conditions of contingency in humanities disciplines; and to be responsive to the diverse aspirations, dispositions, and intellectual interests of those willing to do the time, find the funds, and endure the long haul. This book is a manifesto for meeting the challenge.

This manifesto for a 21st-century doctoral education unfolds in three parts.

Part I advances the mantra that "the times are good enough" to make significant change in how future humanists are educated. As manifestos are designed to do, it surveys particulars related to the current state of higher education in North America, touching on the retreat from commitment to public funding, the din of attacks on the value of a liberal arts education and humanities degrees, and the consolidation of corporatist discourse and practice. Then it proceeds beyond critique, and the nostalgia that feeds a sense of enervation, to suggest why the times are good enough to effect change.

Part II seeks to answer the question, What is the emergent ecology of higher education in which humanities doctoral students will pursue their goals? It explores shifts in the everyday life of academic humanists now—shifts at once quotidian and profound, often troubling and far-reaching. They relate to the evolving concept of the university; the epistemic infrastructure; the new media and modes of scholarly production and communication; the trend toward the "open"; the reorientation of learning environments; and the emergent profile of a possibly posthuman humanities scholar. A manifesto for the sustainability of the 21st-century humanities follows Part II. The manifesto, detailing an agenda for boldly engaging this new everyday, culminates in the call to transform doctoral education.

Part III presents a 21st-century doctoral education in the humanities, elaborating intellectual grounds for transformation as well as the potential effects of change. It makes the case for breathing life into the dissertation by expanding its possible forms, genres, and compositional modes. It suggests changes related to courses and to coursework. In concert with the initiatives of graduate schools and departments across North America, it emphasizes the importance of providing opportunities for doctoral students to gain new skills and competencies increasingly important for humanities scholarship and practice and transferable to other careers graduates might imagine. At its conclusion, it circles around to the issues taken up in Part I by suggesting how a new conceptualization of doctoral education might productively address troubling conditions on the ground.

Manifesto for the Humanities speaks to multiple audiences. It addresses doctoral students, present and prospective. They hear the naysayers and skeptics. They read about the retreat from adequate funding for higher education. They observe and live concerns about student demographics, access and high student debt, corporate discourse and practices. They recognize the undervalued position of the academic humanities in higher education. Part I offers hopeful energy for assessing the current state of the academic humanities and for taking action to map for themselves a doctoral education adequate to the times. The six-part exploration of shifts affecting academic humanities in Part II prepares doctoral students to better understand the current forces affecting the life of professional humanists and the emergent identities and roles through which their life as scholars and teachers in the academy will play out. Again, they know and live parts of this larger story of transformation. Indeed, many of them are out there riding the shifts, if anxious about what is required of them now, and what might be required of them in the future. The manifesto that concludes Part II models one way to integrate an agenda for action with shifting conditions on the ground, even as those conditions continue to morph. In Part III doctoral students gain access to debates taking place in humanities departments across North America broadly, about why, how, and to what ends doctoral education needs to change. Knowledge of the debates, the anxieties, and the possibilities of change, both large and small, prepares them to explore with peers, mentors, and administrators how to move through their program, innovate where innovation is possible, organize for change, and find resources when they are not readily available. At stake here is students' agency and preparation for making change in the academy and in their professions.

Manifesto for the Humanities addresses faculty guiding students through this exhilarating and stressful preparation and administrators charged with ensuring student success, setting policy, and directing resources. In the primer on shifts in the everyday life of academic humanists, they will find useful information relevant to questions their students might raise or projects those students might talk of pursuing; and they will recognize the complex vectors of student anxieties, and their own. Attentive to the broad-based conversation about doctoral education in the humanities now taking place across North America and to foundation support for transformational projects, this manifesto situates local initiatives and conversations in a larger framework of national and transnational trends, debates, and experiments. Faculty agnostic about proposed changes and those eager for them will find here a blueprint encompassing transformation large and small, suggesting how to conceptualize coursework, courses, curricula, capstone projects, and professional preparation. Faculty suspicious of change talk might not be convinced by my arguments, but they may find here more "food for thought" to help them assess whether these changes can contribute to their goals for the humanities in the academy. At stake here is the leadership of faculty and faculty administrators in imagining, working for, and evaluating the efficacy of a 21st-century doctoral education.

Manifesto for the Humanities addresses more generally the public, of which both students and faculty, as well as their friends and families, are a part. I want doctoral students to loan this book to mothers and fathers, partners and friends. I want potential employees of those with humanities doctorates to read this book as well, and public policy analysts and sympathetic politicians. My intention is to convey to people outside the academy what pursuing doctoral education in the humanities involves. I'm not arguing with the liberal arts skeptics here; others have been doing that eloquently and urgently. Rather, I am engaging an audience of generalists who are themselves everyday humanists. They care about those loved ones and friends, and they care about the humanities, even if they may never have articulated exactly why. As potential employers or policy analysts, they care about people with a broad range of talents and a disposition for intellectual inquiry, adaptability, and leadership. At stake here is building a broader community of allies who recognize the prodigious talents and skills that people with doctorates in the humanities bring to the table, allies who appreciate what the humanities contribute to the liberal arts, the public sphere, and the economy and why the work of the humanities is central to the examined and pleasurable and intensely engaged life.

PART 1

The Times Are Good Enough

Let me begin with my mantra. "The times are good enough" to transform doctoral education in the humanities.

I like this mantra. It's compatible with my glass-half-full disposition. It invokes the history of change in the academy over the long span of my career. It prompts a slight uptake in posture, observable nods of appreciation and expectancy, in conversations with doctoral students. It sustains a sense of possibility when confronting the distressing trends of these times of higher education.

And, indeed, the challenges of these times for higher education writ large are contentious, urgent, and seemingly intractable.

My project in this manifesto is to make the case for a 21st-century doctoral education; but I would be remiss if I didn't assay, at the outset and in summary mode, the current times, the realities on the ground, of higher education. The transformation of doctoral education in the humanities is at once driven by and responsive to these conditions. Faculty and administrators are all too familiar with these conditions; they live them. Doctoral students glimpse them early if they don't already know them when they arrive to begin their studies. And so, with the mantra in mind, let me offer an abbreviated list of particulars related to the concatenation of forces that humanists, seasoned and emergent, will want to historicize, track, and engage over the next decade as their careers unfold.

Realities on the Ground

Elsewhere around the world, in China and India, for instance, academic leaders and government officials are investing in higher education to meet the needs of the growing number of students qualified to enter, but unable to find admission into, institutions of higher education. As they do so, they look to the model of U.S. universities, both private and public, to plan for their entry into the global rankings of research institutions. They marshal the means to build competitive research programs, establish partnerships with American universities, launch joint programs, exchange faculty and students. Elsewhere, universities in Europe, Australia, and New Zealand have become competitive destinations for increasing numbers of international students seeking graduate degrees. The shift in the language of instruction to English in many European universities, including the prestigious Milan Polytechnic University, Italy's equivalent of MIT, means that Europe's educational institutions will be far more competitive in attracting U.S. graduate students.[1] Here, in the United States, however, the will to value and support the long-earned preeminence of higher education has been waning.

The story of state withdrawal of support for this remarkable system of public universities has been well and often told. In the post–World War II decades, investment in American higher education grew exponentially. The G.I. Bill made money available for higher education; degrees promised better futures; and those better futures became the testimony to the superiority of the American Way of Life during the first two decades of the Cold War. The military-industrial complex demanded more and better-educated scientists to develop weapons, launch astronauts into space, and produce the new materials that would transform the domestic economy as well. Sputnik in October 1957 launched an education war fundamental to Cold War politics.[2]

The high levels of federal and state investment in higher education did not hold through the 1970s and 1980s, though levels differed across the states. The escalation in the cost of the Vietnam War left less money for "butter." The unrest on campuses soured politicians on investment in the education of the next generations after the Greatest Generation. The oil crisis radically undermined confidence in an ever-expanding economy. The end of the Cold War diffused the sense of intensity to the education war. And the legacy of the Reagan years turned a large swath of the electorate against "big government" spending.

Once considered state-funded, in the last four decades public universities have gone "from state-supported to state-assisted to state-located," as a common refrain across the country goes. My university, the University of Michigan, for instance, is one of the wealthiest Research 1 (as designated by the Carnegie classification) universities. In the current year, "The state appropriation will be around 16% of the general fund budget," as students and parents are informed on the university website section entitled "Understanding Tuition."[3] Across the country, the University of California system has been wracked with budget cuts for the last half decade. At regional state universities across the country cuts have been even more severe.

To deal with escalating costs and decelerating funding, public colleges and universities regularly increase tuition, exacerbating the trend that the cost of higher education increases faster than do wages.[4] To secure tuition dollars, they chase students able and willing to pay higher tuition, including international students bringing a certain kind of diversity to campus, but not economic diversity. Average family income of students across campuses trends upward, thereby decreasing economic diversity.[5] Research accumulates showing that even high-achieving students with high aspirations for earning a college degree reel under the pressures of cobbling together loans, working one or more jobs, and remaining close to families and communities of affiliation. The debt load for parents and students, totaling in excess of one trillion dollars, has become a crisis-in-the-making. In a comparative framework, the New York Times reported on May 13, 2012, that "the size of the average student loan in 2005 was $17,233. By 2012 the average U.S. student loan debt climbed to $27,253—a 58% increase in just seven years."[6] By 2014 it had risen to an average of $30,000. The former promise of higher education has been compromised, rendered unattainable, by the dramatic rise in debt and the rise in the number of "indentured" graduates and parents.[7]

The goal of universities and colleges to attract, enroll, mentor, and graduate more first-generation students, those from underrepresented racial and ethnic groups, those in liminal positions, such as the college-age children of undocumented migrants, among others, becomes harder to achieve. The stark divide between the have-nots and the haves, between those who do not have to depend on student loans and those who have them, negatively affects the accessibility of higher education, especially for underserved populations. This sobering decrease in the percentage of students from underserved communities and low-income families occurs as major shifts in the demographics of the U.S. population point to a time in the near future (projected at 2044) when the United States will become a majority-minority nation (with less than 50% of the population designated as non-Hispanic whites).[8] Universities and colleges thus find plans to enhance excellence compromised by the lack of diverse, experientially earned perspectives around the seminar table, the lab, and the offices of those who set policies, budget priorities, and program initiatives.

Where there is accessibility is in the community college system, which, as Kathleen Woodward observed in late 2014, now enrolls upwards of 44% of all undergraduates across the country, upwards of 50% of students of color in higher education in the United States, and an even higher percentage of low-income students. Yet that system remains woefully "overcrowded and underfunded." Citing the Century Foundation's 2013 report *Bridging the Higher Education Divide*, Woodward challenged educators and the public to acknowledge the potentially "separate" and "unequal" conditions of the community college system and to reflect on the ease with which that system is described as the site of vocational rather than liberal arts education.[9]

And what about graduate education? State legislators often view advanced degrees with suspicion, as an education primarily for students coming from outside the state and outside the country, and as an education whose scholarly and research projects threaten the cultural values of religiously and politically conservative constituents. This situation is joined to the dissipation of the synergistic partnerships that colleges and universities formerly enjoyed with the federal government, the states, industry, and philanthropy to build dependably up-to-date, research-intensive, and successful graduate programs. A 2012 white paper from the National Research Council of the National Academies, entitled *Research Universities and the Future of America*, warned of the inadequacy of current relationships to ensure the vitality of the nation's research universities and the excellence of their physical plants, research agendas, and graduate training programs.[10]

Add to this economic and political situation, the almost-daily assaults on the value of baccalaureate, master's, and doctoral degrees, circulated through the public discourse of economic utility. Pundits and politicians proffer analyses and sound bites about how higher education in the liberal arts is overrated, outmoded, and backward-looking, only tangentially important to meeting 21st-century challenges. They pontificate about how certain degrees are undeserving of public support, not worthy of investment, a waste of time and money. Silicon Valley entrepreneurs and others observe that the real generators of technological revolutions and new-mode jobs of the last three decades didn't finish their undergraduate studies (at Stanford or Harvard).

This argument, based on the exemplary singularity of Sergey Brin, Steve Jobs, Bill Gates, and Mark Zuckerberg, is the impoverished version of the narrative that a college education is no longer requisite to becoming (white male) billionaires.

This question, "whether the debt is worth it," should produce heated debate. Higher education has become increasingly inaccessible for lower-income people and even for many in the middle class. Higher education has changed too slowly; has often not demanded that the climate be inclusive for all students. But many critiques are too formulaic, geared to the sound bite, simplistically fragmentary. They are often lodged by people in power, people with privilege, people quick to distinguish what they term doers from takers, the deserving from the undeserving, the motivated from the unmotivated.

Then too, the impact of politicians and their allies on university policy, value-setting, and governance intensifies. Global warming skeptics continue to attack scientists and the sciences of global climate change, thus exciting the current crop of culture warriors whose distrust of those they label "elites" washes anti-intellectualism with a patina of populism. Culturally conservative activists exert disproportionate pressure on legislators to interfere with STEM (science, technology, engineering, and math) fields in such areas as embryonic stem cell research.[11] State legislators attempt again and again to demand particular changes in state universities, in granular attempts to affect differential tuition for programs, determined by their utility value. And through it all, the discourse of the elitism of higher education feeds the grievance machine of those who distrust the government and decry the erosion of a "real" or "true" America that is no longer.

Within colleges and universities, the effects of 40 years of decreased funding can be glimpsed in the reach of corporate-inflected discourse, policies, and management practices. They can be seen in the rise of the for-profit university. In the nonprofit sector, they can be seen in the big business of college sports; the appointment of business executives as presidents; the positioning of students as consumers; the expansion of administrative positions and bureaucratic practices; the development of patent incubators and intensification of corporately sponsored research; the spin-off of think tanks; the increasing quantification of the impact of scholarship and research results; the emergence in the curriculum of entrepreneurial studies; and the outsourcing of curricula, as seen in the flurry of investment in MOOCs (massive open online courses) a few years ago. They can be heard in the everyday circulation of market discourse: of branding, accountability management, efficiencies of scale, productivity, profit centers, shared services, centers of excellence, outcomes assessment.

They can be observed in the structural inequality of the out-of-balance adjunct system as the cumulative disinvestment in higher education exacerbates the casualization of the academic workforce, a contingent workforce with a demographic that is majority female. As reported by the American Association of University Professors in 2014, "Non-tenure-track positions of all types now account for 76 percent of all instructional staff appointments in American higher education"; and across institutions of higher education in the United States, "More than 50% of all faculty hold part-time appointments."[12] These effects are surely evident in the assaults, from outside and within universities, on academic freedom, the tenure system, and vigorous faculty governance.

No sector of the university is immune from the impact of these large forces, except, perhaps, large athletic programs; and they too are confronting their own scandals. Colleagues in the sciences and quantitative social sciences face the reality of shrinking support for primary research funded by the National Institutes after years of significant cuts and sequestration. Distinguished scientists find grant funding diminished, applications denied, projects delayed. Emergent scientists worry about careers interrupted. Of special concern is the report that "strapped scientists" are "abandon[ing] research and students," as Paul Basken and Paul Voosen reported in the survey of 10,000 scientists nationwide for a February 2014 issue of *Academe Today*.[13] Politicians ride science skepticism all the way to Congress. Local school boards and state legislative commissions neglect scientific expertise in favor of biblical revelation. And on and on.

But the fields of the humanities are vulnerable in their particular ways to the current troubles of higher education. So let me summarize the concatenation of forces, external and internal, affecting the corner of the academy identified with humanities disciplines and humanistic modes of inquiry beyond those disciplines, turning first to the external forces.

For a significant number of commentators and pundits, what humanists do seems elitist, narrow, and irrelevant for the concerns of the day. The humanities are thus consigned to the reliquary of a 19th-century concept of education in which privileged young men inhaled "the best" that had been thought and expressed in the hallowed halls of the liberal arts college. In an era of accountability management and corporate number-crunching, the argument goes, the humanities can't quantify their value. In the current global economy of uncertainty and hardship, the humanities are impractical to study, or just plain expendable. On the way to a job, some say, who thinks about the origins of life, the question of evil in the universe, the history of the Antinomians in the Massachusetts Bay Colony, the sounds of almost-extinct languages, the metrics of medieval verse or Sanskrit epic, or the experience of reading in 12th-century China, 14th-century Spain, 19th-century Peru, or the 20th-century outback of Australia. In the context of what Gary Carnivale of the Georgetown University Center on Education and the Workforce describes as an economic capital concept of education,[14] such preoccupations seem to be much ado about nothing consequential to future careers and to the nation.

Particularly vocal among the humanities skeptics are the public servants. Recall Governor Rick Scott of Florida—the state doesn't need to educate any anthropologists because Florida doesn't need them. Recall Governor Pat McCrory of North Carolina—the state doesn't need to educate any gender studies majors when there are obviously no jobs for which the degree is a preparation. In 2014 McCrory stated over radio: "If you want to take gender studies, that's fine, go to a private school and take it. But I don't want to subsidize that if that's not going to get someone a job."[15]

In part, these dismissals constitute the afterlife of the political and social turmoil of the 1960s, the feminist movement, the consolidation of ethnic studies programs in the academy, and other hot-button issues of culture warriors on the right. In part, they derive from the corporatist logic of utility applied to the academy, with its discourse of comparative usefulness of majors to landing the first job out of school, and its discourse of the nonefficiency of spending so much time studying subjects not immediately applicable to the everyday needs of a job or "strategic" to solving problems. The rush to quantify utility can be observed in the 37 states who by 2015, as reported by Lance Lambert, "have now built—or are in the process of building—systems that can pinpoint what graduates earn," data that can be used to make funding decisions for public colleges and universities.[16] The national conversations about differential tuition and the utility of majors continue in think tanks, legislatures, and boardrooms. Those conversations reproduce for the public at large a narrative of nonutilitarian, nonstrategic humanities education; of disciplines and interdisciplinary fields as lightweight expendables on the way to achieving economic efficiencies, filing entrepreneurial patents, and affirming capitalist values.

And within the academy, the status of the humanities sector is troublingly precarious. Academic humanists have lived with the reality that since the great expansion of higher education in the post–World War II era enrollments have shrunk in economic downturns. But the dramatic rise in the cost of higher education, coupled with the decrease in public funding and the adoption of corporate discourse and practices, now intensifies the doom-and-gloom prognosis of the future of the humanities in the 21st-century university. With the economic downturn of 2008, and in its wake, enrollments in humanities courses and declarations of humanities majors have decreased, dramatically in some units and at particular universities and colleges. For regents and members of university boards, and for administrators, then, the problem of the humanities is that they cannot justify their claims for resources by recourse to course enrollment counts in times of economic distress.

Further troubling to some administrators is that the curriculum in humanities disciplines cannot be easily scaled up. Those pursuing management efficiencies often find the practices at the heart of humanities teaching difficult to translate to huge lecture courses or virtual classrooms of hundreds, thousands, or tens of thousands of students: the expectations of significant and deep reading; the slow time spent developing and supporting interpretive approaches to cultural texts; the writing, and revision, and more writing that is difficult to assess through Scantron technologies. With regard to graduate programs, the difficulty of adequately funding fellowships in departments without grants to support students leads to questions about the value of graduate education considered irrelevant to the pressing issues facing the nation and the world.

The management imperatives of efficiency and quantification render humanities units problems in need of solving. Decreased enrollments and the inability to attract external funding contribute to the mismeasurement of the cost of humanities programs to the university. As a result, in times of severe budget cuts, humanities units are often the first to be downsized; or forced into marriages with multiple partners, willing and unwilling; or eliminated altogether. Small language units have been common targets in projects of efficiency.[17] Just recall the drastic cuts that the University of Albany made in 2010–2011, cuts that ultimately eliminated the Department of Classics and scaled back majors in French, Italian, and Russian to minors. And Albany was only one institution to retrench humanities degrees after the 2008 economic collapse.

Humanities departments have had to adjust. Many departments have pared down the size of doctoral cohorts over the last decade because the costs of educating them cannot be sustained and cannot be off-loaded to grant funding. For some, the size of cohorts hovers at the limit of viability for a "respectable" program. The normal course load for faculty at many places is increasing, dependent on institutional mission, status, and resources. Undergraduate directors are asking faculty to "grow" lecture courses. At some institutions, humanities programs have been delegated to provide general education and skills courses necessary for students in popular undergraduate programs. In other words, they have been managed into the status of "service providers" within the academy.

And there are further issues of academic status particular to humanities units. The pay gap continues to widen between the salaries of humanities faculty and the salaries of those in the social sciences, STEM fields, and professional schools, based on competitive salary setting by disciplines. That gap is exacerbated by another factor, the longer time-to-tenure and time-to-promotion for humanities faculty as compared to faculty in the professional schools, sciences, and quantitative social sciences. Within humanities departments there is also the widening gap between tenure- and tenure-track faculty and those in contingent and non-tenure-track lectureships. Across humanities units, but especially in English and other language departments, large numbers of people off the tenure track, and often on one-term appointment, provide service courses to meet composition and language requirements in the general education curriculum. They work with few benefits, little professional support, and often no job security. This dramatic imbalance in the distribution of teaching across tenure-track and non-tenure-track faculty results in a two-tier faculty, with those in the contingent category earning a median pay per course of $2,700 and an annual average income of $21,600 (according to the 2012 survey by the Coalition on the Academic Workforce).[18]

The demographics of humanities departments also impacts issues of academic status. Humanities departments have a relatively high proportion of female faculty within liberal arts fields. According to a report of the Humanities Indicators, that proportion hovers around 50%, though the figure varies by discipline, with philosophy and religion reporting figures of less than 33% for the 2013–2014 year.[19] The gender demographic in the contingent rank in humanities departments is majority female.[20] No wonder activists in and scholars of higher education talk about the "feminization" of the professoriate in the humanities.[21]

Finally, there are pressing concerns about the realities confronting doctoral students in the humanities, the future professoriate. Since these realities along with the data will be elaborated in Part III, I will be brief here. A large proportion of humanities doctoral students now spend more than seven years earning a degree. Many accumulate substantial debt, the underrepresented students among them even greater debt. When they complete the degree, they confront grim job prospects. The humanities job search for the first tenure-track position now takes three to five years. A modest percentage of newly minted doctorates find tenure-track positions the first year out; a larger percentage by three years out. Many spend one or two or three years in postdoc positions, sometimes with modest teaching obligations, sometimes with demanding teaching obligations. Others spend time in temporary lectureships, joining the contingent faculty. In those positions they work to gain enhanced teaching credentials and publish essays off the dissertation. They also hope for the conversion of the lecturer position to a tenure-track position and for a more robust set of job openings the next year. They hear around them talk of more purposeful and expanded programs in professional development, programs now geared to preparing graduate students for alternative careers inside and outside the academy.

Here then, in condensed form, is my set of particulars about the political economy of the academy and the conditions particular to the academic humanities. This summary sketch does not aim to be comprehensive. Nor are my comments intended as a deep reading of the confluence of forces in play. I tried for that in an earlier draft of this book, but it soon overwhelmed my focus on transforming doctoral education. And besides, over the last decade, in book after book, column after column, and blog after blog, scholars and public intellectuals have chronicled the troubles of higher education. Passionate, and often pessimistic, they have railed at the loss of a vibrant academy and a robust humanities. They have tracked with prodigious research and through trenchant argumentation the "rise" of the knowledge corporation and the "decline" of the U.S. university system after a century of ascendency and preeminence. They have warned about diminished academic freedom and the deplorable exploitation of contingent faculty.[22] These books address the large political and economic formations, with bleak assessments or messianic fervor or frustration at the glacial pace of change. In this book, the focus is on the transformation of graduate education in the humanities even in the midst of these bleak conditions.

There are plenty of reasons for anxiety. There are plenty of concerns to stoke a malaise. There are plenty of critiques to turn on the shortsightedness of politicians, the corporate imaginary, and the neoliberal logic of utility. That's for sure. But critique is not enough now. Intervention is all. Which brings me back to my mantra that the times are good enough. It's a usable slogan, effective in marshaling energy to avoid a sense of despair before the forces out there.

So, what is to be done?

What Is to Be Done?

Academic humanists respond to this query—"What is to be done?"—in various ways. Some put their heads in the sand and bemoan crises that are just too big and intractable to tackle. Well, yes, some of them may be. But, really, there's much to tackle. Some play the victim of an ignorant public and its various representatives who just can't understand the centrality of humanities inquiry to higher education and the world. Okay, where exactly does that petulance lead? And what kind of politics is enacted when faculty expect others to assume that theirs is a privileged position? Others turn back in nostalgia and talk of a time when the humanities were the revered core of a liberal arts education. Not me. No way.

Let's stay in the present moment and go forward from here. To suggest why I cleave to my mantra that the times are good enough, I offer my registry of actions for surviving, even thriving in these times: beware the route of nostalgia; avoid the blame game of theory and identity politics; hold the vision of inclusive excellence in sight; muster data for evidence-based counternarratives to commonplaces about the sorry state of the academic humanities; recognize the larger community of activists throughout the academy and the resources they mobilize for making change happen; remember all the humanists and allies out there; and act to make doctoral education forward-looking for future humanists.

Beware the Route of Nostalgia

Let me talk of my problem with nostalgia. I'll do so by invoking someone writing during what some academics may think of as better times, and writing with something less than enthusiasm for how wonderful they were. And I'll tell a more personal story about why I don't like to linger in nostalgia. After all, those times were a lived experience for many faculty now in the academy, myself included.

First, to Jacques Barzun, as president emeritus of Columbia University, writing about the "higher bankruptcy" of the American university in 1968. In *The American University*, he observed:

> Federal transfusions of cash will keep the great heart pumping; friends will rally round and bring jam (rarely meat); and commencement speakers will administer with a free hand the drug of self-praise.
>
> Then the parts will begin to drop off, as the autonomous professor has begun to do; or go into spells of paralysis, as the student riots have shown to be possible. Apathy and secession will take care of the rest, until a stump of something once alive is left to vegetate on the endowment or the annual tax subsidy.[1]

For Barzun, the metaphor of choice was the university as gangrenous patient, losing limbs and vegetating in an ICU unit.

Two things strike me about Barzun's portrait of the academy. The first is that, amid his doom and gloom, he exudes confidence that the funding of higher education will continue to be robust. It certainly had been the case in the 1960s, when public higher education was robustly funded by state legislatures. When I was a freshman at Michigan in 1962, tuition for an out-of-state student was around $225 per semester, and state funding made up about 80% of the general operating budget. Around 1968 that percentage began its four-decade decline.

The second pertains to his dismissal of the new technological accouterments of the professor's life:

> In another domain the university should have led the way in ascertaining and publicizing the difference between the useful and the deceptive: I mean the clutter of machinery, the so-called aids to teaching. Some are excellent, like the equipment of a language laboratory, various projector devices, and certain films for scientific or medical demonstration; others are fraudulent or futile.[2]

Note the assurance with which Barzun dispatches early technological devices in the classroom and his stunning lack of prescience. Like Barzun, people in the academy are trying to grasp the current state of higher education in the United States and around the globe, to determine what is to be done. Unlike Barzun in the late 1960s, today's faculty and administrators recognize only too clearly that funding is not assured and technology not tangential to the future of higher education.

And for many students, as well as distinguished administrators like Barzun, those good old times were not so good. Let me turn to my story. When

I stayed on for an MA after completing my BA at the University of Michigan in 1966, I found myself in a Department of English whose faculty made it clear that women graduate students were unwelcome and insignificant in the scheme of things. We were tolerated, but not mentored as graduate teaching assistants. We were imagined as future secondary teachers, not future academic intellectuals, and thus not doctoral student material. Legitimate graduate education was for the young men who would be guided by senior faculty and placed in their first job by means of an old-boys network. There was no interviewing at the MLA convention, which was at that time more a learned society than a professional organization. No tension on the elevators or at the phone banks. No frenzied parade around the book exhibit. Jobs were to be had without interviews of the kind routine now. A call here. A call there. The men called other men, asking for the protégé. And the women who inhabited the broader university community? They were wives who wove the web of academic sociality, organizing teas, hosting dinner parties, grading papers, while they provided secretarial support to spouses, typing manuscripts and carefully correcting page-proofs.

And the young woman who left Michigan with an MA in English? I returned to Cleveland to live at home and teach in secondary school. And I soon knew that I couldn't continue on that track, which involved supervising study halls to interrupt the flight of spitballs arcing from ungainly boys to embarrassed girls. To supplement my salary teaching high school, I joined the part-time faculty at Cuyahoga Community College to teach freshman composition. In 1968, I found a place in the Department of English at Case Western Reserve University, a graduate program that welcomed women who wanted to take doctorates, valued us, mentored us, and gave us the confidence to imagine ourselves as future professors. I know my dissertation advisor did. That was the year *The American University* hit the bookstores. The next year, I started teaching Black American Literature and came to understand the importance of literary history to minority communities, of deep reading of noncanonical authors to students' lived experiences.

In 1971, I entered a new kind of job market, and a constrained one. I didn't get a job straight out. I caught a ride to Chicago, combed the yellow pages for universities, made cold calls to see what positions were available, and landed a job as assistant dean of continuing education at Roosevelt University. After a year I recognized that the dean liked his associates and assistants to be female; less competition, less challenge to his authority. Then I got a one-year visiting appointment at the University of Arizona, which turned into a tenure-track appointment. Many of my friends and colleagues in the academy had employment itineraries similar to mine.

In the mid-1970s, when, as an untenured assistant professor at the University of Arizona, I decided with my partner to have a child, we planned for a convenient delivery date. My son arrived on December 31. I returned to teaching within a week and a half. My bid for tenure had failed while I was pregnant and as yet unmarried. In my discussion with the chair about the outcome of the tenure deliberations in the English department, I was told that the decision had nothing to do with my personal life. After a second tenure review the next year, a review on procedural grounds, I did receive tenure. I spent several years in study groups with friends across the humanities and social sciences reading everything that was coming out in feminist theory and retooling myself for a different kind of scholarship. Administrative positions were not an option for many women in the academy then. I sought administrative experience elsewhere, taking a leave to work at the National Endowment for the Humanities in Washington.

When people talk about the "good old times" in the humanities, I'm less than enthusiastic about joining in. Sure, faculty governance trumped administrative fiat; sure, public funding of higher education was more robust and the costs of higher education well within the reach of the middle class. Sure, the humanities seemed in a secure place amid the broader liberal arts. Yet I remember that the academy was not a welcoming place for many, including white women and women and men of color, whether students or faculty; that faculty governance was also faculty gatekeeping; that chairs were often czars of disciplines. I remember a place where arguments for expanding the curriculum into areas of women's studies, black studies, and ethnic studies invited contentious debates and fierce resistance. A time when preparing for courses required not only time and energy and persistence, but also fundamental retraining. A situation in which more than a few people found careers thwarted by tenure committees that labeled them controversial, uncollegial, or unproductive. The stories are there.

The changes came. At the University of Arizona, for instance, friends and I were buoyed by heady talk of continental theory that provided lenses through which we could make sense of the questions we were asking about the difference of women's writing, about the politics of gender, about the workings of ideology in racial formations, and on and on. Those of us involved in building the university's Women's Studies Program were supported in our plans to change the curriculum and introduce new interdisciplinary fields by the Ford Foundation and the National Endowment for the Humanities under the leadership of Joseph Duffey. I and others were tutored by professional organizations such as the American Council on Education on the skills needed for administrative positions so rarely open to majority and minority women and men of color. Elsewhere academic activists were advancing their own agendas; calling attention to processes in need of revision; advocating for new kinds of programs.

My turn away from nostalgia has to do with the fact that, however remarkable the system of higher education in the United States is, and has been, the academy and the humanities are always failing some students and faculty. The history of American higher education has been one of constant change and constant pressure to make the system more inclusive, and more responsive to the aspirations and needs of diverse communities—Jews, women, African Americans, Latinos, Asian Americans, American Indians, first-generation sons and daughters, sexual and gender minorities, people with physical and mental impairments, undocumented migrants. Through successive waves of activism in the academy, enrollment policies shifted.

With regard to the professoriate, substantial change has occurred as well, due to the labors of many people—administrators, faculty, and students alike. Now white women and men and women of color lead major colleges and universities. The numbers and percentages of white women and women and men of color earning doctorates in the humanities continues to rise. An increasing number of research universities and some colleges have been introducing family-friendly policies, enabling men and women in tenure and tenure-track positions to take parental leaves. Revisions of tenure and promotion processes and criteria have brought more transparency at evaluation time. More recently, recruitment initiatives, such as the national initiative called ADVANCE, with its project STRIDE (Strategies and Tactics for Recruiting to Improve Diversity and Excellence), train faculty to recognize forms of evaluative bias and pursue equitable hiring practices.

But this is no time to rest on any laurels. The struggle for inclusion is ongoing. Congratulations are not in order. In the university and in the humanities in particular, there is always more to be done.

As some of the graduate students with whom I work cautioned me to remember, humanities departments are not unqualifiedly progressive, ethically driven redoubts in the contemporary academy. They are not, in and of themselves, an unqualified social good, talking of truth and enlightenment, of meaning and values, of empowerment and consequence.[3] It wasn't that way when I was coming up. And it's not now. The fields of the humanities can talk to— address the needs and concerns of—students from underrepresented groups and first-generation students, students from working-class families, students with disabilities, and LGBTQ students; but they don't necessarily do so.

Now many students feel abandoned altogether as colleges and universities graduate two kinds of students—those without debt and those with debt who have struggled at two or three jobs to make ends meet and bring everything to class required of them. For a good number of students, educational spaces remain alienating environments, unwelcoming if not downright hostile. In the classroom. In the curriculum. In the corridors. In scholarship. Others find themselves isolated, subject to stereotyping on majority white campuses, as evidenced in the fall 2013 Twitter hashtag campaign, #BBUM, "Being Black at Michigan." The campaign and the demands of African American students provoked intense discussions of race and climate, curriculum and support services, classroom attitudes and social relations, and demanded faculty and administrative commitment to timely and creative response.

The relationship some students have with their institutions of higher education can be at once one of desire for what it can offer and antagonism about the costs of that desire in alienation, the devaluation of experiential history, the hostile climate of one's unbelonging, and high debt. Furthermore, as Marc Bousquet argues, a structural disincentive for potential applicants to even pursue doctoral education exists. The result is an absence of promising applicants from certain groups: "The persons unfree to 'choose' the profession are disproportionately Hispanic and African American."[4] This is the case because of what Bousquet terms the "wage discount," that is, the effect of structurally reproducing entrance into a low-waged academic labor force as the endpoint of advanced study.

For many faculty as well, the conditions of academic life are not as enabling and inclusive at campuses across the country as they must become. A large percentage of contingent faculty on non-tenure-track appointments barely make a living wage. A worrisome number of faculty, both tenure-track and non-tenure-track, experience a negative climate. For women, having children "is a career killer," and advancing to the full professor rank a hard slog, especially in humanities disciplines.[5] Faculty in the tenured ranks remain disproportionately white and male with respect to their percentages in the general population, and the fractions of white women and African American and Hispanic women and men remain disproportionately low with respect to percentages in the general population.[6]

So much had, and has, to change to make the academy more inclusive of people and of scholarly questions and of texts and of fields. So many faculty and graduate students had and have to join to make structural change happen. If the good times were so good, why all the struggle for change?

Avoid the Blame Game

That struggle can be obscured in the narratives circulated that play the blame game, whether coming from those outside or those inside the academy. For a few ornery pundits, studying the academic humanities is detrimental to the humanities writ large, an argument made by writer Lee Siegel in a *Wall Street Journal Review* piece in the summer of 2013. The byline for Siegel's piece reads: "Of course it's important to read the great poets and novelists. But not in a university classroom, where literature has been turned into a bland, soulless competition for grades and status."[7] What an argument: kill the humanities to save the humanities. But something like this argument infiltrates the critique of the humanities lodged by public intellectuals and conservative culture warriors.

Inside the academy, a number of humanists have been weighing in with analyses of how the state of teaching and scholarship in the humanities bears much of the blame. Let me take up the critique of one of them. In "What Dido Did, Satan Saw & O'Keeffe Painted" (2013), Mark Bauerlein lambastes "the killing of primary texts—more precisely, canceling the primacy of them" and the elevation of critical activity to the same level as creative activity. He presents these two moves as "a fatal choice . . . with damaging effects continuing today."[8] Bauerlein sees the damaging effects of the theory fetish in recent self-studies by humanists, "The Heart of the Matter" (2013) from the Commission on the Humanities and Social Sciences of the American Academy of Arts and Sciences, a sobering report on the decrease in the percentage of bachelor degrees taken in the humanities; and in Harvard's 2013 report from the faculty on the decrease in the percentage of students majoring in the humanities there. For Bauerlein the paradox is that, in extolling the virtues of humanistic inquiry, advocates for the humanities seem little interested in objects, texts, works, the thing itself. His antidote to the troubles with the humanities is thus the return to the object, the great work.

Bauerlein's is an impassioned argument that the turn to theory and to identity-based research and scholarship directed attention away from questions of value, aesthetics, ethics, and thus the very embodied and intellectual energies that compel students and the public to engage humanistic learning. It's the "No wonder the public doesn't understand or value what we do" argument: humanities scholars have been invested in inscrutable prose accessible to the few, absorbed with political correctness, and carried to a succession of trendy topics. If only so many academic humanists hadn't turned. If only they hadn't wittingly and unwittingly opened the humanities up for the assaults of social conservatives and their political representatives. If only . . . they would have "what," exactly? A return to the "great books" approach to humanistic learning in the academy is not likely to convince state politicians to fund the humanities disciplines and liberal arts education more robustly. Nor is it likely to ground a 21st-century graduate education.

Nor are academic humanists uninterested in texts as texts, or averse to deep readings of what used to be called the great books. Early modernists, whatever their theoretical bent, sleep with the classics, eat breakfast with the great books, make dates with revered authors. So too medieval historians and scholars of the long 18th century. But that is not the only nourishment sustaining academic humanists as they dedicate lives to their questions, topics, methods, and archives. They propose new interpretations to tell new narratives about the meanings, aesthetics, contexts, politics, and afterlives of ideas and genres and metaphors, of discourse and influence and circulation and repurposing.[9]

There are those in humanities departments who counter what they see as a repurposed argument drifting forward from the culture wars of the early 1990s. In *The Humanities "Crisis" and the Future of Literary Studies*, Paul Jay refuses the scapegoating of theory and critique as the cause for the troubles of the humanities and vigorously defends the centrality of critique for both the curation of the objects of humanistic inquiry and for the sharpening of skills. Looking forward while historicizing backward, he issues a salutary call for "professionalism without embarrassment." In the end, he orients his reader not to "a return" but to a 21st-century vision of a humanities energized by multiple reading strategies, motivated by engagement beyond the academy, fascinated by globally distributed and heterogeneous cultural forms, and replete with usable expertise.[10]

I'm with him there. I don't want a return.

And I don't want to participate in bashing what some colleagues see as the latest trends in technologizing the humanities. I'm not with those who link the continued devaluation of the humanities with the rise of "digital humanities." Scholars in the humanities are all humanists in digital environments now, in their scholarship and in their teaching, in their projects of scholarly communication and in their curation of their work. Some are making a contribution by studying digital cultures. Some are pursuing computational approaches to the study of language and history, to inquiry into cultural forms and logics and the condition of the human and the posthuman. Many are creating new archives and databases and developing new platforms. I take up these transformations of the everyday life of humanists in Part II.

For me, the blame narratives are flawed in their targeting of causes. They focus in too neatly on a thread of what is a messy, complicated story. They characterize those people positioned as antagonists in the academic drama as one-dimensional ideologues. They tend to look back rather than imagine forward. They often avoid grappling with large structural issues. I find them "clingy" rather than energizing. But this doesn't mean I'm into avoiding critical attention to practices and projects and modes of communicating scholarly work in the humanities, its discourse, prose, and presumptions. I'm for critique with attitude.

Seize the Opportunities

So what are the opportunities in play now to justify my mantra that the times are good enough to reconceptualize doctoral education in the humanities? They include the opportunity to get into the fray by mobilizing data that tell good-enough stories about humanities teaching and inquiry; the opportunity to participate in and benefit from the activism and advocacy accumulating force across the academy and professional organizations; and the opportunity to join humanists in the academy to humanists and allies beyond the academy.

Marshal Arguments with Data-Based Evidence

Yes, numbers can tell a disturbing tale. Since 2008 they have told the tale of a falloff, sometimes dramatic, in the number of humanities majors. But those numbers tell only a part of the story of the humanities in the academy. Those who advocate for humanities faculty, programs, departments, and disciplinary issues can tell alternative narratives to the commonplace one circulated on campuses and in the broader public.

Michael Berubé and Russell Berman, for instance, both former presidents of the Modern Language Association, have been mobilizing data to this end. Recall the earlier observation that a downturn in humanities majors and enrollments accompanies economic downturns. And then reconsider. No matter what pundits, columnists, and colleagues say, enrollments in many humanities programs remain comparable even now to enrollments in past decades. While enrollments in the humanities trended downward during the recent economic collapse, they are now trending upward, not uniformly across all units but steadily in aggregate.

Berubé brilliantly lambasted, with his unfailing wit, the habitual gloom-and-doom of op-ed pundits and disgruntled academics alike in his July 1, 2013, column in the Chronicle Review. And he did so by doing what they failed to do with exactness: went to "data" and "numbers" and the statistical guru Nate Silver and the authoritative Digest of Education Statistics to ground his argument. His conclusion reads:

> Despite skyrocketing tuition rates and the rise of the predatory student-loan industry, despite all the ritual handwringing by disgruntled professors and the occasional op-ed hit man, despite three decades' worth of rhetoric about how either (a) fields like art history and literature are elite, niche-market affairs that will render students unemployable; or (b) students are abandoning the humanities because they are callow, market-driven careerists . . . despite all of that, undergraduate enrollments in the

humanities have held steady since 1980 (in relation to all degree holders, and in relation to the larger age cohort), and undergraduate enrollments in the arts and humanities combined are almost precisely where they were in 1970.[11]

Responding to a *New York Times* piece on the "small" percentage of humanities majors (15%) graduating from Stanford in 2013, Russell Berman penned a response correcting the slippery statistical presentation:

> In the School of Humanities and Sciences, to which the article refers, 20% of the class of 2013 majored in the humanities and the arts. This surpasses the natural sciences at 15% and approaches the social sciences at 25%. The remaining 40% chose interdisciplinary programs that draw on courses across these clusters. In recent years, the number of humanities majors has held steady, while social science majors have been declining. Yet focusing on majors alone misses the significance of humanities courses in general education. Last year 27% of all course enrollments were in the humanities.[12]

Such retorts keep the focus on what is good enough about the current state of the humanities in higher education. And they insist on resisting uninformed and undocumented platitudes about the humanities. I take heart from the usable data of everyday life.

In the midst of angst about what's wrong with students, theory, and culture-war-era fields, large numbers of students continue to double major in humanities fields. On the Humanities Indicators website, a project of the American Academy of Arts and Sciences, graphs indicate that since 2010 the number of students completing second majors in humanities disciplines has risen significantly (though the percentage of first majors in humanities disciplines has fallen). They indicate that in the community colleges the percentage of associate's degrees earned in humanities disciplines has steadily increased to a 2013 level of near 40%. HI also reports that "the share of college students taking introductory or intermediate Spanish increased more than for every other type of course except freshman composition."[13] In its 2014 annual report, the Linguistics Society of America noted that "the field of linguistics is growing most rapidly for undergraduates, with an increase of approximately 120 more students awarded BA degrees annually for the past 13 years."[14] And by the end of their studies, the IH graphs show, a larger proportion of humanities majors score in the highest brackets of the analytic part of the GRE "than in any nonhumanities discipline."[15]

All across the humanities, capaciously defined, students continue to sign up, sit in, and cross the stage to get diplomas in humanities disciplines. Still. And potential employers continue to insist upon the centrality of critical thinking, capacious reading, appreciation of ambiguity, ability to learn how to learn, and effective communication, to successful careers across the life span.

Perhaps such national media venues as the *New York Times* are so enmeshed in neoliberal analyses of the times, that they reproduce the market-driven narrative of the crises of inutility. They reproduce a stereotype of the current generation of students whom they misrecognize as in it for the buck. Further, they betray presumptions that suggest journalists and commentators might benefit from the project of deep and engaged reading in order to better interpret the alternative stories that data can be made to tell. Perhaps reporters might go looking for historical factors contributing to the shifts in majors: the opening of the academy and the professions to large numbers of white women and women and men of color that gained momentum during the 1970s.

With regard to humanities departments and their status? Data available through *The State of the Humanities: Higher Education 2015*, issued by the American Academy of Arts and Sciences, reveals that there is "very little evidence of decline in the number of humanities departments," though there is some decline in the number of degrees awarded by humanities departments.[16] HI graphs also indicate that "after adjusting for inflation, expenditures in 2012 [related to support for humanities research] . . . were 54.6% higher than in 2005."[17] Moreover, in the current economy of accountability metrics, as Christopher Newfield has demonstrated, some humanities programs *are* profit centers because the costs of mounting English or philosophy or linguistics courses is far less than mounting courses in the STEM fields. Working with cost figures from Arizona State University from 2010, Newfield suggests that the lack of transparency in calculating and publicizing the comparative costs of different programs across the university creates a climate in which the liberal arts can easily be presented and interpreted as a sinkhole of public monies with little benefit to students in terms of jobs and the economy, when in fact they are cost-effective centers within the larger university.[18] Others have cited figures for UCLA and the University of Washington that indicate that humanities departments generate more tuition income than they cost to run.[19]

And with regard to those who would repeat the mantra that degrees in the humanities do not lead to the first job, or may only lead to a job as a barista at Starbucks? A late 2013 survey out of the human resources firm Careerbuilder reported that "nearly half (47%) of college-educated workers said their first job after college was not related to their college major," and, the report continued, "thirty-two percent of college-educated workers reported that they never found a job related to their college major."[20] Another report by urban economists Jaison R. Abel and Richard Deitz in 2013 used data from the U.S.

Census Bureau and the 2010 American Community Survey to run calculations that find that "close to two-thirds of college graduates in the labor force work in a job requiring a college degree, while a little more than a quarter work in a job that is directly related to their college major."[21] These studies suggest that except in certain fields like engineering and other STEM fields, there is no surety that the major leads to a particular job in the field for which the major is said to prepare people. Other data suggest that earning graduate degrees leads to a better match between field of study and career.

These reports tell other stories as well, reminding me that there is a world of data out there—statistics, reports, analytics—through which to tell different stories about the state of the humanities—to ourselves, to colleagues and administrators, and to the public. It is not always easy to sift through the data, the reports on the data, and the further interpretation of the reports. Yes. That's the case. But it is worth the sifting to get a more complex picture about what's happening out there in the academic humanities. It is worth going to the considerable data and reports available through professional organizations and the Humanities Indicators. Turn a critical lens on the hype about data analytics; remember that statistics are an effect of systems of collection; but also take advantage of what data reveal about aspects of the state of the humanities and renarrativize the commonplaces of humanities bashing.

Of course, data itself can't do all the heavy lifting of articulating the relevance of humanities teaching and scholarly inquiry to the grand challenges confronting the world, their value to lifelong learners and learning, their inherent pleasures, their role in sharpening the powers of critical analysis, their centrality to the liberal arts, and their good-enough robustness. But data can be joined to testimonies and experiential histories and stories of scholarly projects to enhance the case to be made about the role of the humanities in the academy and beyond.

In renarrativizing what is happening in the academic humanities, and doing so with intensity, liveliness, and intellectual intimacy, academic humanists engage multiple audiences with sophisticated, evidence-based rejoinders. In doing so, they drive the agenda rather than remain constrained by defensive postures. They also model for faculty colleagues and graduate students the roles of public advocate, educational policy analyst, and engaged scholar.

Recognize the Larger Community of Activists

Every day, across the academy and beyond, there are people out there conceptualizing, preparing for, and enacting plans to intervene in aspects of the conditions sketched above.

There is action out of the national academies. The National Academy of

Sciences, the National Academy of Engineering, and the Institute of Medicine have reported on the state of the university and its funding support, issuing 10 recommendations, the last three of which direct attention to attracting, funding, and graduating new generations of doctoral students, and, most critically, attracting a greater diversity of applicants.

There are the advocacy groups, foremost among them the DC-based National Humanities Alliance, constituted of leaders of all the professional organizations, training faculty to be lobbyists for the National Endowment of the Humanities on the Hill, making the case for public support of the academic humanities and state humanities councils. In the digital humanities community, Alan Liu and others have founded 4Humanities, an advocacy arm of the field energized to move beyond critique. Here is Liu issuing his call for action in PMLA:

> The digital humanities register the crisis of the humanities. For that reason, I and others started the 4Humanities advocacy initiative, "powered by the digital humanities community," so that the digital humanities can try to advocate for the humanities and not just register their crisis. I do not know how much difference that initiative and others like it will make in the meaningfulness of the humanities to the world. But I do know that such an effort—dedicating the digital humanities to the soul of the humanities—is what is meaningful for a humanist, digital or otherwise, now.[22]

Keys words here are "Do not just register," and "act."

There are blueprints for structural change related to the rise of a contingent labor force in the academy, the deprofessionalization of the academic workforce, and the exploitative wage rates for non-tenure-track faculty. The Modern Language Association and the American Historical Association have made advocacy on behalf of the non-tenure-track faculty on the nation's campuses a major project. The MLA website makes accessible information on staffing patterns at campuses through its Academic Workforce Data Center and its Academic Workforce Advocacy Kit.[23] There are as well initiatives to tackle directly the restructuring of the academic workforce through "adjunctification." Under the leadership of Maria Maisto, the New Faculty Majority network brought the conditions of adjunct faculty to the attention of the House Committee on Education and the Workforce in late 2013, with the result that the Democratic staff of the committee issued a report titled "The Just-in-Time Professor: A Staff Report Summarizing eForum Responses on the Working Conditions of Contingent Faculty in Higher Education" (January 2014).[24] Participants in the Adjunct Project compile data on adjunct salaries and working conditions for contingent faculty across the country through a crowdsourcing wiki. The Delphi Project on The Changing Faculty and Student Success "conduct[s] original research on non-tenure-track faculty" and "produc[es] important resources for use by leaders on campuses," including analyses of the relationship between student learning and the status and conditions of adjunct faculty.[25]

Campaigns for unionization target higher wages, better working conditions, secure benefits, and access to professional development opportunities for faculty off the tenure-track and for graduate student instructors.[26] Graduate students at NYU succeeded in organizing the first union at a private university in the United States, signing the first five-year contract in March 2015. Graduate students at the University of Toronto went on strike in early 2015 over wage and benefits issues, eventually agreeing to binding arbitration.

There are calls for renewed commitment to the values of the tenure system and shared governance. The American Association of University Professors tracks and responds to attacks on the tenure system and faculty governance, and incidents of violations of academic freedom across North America. Twenty-three professional organizations signed a joint statement in response to the move of the Joint Finance Committee of the Wisconsin State Legislature to introduce policies in the 2016 budget that would directly undermine protections of academic freedom and faculty governance in the University of Wisconsin system. This statement was followed by one issued by the Board of Governors of the American Association of Colleges and Universities.

And there is the considerable noise of everyday activity. Publishing. Blogging. Speaking to various publics. Making the case all the time and everywhere. Organizing. Testifying. Protesting. Digging into details of budgets and their impact. Digging into data compiled by the American Academy of Arts and Sciences, available on the indispensable Humanities Indicators website.[27] Historicizing structural changes to the funding and administering of higher education. In videos and wikis. At conferences and strikes and teach-ins and performance venues.

There is activism all around. That activism, however fitful, however frustrating, however modest before the large structural trends, is itself a source of energy and a site of agency. It also produces a public goods archive of resources for those seeking to make change: toolkits, task force reports, program initiatives, research, jeremiads, and manifestos. In the midst of debilitating trends and discursive noise, this archive functions as an ideational commons, a cacophonous reservoir of strategic argumentation, unsettling critique, thought-puzzles, extended analyses, improvisational tactics, tutorial education, and innovative programming. It is also a commons of praxis, available for tapping in the project of transforming doctoral education in the humanities.

Remember All the Humanists Out There

Finally, these are good-enough times because there are so many allies out there, people whose work, whose everyday pleasures and lasting legacies, translate the value of the humanities in the world. I like to think they number in the millions.

Of course, some of them are doctorally trained academic humanists in libraries and think tanks, in IT and PR, in administrative positions and presidencies, in contingent positions and tenure-track positions. More numerous are the professional humanists outside the academy. They are the archaeologists and anthropologists who unearth buried pasts and bring cultures of meaning into purview, as do the professional humanists unearthing artifacts from the Roman city Londinium beneath London and the possible plague pit amid the shaft sinkings for the new London rail link. They are the gender studies majors who apply their prodigious skills in analyzing the effects of gender stereotypes, racial discourses, and homophobia, for instance, in the workplace, public health arenas, nongovernmental organizations, law and medicine, among other careers. They are the art historians who build archives, curate collections, educate the public and speak to the creativity of diverse peoples and communities and arts cultures across the globe. They are the philosophers and linguists, cultural theorists and literary historians, public historians and musical theorists who carry their fascination with the humanities into the worlds of work they enter. They translate their love of reading, their visual literacy, and their powers of critical analysis into careers in the profit and nonprofit sectors, into public policy and courts of law.

There are also generations of students of the humanities who continue to follow the interests of their youth, the respite of their wearied, working days, and the unpredictable avocations of their later years. They read voraciously in many genres—novels, memoirs, poetry, biographies, and histories. They pause before a Vermeer, staggered by the quality of light on his translucent canvas. They listen intently to the sounds of a raga, of a reggae beat, of Rachmaninoff's Piano Concerto no. 3, of a wailing sitar or a thundering drum. They sing in choruses or preserve traditions of sacred music. They visit historical sites and wander local historical museums for serendipitous encounters. They ponder the forms of belonging of people in the past or struggle to understand the shifting terms of citizenship in a global world. They too go on archaeological digs, even with arthritic knees. They make gifts to colleges and universities to support humanities programs and students.

There are many who are self-tutored, informally and collectively educated. They turn to cultural authorities for narratives of community and survival, to shamanic storytellers or to stand-up comedians. Others are alumnae of colleges and universities who can remember a particular classroom moment when light broke, or the darkness of doubt descended, or the frisson of a deeper understanding shot through their bodies. Everywhere people thrive on the artists and thinkers who mark worlds of meaning and on the work of scholars in the humanistic disciplines who painstakingly interpret worlds, cultures, events, social relations, and lives in the making. As the American Alliance of Museums observes, far more people in the United States buy tickets to wander museums across the country (around 850 million) than to enter stadia for sporting events and theme parks (around 483 million [2011]).[28]

There are allies all around who understand the value of humanistic thinking and making. They understand that the life of consequence and imagination and curiosity and flexibility and passionate commitment to doing the work of the humanities in the world is another kind of successful life. They recognize that humanistic inquiry is also a kind of training and a way of approaching challenges that are indispensable to the vibrancy and adaptability and capacity of the economy and the ongoing struggle over the meaning, the future, and the ethics of democratic polity. Wherever they find their professional lives, these allies share the passion for doing, learning, reflecting on the many pleasures of the arts and ideas of life, of human sociality, of human aspiration, of transspecies companionship, of knowledge from below.

The diversity of this humanities workforce and its allies helps make the times good enough. Thinking capaciously about community enables academic humanists to resist situating the public as antagonistic to their academic enterprise. Moreover, such a disposition calls mentors and advisers to resist projecting a career outside the academy as a sign of failure. Professionals outside the academy can be identified as potential mentors for doctoral students thinking about multiple possible futures before them. The Modern Language Association has recently acted on this vision of a broader community of humanists through its Connected Academics project, enlisting doctorally trained humanists in supporting students in doctoral programs interested in multiple career horizons.[29] The academic humanities is a vibrant node in a far larger collaboratory of everyday humanists enacting the work of the humanities, and expanding the impact of the habits of scholarly inquiry.

The Times Are Good Enough

There is so much that is good enough in the current climate and economy of higher education in the humanities. I am not glibly arguing that this moment is like every other. As noted earlier, there's been a decades-long retreat from public funding of higher education as a public good, a trend with demonstrable impact on increasing inequality and the erosion of educational access and justice. There's been a seismic shift in the makeup of the professoriate—now disproportionately non-tenure-track, contingent faculty, a seismic shift that Bousquet terms deprofessionalization.[30] There's been the raucous cacophony of the pundits and politicians of utility. There's been an intensification of the chronic condition of the job market for those with doctorates seeking careers in the academy, as economists D. C. Colander and D. Zhou recently observed.[31]

Nonetheless, the opportunities are rich. There are counternarratives to be circulated. There are people and resources to draw on. There is a larger humanities network out there. The academic humanities is a project in process. The changes won by hard work in the past and all the advocacy, innovation, and change now in process sustain a sense of historical perspective and daily purpose.

And thus, my mantra, which to be a mantra has to be said again and again: the times are good enough to work with, although the intersecting complexities of the forces often elude adequate analysis and appear insurmountable. Tales of doom and gloom cannot become an excuse for acting as if change is impossible, or wholly out of any one person's hands. My activist project is the transformation of doctoral education in the humanities. It's in the air. It's on the agenda. It's up for debate.

This is no time for despair, or complacency, about what it takes to ensure a vibrant, disputatious, creative academy. This is no time for complacency about how to conceptualize a doctoral education committed to access, diversity, and excellence. The future of higher education is the future of diversity, human, institutional, and disciplinary. The future of diversity lies in the doctoral training of future teachers and scholars. The future of doctoral training lies in the animation of a 21st-century vision purposeful in its approach to meeting the educational challenges of the times.

The times are good enough. This mantra is a pulse of promise.

PART 2

The Everyday Life of the Humanities Now

Everyday life in the academy has become fluid and fraught. As explored in Part I, support for public higher education, the conditions of employment of the faculty, the economy of prestige, and the bases of public value constitute the many challenges facing higher education in the United States and the humanities in the university. The edifices of matter, thought, social capital, and common goods are being re-formed, sometimes with attention to faculty governance, sometimes with casual indifference to or downright disregard for faculty governance. The particularities of professional practice are rapidly altering, often in ways that call for new technical, theoretical, methodological, and organizational competencies. The identity narratives through which humanists have commonly understood themselves, their roles, and their academic futures seem increasingly inadequate to these evolving practices, and to the culture of sociality and the intellectual imaginary of a 21st-century humanist.

To better comprehend the changing environment in which doctoral students will imagine themselves and their careers in the next decades, let's home in on critical aspects of the everyday life of humanists as they go about their scholarly, pedagogical, and professional activities. I want to look here at large shifts that will increasingly affect the working lives of humanities scholars, seasoned and emergent. These shifts relate to the evolving concept of the university; the epistemic infrastructure; the new media and modes of scholarly production and communication; the trend toward the "open"; the renewed emphasis on teaching, if unfolding through different modes; and the emergent, possibly "posthuman," humanities scholar. But first a caveat. Everything about the academic environment is changing far too rapidly to adequately pin down. At best I can offer only a snapshot at this moment of writing of some movable parts and processes in which academic humanists are implicated and their work lives embedded.

The Distributed University

Where will the university of the next decades be located? Let's start here, with an awkwardly stated, but nonetheless provocative question. This question invites those involved in higher education to think carefully about the complex institutional locus of higher education, and about the architecture and imaginary of its "thereness."

For some 200 years and more, students have settled into the niches of campuses across North America, whatever their size or geographical region, whether less than 1,000 students or more than 50,000, whether rural or urban, whether ivy, independent, or public. Those institutions have had their distinct identities, associated with historical luminaries, the cloak of ivy, land grants, the big name of the state flagship, the urban landscape, the small town, the benefactor. Students graduate certain of the place-based memories of transformative events, favorite or parodied professors, memorable parties or protests, and friendships intimate and transitory. Later, proud or curious alums return to that place, sometimes to join their generational cohort, sometimes to celebrate a child's graduation. They return as well to refurbish a memory palace filled with intellectual, social, and affectively charged recollections. At least this is the powerful mythology of the relation of alums to place-based higher education in North America. For many the myth comes close to the reality. And for many, the experience is different. They carry less than affectionate memories, or the visceral remembrance of alienation. Some secure their diploma and leave campus behind. But even then, the detachment is to place.

Increasingly, however, the place of higher learning is less an effect of geographical particularity than an effect of networks, relationships, and new kinds of academic sociality. The future of doctoral education in the humanities is imbricated in these new-model networks transecting dispersed global hubs. The ethos and sociality of the graduate experience is as well. So let's consider the various ways in which the "thereness" of higher education is shifting.

A number of public and private universities offer a swath of their degree programs online, as Arizona State University does with over 70 undergraduate and graduate programs. Under the presidency of Michael Crow, ASU has expanded its online presence, including partnering with the nonprofit edX to offer to anyone around the world an online freshman year. Open to anyone, without application process, the eight credit-bearing courses will cost in total fees somewhere around $6,000. In such learning models, the campus is dually accessible, offline and online, and attachments mobilized through campus gates and campus portals. ASU is out front in its reach for inclusivity, accessibility, and innovation. As such, it draws applause from those who see its bold experimentation as a breakthrough to conceptualizing "the new American university," to cite Crow's coauthored book[1];and it draws jeremiads of condemnation from many who see it as the harbinger of the end of the university as it's been known and the apotheosis of the corporate university dependent on vast numbers of exploited contingent faculty and algorithmic teaching assistants.

Then there are the virtually placeless universities, the for-profit ventures offering online curricula and a virtual brand. The attraction of for-profits is the delivery of relatively low-cost education at the convenience of students, most of whom work and some of whom have little mobility or live in rural areas. For-profits are also attractive for the instrumental credentials offered to people seeking mobility in the workplace; and that includes graduate degrees. But trends in the recent past put the brakes on the pace of expansion of for-profit higher education, including graduate education. After a stunning expansion, the for-profit higher education sector is currently contracting, due in large part to the scandals related to admissions practices, graduation rates, and loan default rates. The lax standards of support for students and the voracious garnering of the federal government's student loan monies exposed the exploitative ethos of a for-profit sector that approaches students as moneymakers and the federal government as a source of cash investment and the route to profit. Further, the almost total reliance on a part-time faculty without the protections of academic freedom and participation in faculty governance exposes the increasingly exploitative conditions of instructional labor upon which for-profits are built. Nonetheless, for-profits remain a significant sector of virtually administered higher education.

There are also new ventures, nascent, hybrid, and ambitious in their aspirations to model new cultures of higher education through distributed locations and networks. The University of the People, founded by education entrepreneur Shai Reshef in 2009,defines itself as "the world's first non-profit, tuition-free, accredited online university dedicated to opening the gates to higher education for all individuals otherwise constrained."[2] A collaborative venture joining NYU, Yale, and nonprofit foundations, among them the

Clinton Global Initiative, the Haitian Connection, the OpenCourseWare Consortium, and sponsoring corporations, UoPeople offers associate and bachelor's degrees in the fields of computer science and business administration through a fee-based model.[3] Here, the curriculum is assembled through open courseware, and the pedagogical model is peer-to-peer learning.[4] Students are distributed across disparate locations; administrative gears of the enterprise move along global networks; and affective attachments trend toward aspirational horizons rather than retrospective memories of place.

A second model of globally dispersed higher education comes from Minerva Schools at Keck Graduate Institute. The Minerva project promotes a concept of elite, affordable for-profit education (at $10,000 per year), enrolling high-performing students from around the world whom the program grooms for leadership through flipped classrooms and high expectations of intensive in-class intellectual exchange and inquiry. Students and faculty spend each year in a different global city, beginning in San Francisco, moving to Buenos Aires and Berlin, Hong Kong and Mumbai, where in-person classes and access to online open courseware are offered in local space. The achievements of such alternative models to place-based institutions of higher education, the former expanding outward in the catchment of potential students but limited to education in computer science and business, the latter zeroing in on a highly filtered set of admissions criteria and going for small, remain to be seen. Academics and entrepreneurs in these and other ventures have yet to resolve pressing issues of accreditation, degree status, and a sustainable funding model that would make them scalable options.

Bricks and mortar also travel now. Research universities have opened campuses elsewhere around the world. New York University in Abu Dhabi (United Arab Emirates) and American University in Dubai (also UAE) are but two of the 200-plus branch campuses awarding degrees surveyed in 2012 by the Observatory on Borderless Higher Education in Britain.[5] Universities have also established transnational institutes and training consortia, such as Georgia Tech Ireland, a translational research institute joining Georgia Institute of Technology with National University of Ireland, Galway, the University of Limerick, and corporate research divisions to advance basic technology in STEM fields. Some research universities have built entirely new kinds of institutions, such as Yale-NUS (National University of Singapore) College. This liberal arts college is housed on the NUS campus, coconstituted with Yale, but remains distinct from both institutions in its faculty, students, and common curriculum.

These initiatives in distributed higher education of well-known educational brands provide certain benefits for students and for institutions. For universities, the attraction of transnational campuses and programs is the extension of the university brand, which ratchets up prestige factors central to international rankings; expands the pool of applicants and tuition dollars; creates access for students to transnational experiences and learning assets; and opens potential new funding sources deriving from partnerships with private corporations and national research bodies distributing grant support.[6] For receiving institutions, the attraction is the imprimatur of the global brand; access to more capacious research expertise; enhanced training opportunities for students; and the potential for transforming global cities into world-class knowledge economies. For students, in one place and of other places, the attraction can be proximity of educational resources, accessibility, flexibility in certification, and introduction to the practices, fields, and futures of a Western-model higher education and the cultural capital of a global brand.

The potential impacts on higher education of bricks-and-mortar universities building campuses and program collaborations overseas can be troubling as well. To suggest only one of the complex dynamics at play here, think of the promise of adapting prestige models of higher education to local sites, student populations, and cultural milieus. The potential upside includes the intensification of intellectual and research exchange; the preparation of students for the global marketplace and jobs of the future; and the greater diversity of perspectives needed to define, anticipate, and contribute to addressing grand challenges, such as the challenge of educational justice. The potential downside includes the increasing corporate footprint within research and learning environments; the erasure of local traditions of knowledge production; the privileging of certain models of higher education associated with elite institutions in the United States and Britain; the skewing of the concept of a liberal arts education to science, technology, engineering, and business degree programs; the erosion of academic freedom, the tenure system, and faculty governance when foundational values of the U.S. academy do not travel and when large percentages of the faculty are contractual employees; and the exploitative conditions for those laborers who build these bricks-and-mortar campuses.[7]

A more interesting and consequential model of distributed higher education from my point of view involves the consortial networks that join faculty and students across institutions. In Europe, the Bologna declaration brought Eurozone institutions into the European Higher Education Area, facilitating the movement of students from one country to another to pursue comparable academic degrees. In issuing the Salzburg Principles in 2005, the EHEA established a common discourse and a collective vision: "The intention is to allow the diversity of national systems and universities to be maintained while the European Higher Education Area improves transparency between higher education systems, as well as implements tools to facilitate recognition of degrees and academic qualifications, mobility, and exchanges between institutions."[8] In terms of graduate education, the Bologna declaration aims to enhance excellence through comparability and transferability and to realize opportunities for innovative cross-institutional joint degree programs.[9] In this way, students can imagine themselves as entering a far larger "higher education area" than offered by an individual campus and as bearing a credential as recognizable, consequential, and mobilizing as the common passport.[10]

In the United States as well, thought leaders have been calling for intranational research networks, as members of the National Research Council of the National Academies did in their 2012 white paper recommending greater collaboration among constellations of research universities across the United States.[11] That same year, James J. Duderstadt issued "A Master Plan for Higher Education in the Midwest." President emeritus of the University of Michigan, Duderstadt urged "midwestern states, governments, and institutions" to "develop a more systemic and strategic perspective of its educational, research, and cultural institutions—public and private, formal and informal—that views these knowledge resources as comprising a knowledge ecology" and to "shift from Balkanized competition to collaboration to achieve common interests, creating regional partnerships capable of responding to global imperatives."[12]

These trends in shifting the "where-ness" of higher education, by disarticulating teaching and learning from a singular home base, increasingly impact academic humanists. Humanities scholars have long found their intellectual compeers in other institutions in the United States and abroad; they have participated in and led scholarly societies that reach across the globe; they have started and supported scholarly journals and collaborated in large-scale projects of editing or translation; they have taught in study-abroad programs. What is different at this historical moment is the intensification of cross-institutional collaborative activity in the humanities and opportunities for modeling collaborative graduate education.

More or less elaborate, more or less formal transnational collaborations at the humanities program level have launched or are in the pilot phase. Some are "pop-up" programs outside the normative credentialing process requiring contractual arrangements, such as the Tri-national Summer School in American Studies joining students and faculty from Georgia State University (United States), the University of Mainz (Germany), and Beijing University (China) for intensive summer seminars. Some are consortial, such as the Mellon-funded collaboratories organized through the transnational Consortium for Humanities Centers and Institutes, founded in 1988.[13] CHCI has piloted several initiatives. The Medical Humanities Network connects six institutions around the globe "to contribute to the ways medicine and the humanities are taught and practiced."[14] The Humanities for the Environment project designates a five-member partnership spanning the globe focused on "the role of the humanities in a period of planetary crisis and change." And the Religion, Secularism, and Political Belonging project tasks partner institutions to explore "new approaches to religious and cultural criticism and understanding."[15]

Then there are the inter- and intranational relationships joining scholarly inquiry and doctoral training through centerNet, the "international network of digital humanities centers." Linking humanities scholars and students around the world, centerNet provides a commons for "sharing and building on projects, tools, staff, and expertise" and serves as a clearinghouse for information about emergent methods of scholarly inquiry and modes of scholarly communication.[16] As well, the influential HASTAC (Humanities, Arts, Science, and Technology Alliance and Collaboratory), cofounded by Cathy N. Davidson and David Theo Goldberg, mounts innovative annual conferences; networks HASTAC scholars working in digital media; encourages blogging on topics of critical importance to innovative thinking about the future of higher education and the humanities; and administers the MacArthur Foundation Digital Media and Learning Competition.[17]

In the United States, regional initiatives in humanities programs and scholarship are pursuing the benefits of cross-institutional responses to the big challenges ahead in higher education and in the humanities. In the spirit of Duderstadt's call, the Mellon Foundation funded the Humanities Without Walls initiative, directed by Dianne Harris out of the Illinois Program for Research in the Humanities at the University of Illinois, Urbana-Champaign.[18] HWW brings together directors of humanities centers and institutes across 15 Midwestern universities—the flagship state universities of the new "Big Ten" plus Chicago, Notre Dame, and University of Illinois–Chicago—to model innovative cross-institutional collaborations in doctoral preparation and in humanities scholarship on the topic of the "Global Midwest." And, at a more local level, interinstitutional collaboration has begun to organize the delivery of graduate education differently. In the Research Triangle area of North Carolina, Duke University and the University of North Carolina–Chapel Hill have built on long-standing collaborative relationships to initiate what they describe as "the first public-private joint venture in German graduate education in the nation," a venture that "pools" library and faculty resources.[19]

Networks of humanities institutes and digital humanities centers drive the distributed ecologies of advanced learning at the forefront of transforming doctoral education in the humanities. Here are the salient features of their contribution to change. They leverage relationships to offer alternatives to on-campus, course-based teaching and learning. In this way, they expand the number of potential faculty mentors and the size of the cohort of students pursuing mutual interests in fields, topics, and methods. They enact a new mode of scholarly inquiry in the humanities, modeling the benefits (and the difficult work) of building collaborative relationships. They intensify the synergies, intellectual heft, motivations, responsibilities, and routes through which to achieve at once the aims of an individual scholar and the goals of a network of scholars. And they focus considerable intellectual firepower on contributing to the grand challenges confronting the world now: sustainability, the politics of testimony, and the effects of and responses to the radical displacement of peoples, to suggest only a few of them.

On a practical level, networks attract external funding from foundations seeding new modes of scholarly inquiry in the humanities, among them Mellon, the American Council of Learned Societies, and the Canadian Social Sciences and Humanities Research Council. The grant-funded collaborative ventures provide financial support (travel funding, fellowship support) to graduate students involved in large-scale research initiatives, such as the Early Modern Conversions project organized by Paul Yachnin out of McGill University's Institute for the Public Life of Arts and Ideas, funded by SSHRC, and involving 15 partner institutions in North America, Europe, and Australia. Further, they pool resources of all kinds to offer training institutes that enable graduate students to gain new skills and hone competencies. CHCI's Integrative Graduate Humanities Education and Research Training project (IGHERT), for instance, joins faculty and graduate students at four institutions to "engage graduate students in a series of collaborative training and research activities," designed as models for scalable and portable professional development.[20] These initiatives multiply the effects of networking extended across institutions and transnationally. They secure students in expansive intellectual fellowship that can help keep them motivated and affectively grounded in a sense of common purpose.

Bricks and mortar are still the sine qua non housing the people, values, curriculum, and hardware that drive higher education; but they are no longer the only "where" of the university. Indeed, as Cathy N. Davidson observes in *The Future of Thinking*, "institutions" of higher education are better understood "as mobilizing networks."[21] And Rosi Braidotti talks of the university as "a hub of both localized knowledge production and global transmission of cognitive data," a condition that "need not necessarily result in either de-humanizing or disembedding the university, but in new forms of re-grounding and of accountability."[22] Release from a bounded location of higher learning; mobility of faculty, students, curricula, and ideas; interinstitutional sociality; multi-institutional networks of scholarly inquiry—all create what Dan Atkins describes as a "new ecology or culture of learning enabled by cyberinfrastructure."[23]

Given these trends in the multilocationality of institutions of higher education, humanists of the next several decades will find themselves entering a bricks-and-mortar classroom and, at the same time, participating in transregional or transnational activities. They will negotiate teaching and knowledge production in virtual learning spaces via all sizes of screens and formats of connection. Their students will find advising in face-to-face and one-on-one encounters and in face-to-face screenings across vast distances. Those students will share virtual classrooms with students from other universities. Graduate directors, chairs, and deans will imagine and implement new structures and evaluative protocols to seed, support, and preserve innovative programs and new scholarly ecologies.

I started out asking, "Where will one go when one goes to the 21st university?" The answer is multilayered. To the site of bricks and mortar. To a virtual portal. To a network of institutions in globally disparate locations. To a hub in a distributed array of partnerships. To a conjunction of brands. To a sociality of peers, mentors, and strangers. In this succession of answers, the relationship of the materiality of the university, its geographical location, and its named identity disarticulate and rearticulate in interesting, complex, and sometimes troubling ways.

At once here and elsewhere around the globe, mortar and code, structure and network; at once bounded and permeable, insular and collaborative, corporatist and socially responsible; the university morphs into a conjunction of distributed nodes and heterogeneous networks of scholar/learners. The university of today participates in distributed ecologies of inquiry. It is crisscrossed by heterogeneous cultures of learning and teaching. It is animated along interlocking infrastructures that condense time, reorganize space, and realign scholarly identities and relationships. It is entangled in capitalist logics and utopian disruptions.

Knowledge Environments

This is a daunting time, a time of excitement, yes, but also of anxiety about the overload of information and the proliferation of platforms and devices available to humanists in their scholarly lives. Worlds of archives are still out there, in scattered locations, in orderly and disorderly array, to be reached as travel destinations. And worlds of archives, large and small, come online at an ever increasing pace, there to be readily accessed through personal computers, tablets, smartphones, and, now, eyeglasses.

Millions of scanned texts have become fingertip commodities accessible through HathiTrust, a collaboration among Google and more than 80 research universities, whose purpose is to preserve the products of large-scale digitization and to advance the science of shared access within a sustainable governance structure.[1] Millions more items and collections of texts, images, sounds, and videos are accessible to the public through the European Union's Europeana Digital Library, which offers a portal to the holdings of such large institutions as the British Library in London, the Rijksmuseum in Amsterdam. and small cultural centers such as the Musical Instrument Museums Online. In the United States, the Digital Public Library of America, opened in April 2013, "brings together the riches of America's libraries, archives, and museums, and makes them freely available to the world."[2] In pooling and preserving vast knowledge repositories, consortia of universities, museums, and independent libraries have expanded exponentially the scale and capacities of what is commonly called the "public goods" archive, the public heritage encompassed in diverse histories of human thought and imagination and, on and off campuses, the repository upon which the production and circulation of knowledge depends, no matter what the discipline, no matter who the seeker. This remarkable ensemble of public goods repositories, what Margaret Hedstrom and John Leslie King refer to as the "epistemic infrastructure of the knowledge economy,"[3] has been dubbed the 21st-century version of the Library at Alexandria.[4]

This world of public goods is a world in turmoil. Universities struggle to adequately respond to the exigencies of library budgets and the rapidly evolving affordances and capacities of code, data, web, and cloud. Libraries struggle to adapt to a radical sea change in what they do, how they catalog, how they preserve, and whom they serve. Academic libraries confront even more of a sea change as they transform from legacy centers for preservation of books, journals, and special collections into ensembles of legacy centers, accessibility portals, "e-research" hubs, publishing enterprises, cyberinfrastructural nodes, and social centers for new modes of teaching and learning. And they confront the vagaries of their partnership with corporate capitalism in such ventures as HathiTrust, a partnership that demands, as Hedstrom and King argue, attention to issues of access, information quality assurance, social memory (to prevent loss of information on the Web), and information property.[5] Corporate-sponsored and public ventures alike confront thorny copyright issues that have yet to be fully resolved, even as the pace of legal action related to intellectual property escalates. All around, technical, legal, and ethical issues pop up in project-specific terms, as debates around preservation and access, architecture and metadata intrude in daily conversations. Uncertainty, as Hedstrom and King observe, is the lived reality of this epistemic infrastructure.[6]

In effect, this knowledge ecology is a "stay-tuned" ecology, though that metaphor seems so old-media, retrograde in this time. There's always a next story unfolding, of importance to scholars in the humanities: new horizons of intellectual interest, new practices of observation, new methods to drive interpretations; new tools for producing knowledge; new demands for skills and competencies. There's always a dynamic imbrication of disciplinarity and interdisciplinarity, always a residue, a surplus, a surfeit, a resurgence. And there's always the looming insufficiency of human and cyber infrastructures to support the full panoply of scholarly work in its prolific heterogeneity; always the cacophonous demands to keep up and keep up-to-date.

Jerome McGann and Bethany Nowviskie have written eloquently about the formidable challenges of this epistemic infrastructure for academic humanists. Here is McGann writing in 2004 of the prospect for humanistic enterprise in 2053: "In the next fifty years the entirety of our inherited archive of cultural works will have to be reedited within a network for digital storage, access, and dissemination. This system, which is already under development, is transnational and transcultural."[7] And here is Nowviskie writing 10 years later, invoking McGann:

> We humanities scholars and publics stand before the vast, near-wholesale digital transformation of our various and shared cultural inheritance. This transformation—more properly, *these remediations*—are fully underway.

They open new avenues for the work of the liberal arts in all of its spheres: for our ability to gain access to, to analyze and interpret, and most importantly to vouchsafe to future generations, the words, images, sounds, and built and material objects that crystalize in our archives and which we so carefully position to refract little, mirror-like understandings of what it has meant, for the blink of an eye, to be human.[8]

To capture the importance of gaining support and funding for the vast project of digitizing huge swatches of the world's cultural heritages, Nowviskie invokes the term "New Deal."

Humanists have complex and distinctive relationships to digital technologies and digitized archives and databases. And these evolving technologies and proliferating platforms increasingly impact how academic humanists think about their projects of scholarly inquiry and their vehicles of scholarly publication. What follows are brief observations about the relationships of humanities scholars to digital technologies across five domains: digitally assisted scholarship; scholarship on digital cultures; born-digital inquiry, including Small Data and Big Data projects; the Internet of things; and the Semantic Web.

In this time of "information abundance,"[9] *academic humanists are all digitally assisted scholars*, though the range of digital assistance available to them differs radically depending on where they are located globally. This state of interdependency is as true for humanities scholars who describe themselves as doing traditional kinds of humanistic scholarship as it is for those identifying as digital humanists. For 50 years scholarly work has proceeded by means of digital assistance. Over the course of my professional career I've saved versions of essays and books on paper, mainframes, eight-inch disks, five-and-a-half-inch floppies, zip drives, flash drives, and the cloud. I started out on an Osborne, the first portable computer, weighing 40 pounds; and I read green letters on a black background in WordStar. Now digital assistance is second nature as scholarly inquiry progresses through search engines. Through access to digitized archives, collections, and databases. Through an expanding array of organizing and retrieval applications. In the field, humanists keep notes and take photos of documents and material sites on smartphones, tablets, and laptops. They produce endnotes and bibliographies in the freeware of programs such as Zotero. A world of prosthetic assistance and assistants surrounds humanities scholars, even those who take pride and gain pleasure in composing with pencil and paper.

In addition to being digitally assisted scholars, some humanists are *scholars of the digital*. They are found across humanities disciplines, though a good many tend to be identified with media studies. These scholars pursue work on the cultures of computation, including questions of race and gender and sexuality; of political economy and network sociality; of social justice and multisensory aesthetics; of algorithmic values and the affective life of gaming. They explore the logics of digital architectures and the offline labor practices in the production of hardware and software. They examine the subject positions and subjectivities produced through algorithmic processes. Scholars of online composition research the impact and efficacy of online composition in the teaching of college writing. Others explore how issues of design in the building of databases and online archives render design itself a way of knowing.[10] Scholars in my field, life writing studies, explore the persistence of old forms of life writing in digital environments and the emergence of new genres in social media; they explore how technologies impact acts of witnessing to violence and suffering. Political theorists and humanistic social scientists explore online sociality and political advocacy. And humanists in schools of information study, as does Paul Conway, how the process of digitization in such projects as Google Books reveals the traces of the human hands and human labor involved in cultural preservation.[11] Some scholars in these diverse strands of digital studies identify themselves with digital humanities; many do not. Others talk of working on digital environments.

And some academic humanists pursue the strand of scholarly inquiry often encompassed under the rubric of digital humanities (earlier, humanities computing, or what Franco Moretti labels "computational criticism") with its particular relationship of project to technology to data.[12] In response to the persistent query of "what is digital humanities," Donald J. Waters of the Mellon Foundation offers a concise and useful gloss on the definitional imperative. Eschewing a fixed definition, he proposes "a typology of the disciplined methods and tools associated with the application of critical intelligence in various kinds of humanistic research," noting the three central strands that have developed over the last several decades: textual analysis, spatial analysis, and media, but more particularly visual studies.[13] And he cautions that "there is no single set of so-called digital tools, but multiple sets aligned along broad methodological lines."[14] The Mellon Foundation has been committed to funding promising initiatives representative of textual, spatial, and visual media analyses; and to supporting scholars pursuing opportunities to transform how it is that humanists communicate their scholarship, about which I will write in the next section.

For me, it is useful to think of digital humanities scholarship, born-digital, digitally environed, as emerging out of the scholar's relationship to Small Data and Big Data. Increasing numbers of humanities scholars are building small-data archives. Small data are data that accumulate in modest databases and online archives, data that can be grasped holistically by one person. Some accumulations of small data have already been cataloged in University Micro-films and national repositories. Some accumulations, as William G. Thomas, III observes, are "treasures," "wonderful materials in small places around the country and elsewhere" that people want to preserve for posterity.[15] Many are DIY archives; and some of those are accidental archives, dispersed, unsys-tematically assembled, and idiosyncratically curated. Other archives are and will be purposeful, curated, culled; they may have been given a first interpre-tation or come with purpose-built interpretive tools and platforms. Digital humanities centers across the country and the world are centers of support for archive building, as evidenced in the Mapping Colonial Americas Publish-ing project at the Center for Digital Scholarship at Brown and the Slave Biog-raphies project at Michigan State University's MATRIX center. But there are so many more—on the Founding Fathers; on major literary figures, among them Walt Whitman and Emily Dickinson and Christina Rossetti; on realms of documents. And there are more and more resources for scholars assem-bling online archives, such as advice on "best practices in the creation of digi-tal research materials," available through the scholarly organization NINES (Networked Infrastructure for Nineteenth-Century Electronic Scholarship).

Building archives is becoming increasingly important to many strands of humanities scholarship in ethnic studies, studies of marginalized peoples and communities, studies in history from below, and transnational gender stud-ies. In projects of recovery and preservation, scholars assemble digital muse-ums, receiving, cataloging, and displaying stories and objects registering and animating occluded histories. The Chicana Feminists project launched by Ma-ria Cotera and The Women Who Rock Oral History Archive at the University of Washington, spearheaded by Michelle Habell-Palian and Sonnet Retman, are two such DIY archives. And there is the Global Feminisms project at the Uni-versity of Michigan, a transnational project of field-based teams assembling a website of oral histories with feminists of all kinds in Poland, China, India, Nicaragua, Brazil, Russia, and the United States, in order to explore "the his-tory of feminist activism, women's movements, and academic women's stud-ies in sites around the world."

Scholars building small-data archives may or may not position themselves as digital humanists. Some may in fact see themselves as critiquing the dis-ciplinary statuses and identities associated with digital or computational humanities. Some may see themselves as enlarging the umbrella, helping to make the field more inclusive of a diversity of players, definitions, proj-ects, and outcomes. Theirs are projects in decolonizing the archive and the algorithm.

Then there are the humanities scholars working on Big Data, large-scale, large-scope humanities research. Big Data involves huge numbers of texts, far larger than any single person can comprehend and analyze in a lifetime. It ranges from the extensive collections in corpus linguistics to census tracts, from newspaper databases to geographic information systems distantly reading the interconnections of global literatures, and on and on. Digitally environed and digitally intensive scholarship requires methodological flexibility, emerging as it does out of algorithmic numeracy, design architectures in code and visualization, data mining, distant, middle-range, and close reading, comparative analysis, and storytelling. In the 2012 National Endowment for the Humanities report on the first recipients of the "Digging Into Data" grant program, Christa Willford and Charles Henry observed that "'reading' large text corpora by machine," "encompassing an amount of information exponentially greater than would be possible for any individual to take in and process in a lifetime," is "a subject at once intriguing, daunting, and unsettling."[16] Daunting projects extend the repertoire of questions humanists can ask of their objects of study and the scope and scale of the stories they find themselves telling of those objects. In 2013, NEH awarded Digging Into Data grants to support such projects as "Resurrecting Early Christian Lives: Digging into Papyri in a Digital Age" and "Annotating Data Extraction from Chinese Texts."

Debates are rife as humanists pursue and critique this complex constellation of projects, practices, relationships, and implications called the digital humanities. To put it most broadly: Are these projects the future of the humanities or the end of the humanities? Are these projects enabling humanists to add distant reading and surface reading to the commitment to deep reading, or are they the end of deep reading? Are these projects opening the humanities to more diversity or arresting that diversity? Are these projects adding intellectual depth to the academic humanities, or are they merely trendy, often disappointing in their payoff? Is the dazzle of the word cloud generative or just dull?

For many practitioners of born-digital humanities scholarship and their mentees, scaling big extends the theoretical acuity and reach of humanities work. In his early call for the end of the "apartheid" system of literary studies—"on one hand, we have editing and textual studies, on the other, theory and interpretation"—McGann argued that "reality or apparition, a quantum order of bibliographical objects become accessible to us through computerization. . . . The field of textual relations accessible to us through that digital device is statistically significant at a quantum order."[17] At HASTAC 2011, Josh Greenberg argued that Big Data is "something that lets you see broad/big. Something like seeing society."[18] And at the International Auto/Biography Association biennial meeting in Canberra, Australia, in July 2012, Sydney Shep demonstrated how access to large databases demands of the scholar a reconceptualization of the stories data can be harvested to tell, a process that eventuates in rigorous retheorization of terms and social processes, in her case, the transnational social action of the genre of "biography."[19]

Other digital humanists emphasize the interpretive acts required for digging into data, acts central to humanistic inquiry. "In much the same way that encoding a text is an interpretive act," blogger Trevor Owens observes,

> creating, manipulating, transferring, exploring and otherwise making use of a data set is also an interpretive act. In this case, *data as an artefact or a text can be thought of as having the same potential evidentiary value of any kind of artefact.* That is, analysis, interpretation, exploration and engagement with data can allow one to uncover information, facts, figures, perspectives, meanings, and traces which can be deployed as evidence to support all manner of claims and arguments. I would suggest that *data is not a kind of evidence; it is a potential source of information which could hold evidentiary value.*[20]

For Owen, the evidentiary value of Big Data lies not in numbers but in critical numeracy, that is, in how data can be made to give up their numbers to humanistic interpretation. In a 2013 pamphlet from the Stanford Literary Lab, Moretti makes his case for the value of computational criticism by probing the effects of "operationalizing," that is, translating concepts into a staged sequence of computational operations. This process at its most promising can enable humanists to "test" their theories by "building a bridge from concepts to measurement, and then to the world," which for literary studies means moving "from the concepts of literary theory, through some form of quantification, to literary texts."[21] Still others, namely Stephen Ramsay, promote an alternative way of engaging Big Data that he terms "the Screwmenuetical Imperative." This engagement is a kind of idiosyncratic "screwing around," serendipitous romps in which the "algorithmic methods can free us from the tunnel vision that search potentially induces."[22]

Other humanists challenge both the theoretical and the evidentiary value of Big Data as distant reading. In "Diggable Data, Scalable Reading, and New Humanities Scholarship," for instance, Seth Denbo critiques Big Data projects such as the Google Ngram Viewer and Moretti's "Distant Reading" initiative, calling instead for a hybrid mode of humanities scholarship, a "scalable textual scholarship" that maintains the commitment to close reading but situates close reading within "the interrogation of massive text objects."[23] Others metaphorize the seduction of Big Data as a slippery slope that leads to a technologized humanities and a trendy but limited "algorithmic criticism."[24] In his caveats about digital humanities, Alan Liu invokes the phrase slippery "zone" rather than "slope," invoking the metaphor of ice skating, with a nod to Yeats: "Knowledge is an ice-skater's dance on a slippery epistemic surface on which neither the human nor the machine—the dancer nor the skates—alone can stand."[25]

More and more humanities faculty and doctoral students are negotiating the terms, protocols, algorithms, and social relations of this human/machine interface, and the forms and etiquette of the dance. Object and process. An "inexhaustible" refulgence of interpretive possibility, though, as McGann cautions, the interfaces at first promise and then forestall the passionate dance of reading, connecting, and interpreting multiple worlds.

In this churning environment, debates about the place of digital humanities, their provenance and affordances, their value and constraints, continue apace, as any survey of e-journals, e-books, anthologies, and blogs addressing issues of digital humanities reveals. So, too, do debates about what constitutes "scholarship" in digital environments; about the understanding of research outcomes; about the evidentiary value of data; about the methodological relationship of numbers and meaning[26]; about what Christian Sandvig and co-authors pose as the accountability of algorithms.[27] The debates will go on, as they continually go on in humanities disciplines and interdisciplines, around issues of theory, methodology, argument, intervention, and stakes.

To sum up, all academic humanists engage in digitally assisted scholarship. Media studies, including the cultural studies of digital technologies and studies in algorithmic cultures, is now a robust field, departmentalized, professionalized, historicized. Small-data archive-building and curation accumulate apace. Born-digital humanistic inquiry mining Big Data is here to stay, even as it remains contentious, often dismissed as the trendy phase in the turn to quantitative humanities scholarship, often demonized as undermining the status of humanistic learning as practiced for centuries. In addition, two new trends in transformative digital technologies confront humanists.

One is the *Internet of things* with its "ambient intelligence and autonomous control."[28] Of course, this trend is most visible in the business world with its data tracking, data mining, and business analytics; and with its iterations of smartness in a succession of objects that scale downward in size and upward in capacity. As a white paper from one such start-up claims: "The Internet's most profound potential lies in the integration of smart machines and people—its ability to connect billions upon billions of smart sensors, devices, and ordinary products into a 'digital nervous system' that will smoothly interact with individuals."[29] The effects of this "digital nervous system," networking smart people with smart machines, will, in all probability, be felt soon in the world of nonprofit institutions, including higher education and advanced research. Humanists will thus confront the decentering of the individual scholar in scholarship as they take advantage of the knowledge generated by algorithms, things, and networks in a research environment in which the "connectivity of people and connectivity of devices are no longer independent phenomena."[30] They will be able to take new kinds of research support into the field or into distant archives, wearing devices that aggregate data instantly, allowing them to adjust questions, methods, and theories on the go. Moreover, as Jentery Sayers observed at a fall 2014 symposium, "Digital Humanities and Social Justice," at the University of Michigan, the Internet of things may be mobilized by activists to enable new initiatives in multipurpose maker's spaces.[31] One such space is Seattle Attic, "a feminist, woman-centered, trans- and queer- inclusive space for tinkerers, makers, crafters and hackers of all genders." Here learners, devices, and networks join to enable new kinds of creativity and expertise.

A second trend has to do with the *web of linked data*, a phrase coined by the World Wide Web Consortium (W3C), the international standards body.[32] Scholars in the health sciences and computational social sciences have already begun to exploit the capacities of the Web 3.0, often referred to as the "Semantic Web." Here is the early vision of Tim Berners-Lee, often referred to as the "inventor" of the semantic web:

> I have a dream for the Web [in which computers] become capable of analyzing all the data on the Web—the content, links, and transactions between people and computers. A "Semantic Web," which makes this possible, has yet to emerge, but when it does, the day-to-day mechanisms of trade, bureaucracy and our daily lives will be handled by machines talking to machines. The "intelligent agents" people have touted for ages will finally materialize.[33]

At this interface, the generative metaphor comes from linguistics. With its embedded metadata, interoperable connectivity, and natural language processing capabilities, the Semantic Web mobilizes "self-reflexive" software that can search for patterns of meaning and semantic relationships in purposefully and uniformly structured databases. The Semantic Web can be thought of as a network of software "agents" scurrying to find and interpret data and thereby provide the research assistance normally understood to be the province of human research assistants and doctoral students. For enthusiasts, as Phil Pochoda observes, the Semantic Web "permits fine-grained algorithmic tracking and data mining of many of the endless uses and interactions, connections and disconnections obtaining among humans and a myriad of digital products."[34] For those humanists seeking to understand the forms of prosthetic sociality coalescing at the interface of machine and human, the software agencies of the Semantic Web will offer new opportunities for granular and large-scale analysis.

All in all, academic humanists find themselves in a radically new environment for doing the everyday work of humanities scholarship. They look to their institutions to "adapt to, support, or sustain" a robust cyberinfrastructure enabling research and scholarship involving multiple partners, Big Data, and machines.[35] They scramble to find funding for their projects, from private foundations and from an NEH whose financial stability is always subject to political winds. They find themselves to be just one actor in a collaborative team that joins people from adjacent but also distant fields, some from disciplinary units and some from public goods units, many with different statuses in the university.

Further, they have major concerns about the ways in which their projects of and in digital scholarship will be evaluated and credited in the academy. For these projects make trouble for traditional metrics of faculty evaluation and reward systems. They raise thorny questions about the intellectual work of data aggregation, visualization, and curation; the double expectation that one must "publish" traditional scholarly work off the archive as well as produce the archive; and the scholarly impact and value of producing databases upon which other humanists can build scholarly reputations. To address these changing conditions of humanities scholarly production, faculty chairs, deans, and provosts have to adapt hiring practices, tenure and promotion processes, and salary decisions. They have, in the words of the *One Culture* report, to "expand their notions of what kinds of activities constitute research and reconsider how these activities are supported, assessed, and rewarded."[36]

In this evolving environment, academic humanists accrue ever more demanding professional obligations to understand what's going on and to influence how their needs are met and careers advanced. Many scholars play key roles in mobilizing such sites as Critical Commons, "a public media archive and fair use advocacy network that supports the transformative reuse of media in scholarly and creative contexts."[37] Other scholars caution about the potentially disabling relationship of Big Data to the archive. Tara McPherson, for instance, urges humanists to become key players in the transformations taking place with regard to data and archives, and poses startling questions to be insistently posed: "Can we remake the database for our own interpretative genres? Can our analyses and writing more seamlessly live alongside our data and our evidence? Can we combine human and machine interpretations?"[38]

In a less speculative mode, Johanna Drucker enjoins humanists to demand a seat at the table when the details of cyber and epistemic infrastructure are on the agenda, or when tools are in the development phase, for the stakes are too high for complacency or willed disregard or enervating frustration. "The task of modeling an environment for scholarship (not just individual projects, but an environment, with a suite of tools for access, use, and research activity)," she emphasizes, "is not a responsibility that can be offloaded onto libraries or technical staffs. I cannot say this strongly or clearly enough: *The design of digital tools for scholarship is an intellectual responsibility, not a technical task.* . . . The scope of the task ahead is nothing short of modeling scholarly activity anew in digital media."[39] Others encourage humanists to frame sophisticated meta-commentary on the environment itself, from the level of code and architecture to the level of meaning; for, as Liu observes, "Meaning is both a metavalue and a metaproblem."[40]

Humanities scholars, working by means of, on, and in digital environments, with virtual assistance from tools and platforms, and with access to Small and Big Data, algorithms and machines, enter a research terrain of hardware, software, fleshware, network, and institutional structure; of device and cloud; of interdisciplinary potential and disciplinary aporia. They work in collaborative teams, ensembles in which the center of expertise migrates from one person to another. They discover there the complexities of forging practices and ethics to adequately attribute effort to the different parties.[41] They deploy a range of skills: grant writing, project management, coding, perhaps statistics. During the course of large-scale and small-scale initiatives, they morph through multiple identities, becoming at once or by turns theoreticians, database designers, data curators, and managers. They juggle these ever-mobile processes and ever-mobile devices, in the midst of institutions of higher education, which, according to Cathy N. Davidson and David Theo Goldberg, have "within [them] and in [their] relationship to the community beyond, some mobilizing and some (literally) immobilizing aspects."[42] They find themselves located in units where generational identities, methodologies, theoretical investments, technological competencies, careerist goals, and networks of sociality drive colleagues apart and draw them together, often at the same time.

This rapidly changing, radically hybrid, collaboratively configured epistemic environment will tax doctoral students, faculty, and administrators to ply the heterogeneous networks of mobilization, expand the concept of scholarship and knowledge production in humanities disciplines, and rethink the relationship of work in the humanities to the knowledge operations defined as skills, or competencies, necessary for its achievement. The task ahead requires what Nowviskie describes as "*readiness*—both as individual, free scholarly agents and as a federated, broad, and unwieldy system of public higher education—to mobilize and properly equip the next generation of scholars and specialist practitioners to move into [the gulf before us]—actively, capably, confidently."[43]

Readiness for meeting the challenges of this epistemic ecology requires active participation of humanists in vigorous debates about technological affordances and traditions of humanistic inquiry, about the assemblage and preservation of archives and databases, and about the imperative of heritage-keeping and of improvisational and provisional paradigm-shifting. It calls for flexibility in experimenting with disruptive styles of display, in revising the metrics of evaluation, and in valuing the collaborative relationality of its practice. It demands vigilant attention to gendered and racialized dynamics within humanities fields, including the continued challenge of achieving robust diversity in graduate student cohorts and faculty and the gendered division of labor that finds faculty active in digital humanities majority male. It ratchets up the urgency of pursuing a 21st-century vision of doctoral education.

The New Media and Modes of
Scholarly Communication

The new media environment affects the conceptualization, scope, and method of humanistic scholarship, and the means of producing and circulating it as well. Scholarly publication has been the common term of reference for work produced within the traditional publishing system. Faculty commonly conceive of the culmination of scholarly inquiry as the short-form essay and as the more highly valued book or monograph form. But instead of asking, what have you "published," the question might better be phrased as "How have you been communicating your work?" Invocation of the term *scholarly publication* directs attention to the end product of scholarly work, "the article" or "the book" and its materiality. Invocation of the term *scholarly communication* directs attention to the processes of scholarship and opens to a variety of modes, lengths, media, and publication/circulation systems.

All around, the system for publishing scholarly work in book form is in flux. The flux signals both a challenge for academic presses and an opportunity to rethink scholarly vehicles. As former press editor Philip Pochoda observed several years ago, "Now, after half a century of productive publishing, th[e] print-based publishing order is in its final throes of dissolution, having suffered the combined blows of withdrawal of external funding and significant loss of revenue overall; drastically declining demand from libraries and scholarly customers; and, most importantly, the digital revolution which challenges every aspect and assumption of the legacy publishing process."[1] No longer served by the "legacy print system"—which Pochoda described as "a stable, bounded, well-ordered and well-policed publishing model"— academic humanists now navigate an unfolding system "that is inherently unstable and shape-shifting in all its elements, potentially anarchic and boundless, and unimaginably rich in future publishing opportunities."[2] Yes, and also a complex system in search of viable economic models.

For the last decade, press directors, faculty boards, and professional organizations have been analyzing the internal and external trends that have rendered the old funding model untenable. To deal with budgetary constraints and cuts, university administrators have withdrawn or scaled down funding for academic presses, despite their role as a public good serving the academy as a whole. At many institutions academic presses have been shifted from independent enterprises to subsidiary enterprises located in university libraries, now in the business of academic publishing.[3] Academic librarians have readjusted budgets to deal with the high costs of science and STEM journals, an effect of the consolidation of science publications across a small set of for-profit vendors such as Elsevier. And with the pace of technological transformation intensified, library administrators have struggled to balance acquisitions of print materials with acquisitions and preservation needs of digital databases, publications, and platforms. The escalating costs of science journals and the competing demands on library budgets have resulted in diminished sales of academic books in print form, since librarians can no longer purchase every book published in humanities fields by academic presses. Moreover, academic press directors and library personnel running new publication ventures now struggle to adapt to reader habits among professional humanists, develop models flexible enough to take advantage of new possibilities provided by multiple-format publication and print-on-demand publishing, and anticipate the as-yet-unknown impact of open access publishing on sales. And with regard to humanities publication venues for the short-form article: Journals, many located in the publishing wing of academic libraries, are in transition as well, from print to online versions, or some hybrid of the two.[4]

Responding to this unstable publishing environment, the Mellon Foundation has assumed a major role in addressing changes in the scholarly communication system. In 2015 alone, Mellon was funding some 12 initiatives across the United States assessing business models for supporting humanities publishing and open-access journal publishing; developing evaluation guidelines for scholarship in multimedia modes; and developing platforms and software to manage, produce, and preserve digital scholarship. The accumulative goals of these initiatives are to facilitate the transition to and strengthen heterogeneity in the multiple modes and media of scholarly communication in the humanities and humanistic social sciences.

And so to the opportunities in this flux. Rather than bemoan this state of affairs by recourse to a "forced binary" pitting digital against codex genres and forms, and the long book form against other forms, let's reflect on how the continued investment in a singular model of scholarly excellence has consequences.[5] As Abby Smith Rumsey wrote in the SCI8 report of the Scholarly Communication Institute, "Current print-based models of scholarly production, assessment, and publication have proven insufficient to meet the demands of scholars and students in the twenty-first century" (5). And she continued:

> The reliance of faculty on tenure and review models tied to endangered print genres leads to the disregard of innovation and new methodologies. And mobile digitally fluent students entering undergraduate and graduate schools are at risk of alienation from the historic core of humanistic inquiry, constrained by outmoded regimes of creation and access.[6]

Stifling experimentation and innovation. Damping student passion for advanced work in the humanities. Devaluing collaborative modes of scholarly inquiry in the humanities. Digging in rather than digging out to the future.

The traditional model of valuing humanities inquiry and its practices of production will be increasingly inadequate to the many kinds of work future humanists will do, its methodologies, its forms, its audiences, its users, and the entire ensemble of actors involved in producing, circulating, and responding to scholarly communication. As Claire Bond Potter wrote in the April 2015 issue of *Perspectives on History* published by the American Historical Association, "Digital technology is diversifying, not destroying, scholarly publication."[7] So let's rethink the defining place of the book as it signifies in the humanistic disciplines.

First, a shard of historical perspective. In *The Book and the Renaissance* Andrew Pettegree invokes the phrase "the humanist mythology of print" to remind readers that the invention of the printing press was about making money in a new communication environment and making new kinds of readers for reproducible books; and that the ensemble of changes rapidly unfolding was about the transformation of the institution of the library and the shifting notion of scholarly identity. Unhappy scholars, for whom the printing press threatened to debase the world of the mind and the imagination, futilely hoped to stem the tide of high-speed production of multiple copies.[8] For them, this technological revolution threatened their expertise, status, value, and privilege as conservators and minders of received knowledge. Others glimpsed the potential benefits of reproducible type: acceleration of production, portability, accessibility, and diversification of centers and purveyors of knowledge, among others.

And next, a bit of bookish deconstruction. The book as it's been known may not have been the book as it's been known. In the Vimeo production *This Is Not a Book*, Alan Liu unsettles common wisdom, situating the physical book as "not a book," just as an e-book is not "a book" in the discourse of those who bemoan the end of the book.[9] Unpacking the common definition of "the book" as a physical object, Liu suggests that what is most critical to people's understanding of the book is its status as a long form of attention, identified with the idea of permanence, standards of excellence, and authoritativeness. Liu's thesis is that the physical book is not a book either, arguing, vis-à-vis book history, that the materiality associated with the book is "historically situated, contingent, ephemeral, and highly irregular." Indeed, he observes counterintuitively, "The long form book is not standard, regular, and authoritative"; rather, "The more authoritative the book, the more it is likely to be read discontinuously."[10] Thus, he proposes, the printed book is "only a physical metaphor for the book," concluding that, increasingly, Big Data and digitally environed projects will enable scholars to discern long forms of attention from the past in new ways.

And now for a glimpse of bookish persistence. Many academic humanists struggle with the loss of materiality of the traditional print book, so much a part of the scholarly imaginary. So it might be salutary to keep in mind the ways in which the desire for the physical form of the book returns as a kind of repressed. Here's one such expression of that desire. In a March 2012 online journal, Craig Mod composed a multimedia essay entitled "The Digital-Physical: On Building Flipboard for iPhone and Finding the Edges of our Digital Narratives."[11] Mod wrote of the "feeling of thinness that I believe many of us grapple with working digitally. It's a product of the ethereality inherent to computer work. The more the entirety of the creation process lives in bits, the less solid the things we're creating feel in our minds."[12] In response to this unbearable feeling of thinness, Mod created an eight-pound book with hard edges, a physical book assembled out of "git" comments and design sketches involved in building a digital tool. Intriguingly, the physical book form becomes a platform visualizing the flow of work and the participation of team members in a born-digital project. In the end, Mod writes, "What projects like this speak to is the unique and increasingly important value we can give data by abstracting physicality. . . . Creating that space. Capturing a journey effortlessly in bits, and then giving it *edges*. This dance makes our digital experiences more understandable, parseable, consumable."[13] While the book, as Mod observes, cannot capture the emotion of putting the Flipboard app together, it can capture in its visuality and weightiness the "activity" of the project.

Finally, a bit of debunking with regard to the value of weight. Across the years I've certainly read many good, some great, books. But I've read bad books, predictable books. I've read books whose successive chapters end up saying much the same thing again and again, but about different objects. I've read books with one or two good chapters. I've read books that don't cohere into a long argument. I've read books whose argument could have been condensed in one long essay. As Paul Conway observed to me, "The only argument for the long-form book is that the knowledge transmitted and the rhetorical method for doing so requires a long form." Indeed, he insisted, "Many long-form books are really a sequence of arguments that could be packaged/ parsed into appropriate and accessible segments."[14] In addition, I've known scholars over the years whose métier would have been the long-form essay, if there had been venues for publishing such an essay. I've known scholars whose accumulated gravitas in a field is the result of the sedimented impact of a succession of essays that kept probing different topics or archives or theoretical frameworks; scholars, that is, for whom the long-form book was constraining as a project. I've known scholars for whom the book could only work if it was pieced together experimentally, rather than formulaically. The opportunity now available is the opportunity to dislodge the hold of the book form and pursue a diversity of scholarly projects and products.

The long-form physical book is, and will remain, a particular container for circulating knowledge and a measure of excellence in the corner of the academy that is the humanities and humanistic social sciences. But the physical book will be only one form of "bookishness," to invoke Tara McPherson's rakish term; and that bookishness will take a variety of forms and unfold through a variety of media and modes.[15] Going forward, humanities scholars will communicate their work in a complex, shifting environment with its new ecology of bookishness.

To effectively negotiate this scholarly communication system, academic humanists will expand their familiarity with all kinds of tools and platforms useful in pursuing their research and composing their scholarly products. They will assess a multiplicity of scholarly vehicles, including but not limited to the common article and book forms. Many will migrate to makers' spaces and collaborative, born-digital projects. They will discover new relationships with readers. They will become familiar with layered practices of scholarly authorization. They will attend to evolving evaluative criteria for judging scholarly achievement.

Familiarity with tools and platforms. The terms of reference are no longer just pen/paper, or computer/pdf files. They encompass platforms, protocols, affordances, modes of visualization, and management systems for pursuing and composing humanities scholarship. Websites of reference include BambooDiRT, a portal providing information and links to digital research tools out there for humanists to use in their research and authoring activities.[16] Programs and apps of reference include Zotero, "the only research tool that automatically senses content, allowing you to add it to your personal library with a single click," and Scribd.com, a site onto which to upload text in various formats for comment and for building communities of reading.[17]

Then too, there are the authoring tools and environments about which to become familiar. With freeware, such as the blog site WordPress. With PressForward (developed out of the Roy Rosenzweig Center for History and New Media), a site for "scholarship and publication, the Web Way."[18] Press-Forward culls the Web for the best online scholarship, "including scholarly blogs, digital projects, and other web genres that don't fit into traditional articles or books."[19] With Scalar, an authoring and publishing tool developed by McPherson and her collaborators in the Alliance for Networking Visual Culture out of the University of Southern California, and funded by the Mellon Foundation and the NEH. Scalar joins multiple software packages together into one platform, enabling scholars to author works that incorporate visual, aural, textual, video, and database materials.[20] And in the future, with Cairn, a platform in development by Cheryl Ball at the University of West Virginia and Andrew Morrison at the Oslo School of Architecture and Design in Norway. Funded by Mellon, Cairn will be "an online, free and open-source system that will help editors of scholarly multimedia journals, books and data sets engage in building and reading multimedia-rich, peer-reviewed content."[21]

And these are only a few of the tools, sites, and authoring platforms that support faculty as they pursue research projects and compose their work for publication. Some will be displaced by the next "big thing." Some will fizzle. Some have legs and will keep going. Just trying to stay abreast of what's out there becomes a dizzying affair.

Familiarity with new forms of bookishness. No longer must scholars think of communicating their work in only two vehicle lengths, the printed article and printed book; for, as Pochoda observes: "The digital regime, in principle, permits publication in any length and in a wide and expanding variety of digital (as well as print) containers."[22] Indeed, right now academic humanists can produce books in digital and print versions simultaneously. They can write in lengths that are longer than the normative article form and shorter than the normative monograph form. Middle-length and middle-state publishing ventures address this glaring lacuna in scholarly communication in the humanities. The Trio Series at the University of Chicago Press is one such venture, publishing long essays "address[ing] an important theme in critical theory, philosophy, or cultural studies through three extended essays written in close collaboration by leading scholars." The 2015 book entitled *Nothing*, for instance, offers "three inquiries in Buddhism."[23] The Palgrave Pivot imprint publishes scholarly work "at lengths of between 25,000 and 50,000 words—longer than a journal article, but shorter than a monograph." David Elliott's *Fukushima: Impacts and Implications*, published in 2012, was a winner of the CHOICE Outstanding Academic Titles award in 2013.[24] There are opportunities for humanities scholars to participate in experiments with repackaging, such as the Princeton Shorts series. There are quick print opportunities to repurpose earlier work into new collections. There are experimental presses, on the model of Phantom Limb. There are write-on-demand mash-ups on hot topics in e-book format. There are born-digital journals, such as *Kairos*; and online websites deploying born-digital publishing platforms, such as Scalar, mentioned above. And at the other end of the spectrum that runs from long-form book to microforms, there are short forms, such as blogs and apps.

In this ecology of heterogeneous "containers," the notion of the fixedness of the scholarly product seems more opaque than it does in the traditional print landscape. Paul Conway observes that the book is "taking multiple forms as a curated object, fixed, done, set and then handed off to preservation services (such as libraries) for long term care." Thus, even while the "long form curated object" may be "digital, paper, and a combination of the two . . . the notion of fixing the argument—a long one at that—will persist."[25] But, increasingly, as a prequel to that fixing, there is elasticity in the publishing system. At the 2011 HASTAC conference, Daniel J. Cohen remarked that inertness as an assumption of scholarly publication is becoming a bit outré. He challenged those assembled, by asking: "How can we wean ourselves from the inertness of knowledge, the sense that once it's in a book, it's done."[26] He answered his own question by suggesting that there's "sort of" publishing, the publishing of bits and pieces of scholarly and theoretical work, some of which will be in blogs, some in other forms.[27] In sort-of publishing, humanities scholars circulate pieces of their ideas publicly, inviting or inciting response. In this way, they test their arguments, curate early and intermediate stages of ideation, and attract potential readers on the way to preparing their work for a more fixed form of publication.

Familiarity with new genres of born-digital scholarship. Adjusting to the new platform environment, academic humanists discover how it is that new modes and media of communicating scholarly work alter the conceptualization of what to compose, what to communicate, and how best to display and array arguments, evidence, and archival materials. Indeed, the value of humanities scholarship lies in the interpretive capacities to illuminate; and new modes of scholarly composition and communication enable those who adapt them to expand interpretive capabilities.[28] Always eloquent in her reflection on the processes and practices of authoring platforms, McPherson early on "recognize[d] certain genres or types of scholarship well suited to database platforms," among them "the animated archive, the experiential argument, the interactive documentary, and the spatialized essay, as well as various forms of simulation or visualization."[29]

In born-digital multimedia platforms, modes of unfolding scholarly analyses and their vehicles of presentation may be progressive and iterative and recursive and interactive, all at once, as McPherson argues of the epistemological shifts attending multimodal scholarly communication. They may, paradoxically, be approached and navigated as long form and middle form and short form simultaneously, depending upon how readers/users move through them—upon whether they browse or follow a map or read text or listen in. They may be experienced as conjunctions of deep, surface, distant, and affective readings.

And with regard to born-digital projects, "doneness" can be a more complicated state to reach. Matthew G. Kirschenbaum introduced a special section of articles in a 2009 volume of *Digital Humanities Quarterly* by asking: "What is the measure of 'completeness' in a medium where the prevailing wisdom is to celebrate the incomplete, the open-ended, and the extensible." Essays in the special section took up questions of doneness in born-digital projects involving emergent tools, platforms, and interactive websites. Here the complexities of doneness circle around versions and releases and going live-ness, and extend to issues of "digital preservation and version control."[30]

Familiarity with potential new relationships with readers. In this ecology, humanities scholars enter new relationships with readers, whom they may engage at all stages of authoring their work. Readers—or "users"—may become active interlocutors, who, as Rumsey notes, "are each and every one potential authors and publishers as well as readers."[31] She notes that as "users of content, "the new audience expects not only to read, but to listen, to look, to download and re-use."[32] In circulation, scholarly content will travel through networks that include not only scholar-peers but a broader array of graduate and undergraduate students; scholarly networks that are not only institutionally based but globally networked in their configuration. It may even reach different kinds of "readers," different kinds of publics.

And readers will be differently positioned vis-à-vis the object before them. Reflecting on the experience of authoring *How Text Lost Its Source: Magnetic Recording Cultures,* a Scalar dissertation, Jentery Sayers noted the potential for readers to "select how a book's content is viewed." "These views," he observed, "range from 'text-only' and 'media-emphasis' to a radial visualization, a force-directed graph, and a history browser. Again, this array of perspectives brushes against any totalizing account of media history. . . . It also destabilizes a scholar's authority over an audience's interpretation as it allows them to arrange and re-arrange content."[33] Readers gain agency to take their own route through a born-digital scholarly site. This release from the author's directed itinerary may enhance readers' pleasures of discovery, or intensify the indeterminacy of readers' versions of the argument, stakes, and impact of the scholarship. Effectively, the multiplicity of readings, viewings, and/or hearings readers pursue decenters the knowing "I" assumed to lie at the center of humanistic inquiry and distributes knowledge making across readerships and networks of relationality.

Familiarity with evolving processes of scholarly authorization. And what of the evaluative systems for vetting scholarly work? The traditional vetting system of peer review rests on the assessment of scholar-experts reading blindly, without knowledge of the identity of the author. That system is still standard in submission of manuscripts to most journals and presses, whether publication comes out in print or e-book format. But the addition of so many other possible containers or vehicles for scholarly work complicates the system of peer review, implicating evolving processes of authorization and evaluation. Kathleen Fitzpatrick, director of scholarly communications at the Modern Language Association and author of *Planned Obsolescence: Publishing, Technology, and the Future of the Academy*, offers trenchant analysis of the contemporary state of play in review practices, calling attention to the ways in which new platforms, among them blogs and social media, enable online publication that circumvents customary norms of authorization and the ways in which versions of "bookishness" can now enter multiple review systems, some traditional, some hybrid, some experimental.[34]

Fitzpatrick herself participated in a mixed review process in the publication of *Planned Obsolescence*: New York University Press sought traditional peer review from experts in media studies; and Fitzpatrick mounted an open version of the manuscript in MediaCommons, soliciting peer-to-peer review from anyone who registered as a reviewer on the site. Moreover, within the book she advanced her argument for open peer review in the chapter entitled "Beyond Metrics: Community Authorization and Open Peer Review." Subsequently she codirected a Mellon-funded project assessing issues related to the values, practices, labor, and platforms necessary to implement peer-to-peer review systems.[35]

With regard to born-digital work, new models for review are emerging to evaluate developmental stages of projects using Big Data and producing substantial metadata, websites, and new tools and platforms. Among them, NINES (Networked Infrastructure for Nineteenth-Century Electronic Scholarship) has attempted to instill a peer-review ethic in its digital objects aggregation project. And centerNet's Digital Humanities Commons matches scholar experts with particular interests to projects around the globe and seeks peer reviewers for projects in the making. But the diversity of projects, the reach of multidisciplinary collaborations, the pressures of ensuring preservation, all require far more extensive, complex, and differentiated review mechanisms. Again, it's a one-size-does-not-fit-all moment.

Attention to evolving evaluative criteria for judging scholarly achievement. Humanities faculty and university administrators responsible for tenure and promotion decisions have a long history of evaluating the printed article form and book form. And though there is often contention around on-the-ground evaluations of import, quality, and intervention within disciplines and across disciplinary boundaries, there is little contention about how one goes about evaluating those forms. This is true of the e-book form as well as the printed book form, the online journal article as well as the print journal form. Add to this mix multiple new containers for born-digital work and the challenges ahead become formidable, due to new forms of expertise required to evaluate them. As Jennifer Howard explores in the *Chronicle for Higher Education*, the environment for reviewing digitally environed scholarship has yet to mature.[36]

In that piece, Howard cites Brett Bobley, director of the NEH's Office of Digital Humanities. Bobley writes:

> In the past, an edition was judged almost entirely on the scholarship (rightly so). But in the digital realm, we also need to judge it on their digital infrastructure. Do they have useful metadata? A sustainability plan? Are they conforming with library/archive standards? Do they have an API (application programming interface) to enable others to repurpose the data or mash it up with other data? Etc. These are all important issues.[37]

As with review processes noted above, there are evaluative models out there. PressForward at George Mason assesses quality blogs; and some journals provide website reviews, such as *Digital Humanities Quarterly*.[38] There are also recommendations for the components of adequate review. Julia Flanders, editor of DHQ, cited by Howard in the *Chronicle* piece, observes that "the key elements are the content, the digital tools used to build it, how its data are structured, and the interface."[39]

Sounds like a plan! But the number of humanists prepared to evaluate new modes and media of scholarly communication on departmental review committees and the faculty at large is still modest. Those tasked with evaluation look for guidance from peers in the field of digital humanities and from professional organizations, such as the Modern Language Association and its *Guidelines for Evaluating Work with Digital Media*.[40] In the meantime, pressures are considerable on scholars working in new modes and digital environments: they now have to explain what is scholarly about their work; situate the work; justify it; and document their role or roles in the project. They have to ensure that department chairs and review committee members have available guidelines in hand when they do their evaluations.

Moreover, faculty interested in pursuing new methods, modes, and media of scholarly inquiry and communication continue to confront the problem of conventional expectations about what "counts" as scholarly work. Many faculty who pursue, or consider pursuing, new digital methods and digital modes of communication find that such work must be "in addition" to producing work in conventional containers of printed book and article forms. To engage this issue, the Five College Digital Humanities consortium launched an initiative in 2015 titled "The New Rigor." Its purpose is to bring various stakeholders together—faculty, staff, students—to "start from scratch" and model a "structure of evaluation or assessment—in terms of peer review, tenure and promotion, or student research experience" that "would encourage [faculty] to do digital work."[41]

New terms of reference. New forms of bookishness. New genres of scholarly productivity. Potential new relationships with readers. Evolving practices of peer review. Evolving evaluation criteria in tenure and promotion.

Academic humanists confront a fluid, and demanding, publication/ communication scene. The multiplication of the vehicles, media, speed, and sociality of scholarly communication enables humanities scholars to work in the form of communication most compatible with their particular project, flexible imagination, scope of interest, argumentative mode, and desire for impact and visibility. Sometimes scholars choose one form or mode over another; sometimes they move between and ply the terrain of digital-physical bookishness. Sometimes they take the plunge. In this complex, shifting environment, then, traditional forms of bookishness will persist alongside new forms of bookishness. The book as it's been known will no longer be the sole "gold standard." The currency of humanistic scholarship will be multiple.

This evolving ecology of scholarly communication puts every aspect of scholarship into play: its germination; its unfolding through particular forms of interpretation, argumentation, and presentation; its environment of composition; its media of presentation; its preparation for circulation; its address to readers; and its circulation and, increasingly, its reuse. It often involves an ensemble of actors: individual scholars, libraries and librarians, publishers, computer technicians, administrators, funders, and heterogeneous users. In this context, scholars are multipositioned as authors and also collaborators, project managers, publishers, disseminators, and curators of their work.[42] As Pochoda sums it up: "No traditional publishing role, much less traditional publishing entity, seems stable or settled in the fully digital universe: the digital system, by its nature, empowers its components to shed rigid identities and labels and be not a this or a that but both, and more, simultaneously and sequentially."[43]

Long forms and short forms, experimental forms, middle-state forms and as-yet-imagined forms. Multimedia forms, at once haptic and visual and textual and aural. Forms distributed, in process, and interactive. The everything-that's-in-play unsettles those who are used to the traditional legacy-print system, those who are experimenting with or immersed in new modes and models of scholarly communication, those who are tasked with evaluating the quality, reach, and impact of a scholar's work, and those just beginning their doctoral studies. Questions about what the evolving terrain will look like and how to successfully navigate its complexity can only multiply. Here are just a few, articulated in a 2012 meeting of participants in the Scalar project at USC. How long is long? How short is short? What's the relationship of genre and longevity? What happens to born-digital scholarship inadequately preserved and curated? What's the role of the ephemeral in humanities scholarship?

And there are so many more: How might doctoral students prepare to experiment in these genres and faculty prepare to guide them? How do faculty and students learn to navigate them, read them? What is becoming of reading, for faculty and for students? Following the funding: who is going to ensure the longevity, the preservation, of online scholarly presentations and publications? And how are continuing questions of evaluative criteria going to be addressed? There are anxieties to be confronted and perhaps allayed, perhaps intensified. And there are intellectual rewards to be reaped in this new ecology of scholarly communication.

The scholarly communications system is a system in radical transition. But it is one of exciting opportunities. Cohen, at once optimistic and cautionary, gets my last word here. "Surely," he observes,

> we can reorient ourselves to our true core values—to honor creativity and quality—which will still guide us to many traditionally published works but will also allow us to consider works in some nontraditional venues such as open access journals, blogs or articles written and posted on a personal website or institutional repository, or non-narrative digital projects.[44]

Cohen's challenge leads me to the next discussion—humanists and the open-access movement.

Going Open

Time was, the afterlife of humanities scholarship lived out in the copies of books stored on some number of library shelves. It left traces in print on catalog cards, visible to the browser through Dewey's decimal system. If authors had no copies left on their personal bookshelves because they'd given them away to friends and relatives, they might luck out and find one in a used bookstore somewhere. Then books became accessible through search engines and digitized library catalogs. But they had yet to become searchable themselves or accessible for download.

Now out-of-print books come to readers through academic presses that digitize and deliver back catalogs in digital form for a fee. And the afterlife of journal essays is lived out in such platforms as JSTOR and Project MUSE, accessible to academics through gated library subscriptions. Now too they come to readers in multiple forms of open access, though scholarly books can still be locked up through draconian copyright restrictions. Google Books delivers whole books out of copyright and snippets of books in copyright. Some presses strike deals with Google to deliver back catalogs openly through Google Books. And, if copyright has reverted back to the author, institutional repositories at colleges and universities make out-of-print books by faculty openly accessible under specified conditions.

Increasingly, scholarly work, in book and article forms, can live "open" in its two primary modes of green and gold open access. Green open access is the term of reference for the decision by authors to retain copyright and archive their publications or data sets through well-managed institutional repositories. Articles can be made openly available in preprint or postprint versions, immediately accessible or accessible after an embargo period, commonly but not uniformly 12 months. Gold open access is publisher controlled. Going gold involves publishing in journals in which all content is freely provided or in for-profit journals with an open-access option. In both gold cases, journals require a payment fee or article processing charge (APC) for publishing open access, commonly running from $1,000 to $3,000. Gold model payments made by authors or their organizational proxies commonly come out of grant monies, though sometimes they come from funding agencies directly.[1]

Through these evolving arrangements, scholars can now share their work before it is ready for publication, multiply the networks for work upon its publication, stretch its impact through multiple formats, and extend its afterlife. They can go open for professional ends: to get work out sooner, gain a wider audience, extend its impact. They can go open for field-related ends: to excite other scholars, invite them to the conversation, intervene in debates. They can go open for the benefit of others: to make work easily accessible to emergent scholars nearby and around the globe. They can go open for utopian ends: to address issues of educational injustice related to the disparities between haves and have-nots, and the resource-rich and resource-strained institutions in this country and around the globe.[2]

The call for "maximum access and optimal re-use," as Tom Cochrane observes,[3] has been in the air ever since Tim Berners-Lee invented the World Wide Web in 1989. That call is the effect of multiple intersecting forces: *the imaginary of the knowledge commons, exigencies of professionalism, the politics of government funding, and the transition in the scholarly publishing system* noted in the previous section of this book. The *imaginary* of what Michel Bauwenson terms a "commons-based knowledge society"[4] derives from the affordances attached to networked cyberinfrastructure: the communicative capacities of digital technologies and the ease of archiving and aggregating the Big Data of research for repurposing and reuse. It also derives from the utopian commitment to meeting grand challenges—of climate change, health delivery, disease eradication, economic development, and educational and social justice and the animating vision of a modern-day distributed Alexandrian library, whose common goods can be freely accessed and opened not just to academic researchers but to everyone around the globe with a connective device.

The *exigencies of professionalism* revolve around the faculty desire for impact and an extended afterlife to scholarly work; the increasing pressure to quantify excellence in scholarly output; and the urgency in STEM and medical disciplines to distribute research findings quickly, in the competition for prestige through grant funding, patenting, and technology transfer. The *political* forces encompass the pressure on federal government agencies, as the principal funders of STEM and medical research, to assure taxpayers that their monies are well spent and the knowledge they paid for is accessible; and the national interest in maintaining competitive advantage in the global marketplace of patents, inventions, and new technologies.

Finally, there is the impact of the *three-decades long churning of scholarly publishing systems*. Researchers in science and STEM fields, and quantitative social sciences, have struggled through dramatic changes in journal publication.

Humanities faculty and qualitative social scientists have struggled through pressures on book publication. These systems in turmoil are distinct and linked. Let me explore the trend to open access in the sciences before turning to trends in open in the humanities.

"The mid-1980s to 1990s," Paul Conway observes, "was marked by massive price inflation as for-profit journal publishers moved aggressively toward electronic publication."[5] Scientific researchers grew restive with commercial control of access to their work and with the rapacious pricing by for-profit publishing giants, foremost among them Elsevier, which maintain a near monopoly on the prestige market for results of research in STEM and medical fields. Thus, the decade from the mid-1990s to the mid-2000s, according to Conway, "was marked by recognition, diagnosis, and possible solutions to the problem, and the identification of OA as a viable option."[6]

By the early 2000s, restiveness turned to advocacy. Calls for an alternative system for circulating new knowledge gained purchase and momentum.[7] In quick succession, three influential and widely referenced statements defining open access and issuing the call for open in the STEM fields and sciences generally appeared: the Budapest (2002), Berlin (2003), and Bethesda (2003) statements. Here is the Budapest statement, giving an account of the benefits, for authors and readers, in having open access to research findings: "Many different initiatives have shown that open access is economically feasible, that it gives readers extraordinary power to find and make use of relevant literature, and that it gives authors and their works vast and measurable new visibility, readership, and impact."[8] And here is its call for action:

> To secure these benefits for all, we call on all interested institutions and individuals to help open up access to the rest of this literature and remove the barriers, especially the price barriers, that stand in the way. The more who join the effort to advance this cause, the sooner we will all enjoy the benefits of open access.[9]

Since these calls, Conway continues, a "third decade has been marked by acceptance (momentum) of the OA models, but also increasingly complicated strategies to break the hold of commercial publishers and to create an economical and politically-acceptable OA regime."[10] After a decade plus of manifestos, the trend toward open is well launched, if not untroubled.

Across the globe open access has become a mandated feature of research in medical fields, though no uniform mandate has emerged. In the United States, the National Institutes of Health set its public access policy to meet the mandate of Congress's Omnibus Appropriations Act of 2009, requiring "that NIH-funded researchers submit a copy of their refereed journal articles to PMC (formerly PubMed Central) upon acceptance for publication, to be made publicly available no later than 12 months after publication."[11] When, in early 2012, a bill to roll back the mandate was introduced in Congress, an outpouring of support for open access in higher education ensued. Among those weighing in were 11 university provosts in the CIC (Consortium of Institutional Cooperation, composed of Big Ten universities plus the University of Chicago). Collectively, they issued a statement entitled "Values and Scholarship" that reaffirmed the importance of open access for the advancement of "the public good."[12] "Toward that end," they wrote, "our scholars seek to share information broadly as the most effective way to assure excellence—not just for themselves, or for a particular university, but for the relevance of their disciplines and the world-changing outcomes each can produce."[13] In mid-2012, the Faculty Senate at the University of California, San Francisco, arguably the most prestigious life sciences center in the country, voted "to make electronic versions of current or future scientific articles freely available to the public."[14] UCSF was among the first of the Research 1 public universities to do so. And on February 22, 2013, the Office of Science and Technology Policy in the White House issued the directive "Increasing Access to the Results of Federally Funded Scientific Research" to ensure that "the direct results of federally funded scientific research are made available to and useful for the public, industry, and the scientific community. Such results include peer-reviewed publications and digital data."[15]

At the same time, research scientists, engineers, and mathematicians have been protesting against the high cost of publication in their fields. In early 2012, thousands of researchers in the United States and abroad signed the "Cost of Knowledge" statement calling for a boycott of Elsevier as the foremost publisher of leading science journals. The statement denounces "a system in which commercial publishers make profits based on the free labor of mathematicians and subscription fees from their institutions' libraries, for a service that has become largely unnecessary."[16] On April 10, 2012, the *Guardian* in England weighed in on the deleterious effects of the prohibitive pricing of journals:

> In the arid language of modern economics, information is "non-rival," which is to say that one person can have more without another having less—so there ought to be no need for anyone to be locked out by subscriptions. . . . The rationing of reading is always objectionable, but the consequences are suddenly graver because of text-mining technologies. These look across studies to uncover truths invisible to the human eye— truths which might sometimes save lives—and yet papers that languish behind pay walls are not available to be crunched in this way.[17]

By August 2015, 15,185 researchers from around the world had signed the pledge, many committing not to publish in Elsevier journals; not to referee for said journals; and not to do editorial work for them. The rationing of reading; the firewall around data; the inflation of pay-to-publish economics; the exploitation of scholarly labor—these are the terms through which scientists, engineers, and mathematicians articulate their continued frustrations with the scholarly publishing system.[18]

Across campuses, in buildings housing literature, language, history, anthropology, classics, and philosophy departments, humanities faculty and qualitative social scientists have been confronting changes in the system of book publishing. The journal publishing system in the humanities and humanistic social sciences differs from the system in the science and STEM fields. Comparatively, journal publishing in these fields tends to be a shoestring affair, dependent on universities to provide some space, sometimes release time for editors, some administrative expertise of library and press staff, and some modest budgetary commitment to supplement subscription fees. Individual subscriptions are also modestly priced. Or they are a benefit of membership in professional associations. In this system, there is no incentive drawing for-profit publishers into the market. The turmoil in the humanities and humanistic social sciences involves the publication of the book.

In the previous section, I sketched the dynamics of this changing publishing system. Here, it is important to reiterate that the crisis in academic book publishing is related to but also independent of the crisis of the exorbitant cost of science journals published by for-profit corporations. Library funds formerly designated for the purchase of academic press lists have had to be diverted to cover the rising costs of journals in the science and STEM fields. Standing orders for purchases of academic press books have dwindled to between 200 and 300 per book. But there are other contributing factors to the turmoil of the system, among them the impact of digitization on academic book publishing, the online sales of used books, the changing purchasing and accessing habits of scholars themselves, and the shift from positioning academic publishing as a public good to approaching it as a break-even or profit-making venture. With regard to book publishing, the critical issues thus revolve around an unsustainable marketplace, an inadequate business model, and a paucity of alternatives. In this roiling environment, the call for open access as a solution to a problem and as a social good adds more confusion than light to efforts of evolving sustainable publishing models.

Thus, while the sense of urgency and the immediacy of relevance are palpable in the sciences, in the humanities the move to open access has had slower uptake. Slow uptake is an effect of the attenuation of urgency in the life of tenured academic humanists and the relative scarcity of data-driven research with potential immediate benefits for the public and the field. Scholarship in the humanities often moves in slow time, compared to that in STEM and medical fields. If it is successful, it eventuates in potentially paradigm-shifting books, pieces of it to be spun off along the way in journal articles. Rarely are preprints of those articles mounted on websites. Mostly, humanists are habituated to waiting six months to a year for peer reviews of book and article manuscripts, and two years from the time of contract to publication.

In a 2005 piece entitled "Promoting Open Access in the Humanities," Peter Suber, now director of the Harvard University Office for Scholarly Communication, cataloged multiple features of work in the humanities that make open-access publishing less attractive for humanists, among them less pricey journal subscriptions noted above; less access to grant-funded research that bears the costs of author processing charges; less political pressure from a taxpaying public that rarely thinks of humanistic scholarship as life-saving; less demand for access to preprint articles; high copyright fees for the use of visuals and printed material such as poems; and the secondary status of articles versus books in the humanities, for which faculty somehow imagine royalties as compensation for the slow time it takes to bring them to publication.[19] And, of course, there have been no external mandates that humanities scholarship must be deposited in institutional repositories. Despite these formidable obstacles to an altered imaginary of professional practice, however, Suber made the call for humanists to change their publishing practices, beginning with journal articles, which he described as "the low-hanging fruit for open access" in the humanities.[20]

Five years later, Daniel J. Cohen, formerly of George Mason University's Roy Rosenzweig Center for History and New Media and now the director of the Digital Public Library of America, impatiently promoted open-access thinking in the humanities. Cohen made a trenchant case for open-access initiatives by factoring in the "hidden cost" to humanities scholars of presenting one's work in the closed publication system. The case invokes economic terms humanists rarely consider when talking about publishing. "*The largest hidden cost is the invisibility of what you publish*" (emphasis his), he observes: "When you publish somewhere that is behind gates, or in paper only, you are resigning all of that hard work to invisibility in the age of the open web. You may reach a few peers in your field, but you miss out on the broader dissemination of your work, including to potential other fans."[21] This cost is a high one to pay for maintaining the status quo of traditional publication formats, venues, and values.

Ten years have passed by since Suber's call and five years since Cohen's trenchant riposte about publishing behind a firewall. Initiatives in open-access journal publication are developing rapidly, if at different paces and through different practices around the world. During those years, humanities faculty, a good number of them working in media studies and digital humanities, but also faculty working in a diverse range of other fields, have been changing the ways they communicate their work by pursuing open-access options. As scholars change their habits and dispositions with regard to communicating open, there are, of course, concerns, issues, constraints, and contentious debate. For a detailed exploration of open access in the humanities, readers can turn to Martin Paul Eve's 2014 *Open Access and the Humanities: Contexts, Controversies and the Future*. Written by this cofounder of the Open Library of Humanities (OLH) and published by Cambridge University Press, Eve's book is, to be sure, available in an online open-access version and for purchase on the press website.[22]

Here I want to explore how initiatives in open access are playing out in four arenas of scholarly publishing, briefly discussing *short-form writing, journal publications*, and *dissertations*, and lingering on *long-form books*.

New media writing. The arena in which open-access values predominate and practices operate at this moment are born-digital forms, embedded in the platforms of social media. While earlier generations of humanists commonly shared, and still share, early versions of their work in conference papers, now more and more faculty and doctoral students have taken to blogging, tweeting, and contributing to scholarly and professional conversations on "commons " sites such as the MLA Commons.[23] This short-form writing is scholarly activity with attitude and often substantial intellectual heft. It is termed "gray literature" on such sites as PressForward. "An experiment in new methods for capturing and highlighting presently orphaned or underappreciated scholarship," PressForward has launched a set of journals on the open Web, including proceedings of THATCamp unconferences; Digital Humanities Now, "an experimental, edited publication that highlights and distributes informally published digital humanities scholarship and resources from the open web"[24]; and *Data Curation Now*, a journal format to "identify and disseminate the 'gray literature' of white papers, project reports, and online writing that are so important to the field of digital libraries."[25]

Journal publications. The current state of journal publishing is in transition and transformation. Professional organizations are taking steps toward open. In the United States, the Modern Language Association now publishes accepted essays for its online journal *Profession* on a rolling basis throughout the year as well as issuing an annual e-book; the rolling version and annual e-book version are available to anyone accessing the website. Governments elsewhere around the world are affecting the trend to open in journals. In Brazil, for instance, academic journals seeking a rating of excellence from the educational board overseeing research, including journals in humanities fields, require contributors to include a statement in their submission materials permitting the journal to make the work available online. Particular fields are trending open. Open-access journals are increasingly common in digital humanities, among them the prestigious *Journal of Digital Humanities* and *Digital Humanities Quarterly*. And new "boutique" presses are spinning off innovative open-access journals to complement their commercial publications, such as the line of journals at the independent Intellect Press. And these are all initiatives conforming to the tradition of peer review. As of the summer of 2015, 517 peer-reviewed, open-access journals in languages and literatures and 152 in arts in general and arts and architecture, as well as 100 in Media and Communication, were listed on the DOAJ—Directory of Open Access Journals—website.[26]

Humanities scholars are publishing in open-access e-journals. They are conversing with journal editors about routes to open access, gaining knowledge about the repertoire of options available out there: full open access; or subscription for immediate use/free after embargo; or free from Web but printed for a fee.[27] They are advocating for limited embargo periods with journal publishers and editors, say, for a one-year period, so that their essays can be made openly available on their professional websites or in institutional repositories relatively soon after publication. They are securing their own copyright to their material. They have also launched their own peer-reviewed, open-access journals, such as the *Medieval Review* (open-access rolling reviews of new work out of Indiana University), *Southern Spaces* (an online, multimedia, open-access journal out of Emory University), and *Networks and Neighborhoods* (from the independent, antigatekeeping Punctum Books).[28] Or they have developed online, open-access components to traditional print journals, as in the semiannual *Postmedieval Forum*, described in its purpose statement as "a vibrant space for public, open, and spirited conversations relative to the content published in *postmedieval* and to pressing issues and questions circulating in medieval and early modern studies more broadly."[29]

An increasing number of humanists, then, are walking the walk of open-access values, despite what are still significant constraints in play. A major obstacle concerns article processing charges (APC). In the current environment of financial constraint, some journals are resorting to APCs as a mechanism for dealing with costs (processing, editing, formatting, packaging, and circulating scholarly research) that persist through the transition from paper to digital distribution. For-profit journals, therefore, may offer the option of publishing open access but set a steep price on that choice. So too with academic journals, as I was dismayed to discover when I learned that my desire to publish an article open access would cost me, or my university, $3,000. Gold OA options thus remain problematic for faculty in the humanities. It is costly for humanists to bear exorbitant APCs, because they rarely have grant funds available to cover those charges. And in many, though not all, colleges and universities, there is little to no funding available to humanities faculty to cover the charges, especially since there may be no college or university policy, in addition to policies developed to address government mandates and funding agency directives, that covers accessibility of nonfunded research output.[30] And yet there is activism and advocacy afoot, as humanities faculty raise the issue of APCs with their chairs and deans and provosts.

There are challenges as well for journal editors desirous of taking journals open access. This is particularly the case for nonprofit scholarly and professional associations trying to shift to gold OA. Those associations have depended for years on subscription fees to support their journals. Moreover, as premier, high-status publication venues in the disciplines, the journals are viewed by members as a significant benefit of membership. Associations thus face a double threat in pursuing the ideal of open access: the significant loss of subscription fees and the preference of members for embargos on open access for a fixed period. Even in this difficult economic and political situation, however, humanists are making the case for a future that trends toward open.

While the trend toward open in journal publishing shows no abatement, it remains the case that going open is not always an easy choice for humanists. Many humanities faculty are understandably concerned about the economic health of journals. They express allegiance to journals, ones for which they have done reviewing, ones they have helped launch, ones in which they have published, ones on whose editorial boards they serve, ones that have brought legitimacy to their field. Given the disproportionate share of library budgets dedicated to the big sciences journals, humanities faculty feel the threat to their venues of publication and want to see those journals find funding, survive, hang on, rev up. They know their professional lives depend upon them and, at least in the short term, upon the subscription model through which journals support themselves. As Chris Wickham, coauthor of the British Academy report on "open access journals in Humanities and Social Sciences," observed, there is a "felt need to protect journals from going under because no-one needs to buy them because all the research is already free."[31] This commitment to journal survival is important; but far more research based on the actual figures of subscription holders and readers/users is required to assess what the real impact of going open is on journals, both traditional print and online and some hybrid of the two. And there is evidence that many scholars keep up subscriptions to journals that are open to them through JSTOR and Project MUSE; that many value free and subscription access simultaneously.

Dissertations. At this point in time, many journals, and their faculty boards, adopt an embargo policy that establishes a fixed period (of months, years, or specified date) during which the journal is not openly available to readers who have not paid for a subscription. Other scholars advocate short embargo periods. There are good reasons for such an embargo for journals, among them subscriber benefits, subscription income for nonprofits, and a sense of exclusivity for a tight community of readers. But embargoes remain a contentious issue, as they certainly are with regard to a third arena of open-access publishing in the humanities—digital versions of dissertations, an arena that affects newly minted doctorates and junior faculty on tenure-track appointments expecting that their dissertations must be revised into a first book as a requirement for advancement.

I'm among those who advise against a long embargo period on dissertations. Sure, those in support of shorter embargo periods need to be mindful about the ability of senior scholars to risk new experiments in scholarly communication and open access without the threat to careers that doctoral students and emergent scholars might confront and/or imagine. Nonetheless, it is worth noting shifts in the practices and venues of scholarly work in the humanities, which will continue to be more fluid, more responsive to open forms and preprint iterations. But most important, it is worth registering that arguments in favor of long embargo periods reinforce what I see as the fantasy that the first book is just the dissertation in need of some tweaking. Reinforcing the twinning of dissertation and first book does a disservice to early scholars, to those with aspirations to do something different, something hybrid, and to those who want to get their ideas out and in the conversation.

There are certainly collective voices out there making the case for longer embargo periods. In response to university mandates that students submit their dissertations in digital form to open-access university repositories, leading scholarly associations have issued endorsements of embargoes on dissertations for up to six years. In 2013 the American Historical Association and the Organization of American Historians publicly endorsed such embargoes; and in spring 2014, the Medieval Academy of America followed suit, circulating its "Statement on Online Dissertation Embargoes," which strongly argues for student choice in the matter.[32] And mentors offer arguments in defense of embargos of humanities dissertations that speak to concerns for emerging scholars, including anxiety about the potential misuse and appropriation of intellectual property; concern about resistance of academic presses to contract a manuscript, a significant proportion of which has already appeared in print; and the indeterminate status of an openly accessible dissertation as a "publication."[33] Yet subtending all these concerns is the assumption that there is a close relationship between dissertations and first books, which, as I noted, is misleading in most cases. Moreover, the arguments don't factor in how press editorial practices have shifted in response to the emerging ecology of academic publishing and how editors seek out exciting new voices through available sources of scholarly communication. As a 2013 statement from the Harvard University Press Blog entitled "On Dissertation Embargoes" reads, "If you can't find it, you can't sign it."[34] Nor do those who argue for long embargoes acknowledge that some graduate students come in with expertise in and desire to share pieces of their scholarly writing in short-form modes; that some graduate students imagine addressing a larger public in their work; that some conceptualize innovative projects that invite interactive exchange with readers/users; that some might benefit by learning to live open early on.

The long-form book. With regard to the long form, that book which has been the traditional gold standard in humanities disciplines, there are initiatives as well. Humanities scholars are collaborating in new publishing ventures or negotiating with academic publishers for multiple formats of production, as in a combination of paper, print on demand, and open-access download. A sampling of books living open follows.

A number of humanities scholars have begun to publish their work through Open Humanities Press, the initiative of a group of self-organizing scholars around the globe pursuing new ways to publish the latest work of well-known scholars in a publicly facing, open online venue. The goals of Open Humanities Press are to "Advocate Open Access in the Humanities; Foster Community; Promote Intellectual Diversity; Improve the Experience of Academic Publishing; Explore New Forms of Scholarly Collaboration."[35] Editors have set as one of their series the provocatively titled "Liquid Books," an oxymoron that upends the humanist's imaginary of "the book" as solid, fixed, complete. As Gary Hall observed in "Radical Open Access in the Humanities," "Books have always been living and liquid," and now are "open to be annotated, edited, updated, reimagined."[36] Or there is the independent, renegade publishing venture noted above, Punctum Books. The international collective of scholars announces:

> **Punctum books** is an open-access and print-on-demand independent publisher dedicated to radically creative modes of intellectual inquiry and writing across a whimsical para-humanities assemblage. We specialize in neo-traditional and non-conventional scholarly work that productively twists and/or ignores academic norms, with an emphasis on books that fall length-wise between the article and the monograph—id est, novellas, in one sense or another.[37]

Punctum goes further to talk of "tak[ing] in strays" and "the imp-orphans of your thought and pen" and "little vagabonds," its jaunty self-description hinting at desires for fragments, clusters of ideation, scholarly riffs.[38]

Individual scholars are negotiating with presses for the simultaneous appearance of a book in open-access and commercial print versions, as did danah boyd. Principal researcher at Microsoft Research, research assistant professor in media, culture, and communication at New York University, and fellow at the Berkman Center for Internet and Society at Harvard, boyd negotiated with Yale University Press to have *It's Complicated: The Social Lives of Networked Teens* (2014) appear as a free download on her personal website the day the book appeared in the commercially marketed print form from the press. The copyright page tells readers: "For a digital copy of the work, please see the author's website at http://www.danah.org/."[39]

For even more variety in the way in which humanities bookishness lives in open, there is MediaCommons Press.[40] On *The Piracy Crusade* page is a link to a site hosting the "original manuscript" of the book by Arem Sinnreich, subtitled *How the Music Industry's War on Sharing Destroys Markets and Erodes Civil Liberties*.[41] The original manuscript was posted on MediaCommons Press for open peer review through the CommentPress platform. In his introduction to the online version for open comment, Sinnreich, attentive to issues about the labor of reviewing and the importance of its recognition as intellectual contribution and impact, informed reviewers: "All public and private commenters will be explicitly thanked in the Acknowledgments section of the printed book."[42] In late 2013, the University of Massachusetts Press published *The Piracy Crusade* under a Creative Commons 3.0 Attribution-NonCommercial-ShareAlike license. The license enabled Sinnreich to leave the original text online and openly accessible even as the book is available for sale on Amazon. com in hardcover, paperback, and Kindle versions. The website for *The Piracy Crusade* at MediaCommons Press announces that "in Spring of 2014, the published version of the book could be accessed in PDF format for free."[43]

The site presents other projects in various iterations of open. Chapter 6 of Thomas Streeter's *The Net Effect: Romanticism, Capitalism, and the Internet*, already published by New York University Press, is available for free download. There is a short "bio" of the open peer review stage of *Learning through Digital Media: Experiments in Technology and Pedagogy*, edited by R. Trebor Scholz, and the link to the published book website with its learning toolkit and constituent essays available for download or purchase.

For another iteration of open-access book publishing, consider the history of *Debates in the Digital Humanities*, edited by Matthew K. Gold for the University of Minnesota Press. *Debates*, in its first iteration of bookishness, appeared in print form in 2012, a compendium of essays and reproductions of born-digital formats, as in blogs and tweets. Its review process combined peer-to-peer open-access review and traditional blind peer review. Then in 2013 the "book" appeared in its open-access version of bookishness, an interactive

version of the printed *Debates* presented through a "custom-built social reading platform."[44] About this platform, the website announces: "The platform
marks a significant shift for *Debates in the Digital Humanities*, from a single
printed edition of collected essays to an expanded, ongoing digital publication stream."[45] Bookishness here morphs into open-access stream.

This riff on bookishnesses offers a glimpse of future possibilities and also
a cautionary tale of streams interrupted. On the site, Gold announces on January 3, 2013, the future appearance in 2013 of an "expanded edition" that will
contribute a "new cluster of essays."[46] But, in late 2014, this new iteration of
streaming bookishness had yet to appear. Now it's not as if journal issues in
traditional print formats aren't delayed in their publication date. Delay is not
an argument against these experiments. What this site signals is a stay-tuned
open-access process, a flexibly contented "publication," and a conception designed to track the movement of a field in real time. Such ventures, whether
carried through or still aspirational, become indicative of the fluidity of the
moment and the complexity of inhabiting a scholarly world in which multiple
concepts operate and commingle.

These are all versions of bookishness. Books digitized in accessible repositories. Books in dual or triple styles of dress. Born-digital bookishness.
Bookishness in stages of assuming form. Bookishness as ongoing stream.
Bookishness as augmented multimedia distribution. All versions of open negotiated between authors and publishers.

The possibilities are out there. So too a number of concerns and constraints. Humanities scholars voice a concern that placing a book in open-
access format undermines the financial gain that comes through royalties
for all the hard work of researching, writing, and revising the manuscript.
In 2005, Suber offered two counterarguments: one, that there is little available evidence that sales of a book are suppressed by having free access to the
book in, say, a pdf format.[47] Indeed, one might argue that wider accessibility
to one's work might increase sales. And two, very, very few scholars in humanities disciplines earn significant money in royalties from book sales, un-
less they produce a crossover book with commercial success. Stars and some
textbook authors, no doubt, do make money. But for most scholars, it's a matter of weighing potential greater impact and engagement with one's work,
and thus a reprieve from oblivion, against potential minimal income. And,
given that the average sales figure for printed books in the humanities from
academic presses, as noted earlier, is around 200–300, minimal is becoming
more minimal, if that's grammatically possible.

Presses and libraries face concerns related to finding an economic model
that accommodates open access while ensuring the sustainability of the
academic press. In response they have conceptualized new models for the

production of humanities monographs. One potentially paradigm-shifting venture is Knowledge Unlatched (KU), a project out of the United Kingdom involving libraries around the world that bundles participating libraries into a consortium that agrees to pay publishers a common title fee in exchange for new monographs being available in open-access venues. KU has completed its pilot phase, and is now testing scalability, based on the following model: "The Knowledge Unlatched model depends on many libraries from around the world sharing the payment of a single Title Fee to a publisher, in return for a book being made available on a *Creative Commons* license via OAPEN and HathiTrust as a fully downloadable PDF."[48] In this model, humanists are not asked to bear the cost of the fee to cover editorial and publishing costs; instead, that cost is shared by libraries, the more involved, the less the fee. A report on the pilot project describes how KU tested its economic model and assessed its value for authors, libraries, and publishers.[49]

Finally, humanities scholars and presses confront the problem of securing permission rights for digital versions of books and essays or for born-digital projects with embedded images, audio, and video. This constraint is what the authors of the "Code of Best Practices in Fair Use for Online Video," published online by the Center for Media and Social Impact at American University, refer to as "copyright uncertainty."[50] Indeed, copyright restrictions deeply embedded in the products of humanities scholarship continue to trump author prerogatives and constrict the boundaries of fair use. However, the boundaries of fair use, of reuse and repurposing, are slowly, and sometimes dramatically, expanding in some quarters through favorable court rulings regarding HathiTrust, due, in part, to activism on the part of scholars.

After forming in early 2014, the Author's Alliance, whose motto is "Promoting authorship for the public good by supporting authors who write to be read," filed an amicus brief on behalf of the defendant in the *Author's Guild v. Google* lawsuit directed at Google's Book Search project, arguing that "the dismantling of Book Search would be harmful to our mission of helping authors reach readers."[51] The Author's Guild, a long-lived organization dedicated to serving authors who make their living from writing and advocating for their interests in copyright protection, has filed a series of lawsuits seeking to strengthen that protection and limit the scope of digitization projects.[52] In an adversarial position, the Author's Alliance advocates for more flexibility in copyright law to address the needs of those who do not want their work to fall into oblivion, and "provide[s] information and tools designed to help authors better understand and manage key legal, technological, and institutional aspects of authorship in the digital age."[53] In the summary judgment issued by the U.S. District Court, Southern District of New York, Judge Denny Chin found in favor of Google and its Google Books project and against the plaintiffs, determining that "Google's use of the copyrighted works is highly transformative" and thus within fair use guidelines and so protected under copyright law (19) and that "Google Books provides a way for authors' works to become noticed, much like traditional in-store book displays" (25).[54] Such significant changes to the ecology of open-access book publication take place through the hard work of committed humanities scholars, as well as other academics, who organize, advocate, and register their arguments for more flexible copyright law and practices.

As discussion of these four arenas of scholarly communication makes clear, the desire to reach more readers is intensifying, the requisite changes in scholarly practices profound, the effort needed for faculty to move to open access formidable, the activism on the local level and the national level essential, the trend toward open in the humanities unstoppable.

Going open will not be easy for humanities faculty. First of all, there are the needs. To go open, humanities scholars need new tools, new platforms, and new models for assembling journals and books. They need new networked publishing structures, structures that organize ongoing "open review" as part of the process of scholarly writing, revision, and communication. They need a licensing infrastructure to facilitate open access and redistribution and reuse infrastructure. They need a robust cyberinfrastructure. They need flexible academic press policies. They need an expanded culture of peer review, at once traditional and peer-to-peer. In sum, they need people to contribute their expertise, time, and technical and editorial acumen to satisfying these needs.

There are two initiatives out there to support faculty with interests in going open. To contribute to changing the system, to how faculty research, write, make open, and revise scholarly work in the humanities, Kathleen Fitzpatrick established MediaCommons, a digital network for scholars. To provide licensing infrastructure, others pioneered "Creative Commons licenses" through which faculty retain copyright to their work and take responsibility for deciding how and where to make it accessible to others for copying, distribution, attribution, and reuse. Creative Commons is a nonprofit organization dedicated to the Internet commons; it "develops, supports, and stewards legal and technical infrastructure that maximizes digital creativity, sharing, and innovation."[55] Although there have been obstacles to a large-scale move to Creative Commons licenses, there are signs that academic presses and scholarly associations are beginning to resolve these issues and to build Creative Commons licenses into their contracts.

Then there is the imperative of advocacy, arguments that evaluation criteria need to be attuned to and adequate for hiring, tenure, and promotion processes in the changing ecology of open; that open-access journals are not by definition less rigorous in their review processes than traditional print journals; that books can prosper in open mode; that extending an embargo beyond a year is a mistake; that short-form writing loosens up the voices of humanities scholarship. In other words, that excellence can live open. And that part of the academic mission is making knowledge available to everyone.[56]

Ultimately, this new ecology of value in the academy will tax humanists and their self-understanding. Faculty have been educated to normalize the constrained spaces of a closed system of scholarly publication. Now they are confronting the possibilities of release from certain of those constraints. Making work open access, publishing in open-access journals, making research data and archives open access, all these decisions involve a transformation in the notion of "value" and valuation, the sense of an individual's value, the understanding of the relationship of value to venue, and the understanding faculty have of their value to their institutions.[57] Intellectual labor is the measure of value in times of judgment, at tenure and promotion, in annual reviews. Intellectual labor is also a gauge of professional value.

For many humanities scholars, intellectual labor is also the gauge of commitment to expanding access and diversity, recognizing marginalized communities of practice and knowledge-production, extending inquiry into communities through publicly oriented scholarship. Yet, Cohen observed, in "Open Access Publishing and Scholarly Values," that "humanities scholars in particular have taken pride in the last few decades in uncovering and championing the voices of those who are less privileged and powerful, but here we are in the ivory tower, still preferring to publish in ways that separate our words from those of the unwashed online masses."[58] Decisions to publish open, for an increasing number of humanities scholars, are decisions more closely aligned with scholarly commitments.

With the move to emergent scholarly communication platforms, modes, and media, and the adoption of open-access processes and publication arrangements, and with the archival capacities of institutional repositories and the public facing networks of social media, humanities faculty will have to take their emergent role as curators seriously. So let me conclude this discussion of communicating open with some observations about the faculty role of self-curator. There was a time when humanities scholars celebrated when offered a contract by an academic press; negotiated modest royalty rates of something between 5% and 10%; filled out marketing forms; provided the revised version of a manuscript; and then settled into expectations that the press would sell a certain number of books to libraries across North America, send copies of that book to a set of reviewing journals and magazines, and then forward the reviews as they came in.

Then college and university libraries stopped buying entire lists in the humanities from academic presses, in part as a budgetary response to escalating costs of science and medical journals and in part as an acknowledgment of the declining value of redundant book purchases across the academic library universe. Lower per book sales ensued. To economize, university press publishers outsourced editorial work and curtailed marketing efforts. Reviewing venues contracted in number. And scholars, still overwhelmed with the number of books produced each year, no longer purchased paperbacks as liberally as they had in the 1970s and 1980s. By the late 1990s academic authors recognized they had to be proactive about marketing their books to other scholars. Unwillingly, many authors, and I include myself here, began this early project of curating their work—displaying it to others in flyers distributed at conferences or mailed to colleagues on lists purchased from professional organizations. Now self-curatorial practices have become far more extensive. Now faculty attend seminars on online profiles; and then put on to-do lists the authoring or updating of an array of professional profiles on multiple websites and in multiple platforms. They disseminate fragments and versions of their work through social media. Some get "a following." They display, and mount excerpts from, publications to whet appetites. They place essays for which they retain copyright online. They deposit print versions or digital files of the books and articles for which they hold copyright in institutional repositories.

All of this activity takes time; but self-curation can serve not only to brand faculty—a nagging feature of corporate-speak, I agree—but to serve other purposes, some of which I like to think of as noble. For me, it is a way to respond to queries I often receive from graduate students around the world. They ask if I can tell them what I said about women's autobiographical writing in my 1987 book. They have no way of getting access to a copy. I can barely remember what I said then, and would have to spend hours trying to summarize the argument in a couple of e-mail paragraphs. But I can put my out-of-print book on academia.edu or in Michigan's Deep Blue institutional repository so that those graduate students can get access to it free, online. It's a win-win knowledge exchange, an open exchange going both ways, and an exchange that is supported as a matter of policy and practice by my university.

There's a bumpy ride ahead, to recall the quip from Bette Davis in *All About Eve*. Academic humanists can find themselves out of their comfort zones— what with consulting the copyright infrastructure available on Creative Commons; staying abreast of legal decisions regarding fair use; gauging the affordances of multiple forms of bookishness; overcoming hesitancy to let work live open; rethinking their relationship to cultures of urgency; crafting new kinds of documents when preparing for forms of evaluation; and making curatorial to-do lists. Scholars, publishers, and institutions confront thorny and evolving issues of copyright; and as new obstacles arise, new modes of adaptation and innovation follow. Administrators—research officers and graduate school administrators—chase after changes, develop policies, confront funding mandates. And nationally, governments adopt different mandates with different consequences for the production, circulation, and reception of knowledge.

Here are moving parts again, the moving pieces of open access as possibility, initiative, obligation, and ethos, and the moving pieces of mixed practices, mixed media, and mixed economic models. But I'd rather be in the vehicle than on the sidelines. In the vehicle, faculty can respond to change and make change, in the new ecology of publication structures, in the infrastructures of open-access licensing, in changing self-understandings and evolving narratives, and in reconceptualizing doctoral education. And just maybe, the investment in transforming doctoral education can contribute, if in a small way, to advancing the cause of educational justice on a global scale by optimizing the utopian vision of a "commons-based knowledge society."

Learning, Pedagogy, and Curricular Environments; or, How We Teach Now

Small liberal arts colleges have always valued teaching: that is what they do, that is their mission, their brand. It is what students and parents value; it is what they purchase; it has purchase. The hundreds of small liberal arts colleges, nested inside cities, distributed across country roads and small towns, distinguish higher education in the United States from that in all other countries. I come from the state of Ohio; and I knew growing up the names of the many fine liberal arts colleges in small Ohio towns: Oberlin, College of Wooster, Ohio Wesleyan, Kenyon, Denison, and the many religiously affiliated colleges across the state. In these intimate environments, a premium is placed on faculty contact, mentorship, advising.

Over the last five decades many liberal arts colleges have changed their expectations of faculty. Now they are expected to be totally dedicated teachers in the classroom and published scholars who compete for prestigious fellowships. At the wealthiest colleges, teaching loads have been adjusted accordingly. Some colleges now recruit faculty with the promise of a 2/2 or 2/3 teaching load. And the branding has been reoriented. Prospective students are promised access to research active faculty in student-centered classrooms and intimate campus settings.

Research universities have been another matter. In the mid-twentieth century great research universities restructured to support research, incubate new products and technologies, produce cutting-edge scholarship across all sectors, educate the next generations of faculty/scholars, and model a higher education system designed to provide a competitive edge in a world divided by the hot ideological warfare of the Cold War. Research universities attracted eminent faculty researchers, sought Nobel Prize winners, and recruited early-career faculty with great scholarly promise. Their ambitious faculty sought as much external funding to support their research as possible. And along the way, faculty and administrators privileged the research mission of the university at the expense of the teaching commitment to undergraduate education, in a hierarchy of effort reaffirmed in successive stages of faculty evaluation. Throughout the 1970s, 1980s, and 1990s the "publish or perish" mantra defined life for faculty in the research university. It sounded sotto voce through departmental corridors. Criteria for tenure and promotion ratcheted up. In the humanities, the published monograph became the sine qua non of successful tenure bids, and at elite universities criteria expanded with expectations of a second book on the way.

Let me linger for a moment, here, on "the book" mantra. "The book" ecology encompassed a myriad of forces and activities: the expansion in the number of academic presses, a marker of seriousness as universities chased greater prestige and higher rankings; the expansion of lists by presses, and the ability of universities to quantify for other universities and the public the substantial achievements of their faculty; the pursuit of niche excellence and special series; the willing faculty whose service as press readers weighed as national or international recognition at the time of faculty evaluation; the traditional publication culture, dependent on a secure line in library budgets for the purchase of all humanities lists from academic presses. And it's also important to note that along with distinction, prestige, and impact, the expectation of "the book" was a quantifiable, and seemingly neutral, measure of achievement in a tenure system reoriented, from the early 1970s on, to the principle, if not always the realization, of equitable criteria in evaluation and advancement.

By the 1990s, senior faculty in the humanities expected to spend their time researching and writing their monographs, enacting with even more intensity the "solitary genius" model of scholarship. By then, the faculty reward system reinforced the value of teaching less, teaching fewer students, teaching graduate rather than undergraduate students, upper-division rather than lower-division courses, seminars rather than lectures, of buying time out of teaching altogether. By then, faculty in humanities units evolved into a two-tier faculty: the tenure and tenure-track faculty with a 2/2 teaching load and the contingent and full-time non-tenure-track faculty with higher teaching loads. By then, students in their first year or two rarely took classes with tenured or tenure-track faculty. By then, graduate programs had expanded to bring greater prestige to humanities units and to provide a corps of faculty-in-training to staff lower-level undergraduate courses. And tuition continued to rise, and public funding to erode.

The pattern could not hold. Administrators and faculty came to recognize that the escalating cost of an undergraduate education brought an obligation to provide students access to senior faculty in undergraduate classrooms and an education whose immediate and long-range value justifies its cost. They experienced increasing anxiety about the mounting pressures wrought by successive waves of technological innovation, and anxiety as well about the technological skills that students brought with them to college, the aptitudes and dispositional effects. They felt unease that the balance of teaching and research missions had become radically out of kilter. They acknowledged the need for major rebalancing. Gradually through the 1990s and with greater urgency in the 2000s, provosts, deans, department heads, and directors of undergraduate studies directed more attention to the undergraduate experience, attention now informed by research on learning and teaching and by the new analytics of student trends and achievements made possible by Big Data computation. Increasingly, externally imposed and internally adapted initiatives in assessment of learning outcomes motivated discussions of the value-added of courses, curriculum, and degrees. Of course, there's a troubling aspect of many assessment initiatives: the overinvestment in metrics of student satisfaction and measurements of utility with regard to degrees and curricular offerings. Nonetheless, the attention to undergraduate education is bringing with it exciting new initiatives and thoughtful reconceptualization of general education in the bachelor's degree.

The renewed commitment to undergraduate education, however, is not a return to teaching as faculty in the humanities have understood that activity up through the 20th century. The churning on the teaching side of things in the academy is no less daunting than the churning related to how humanists pursue and communicate their scholarly interests. Daily, faculty at research universities and at small liberal arts colleges alike confront the ways that social media, technological prostheses, and cyberinfrastructural environments compel and complicate how they teach. Nothing about teaching remains undisrupted. How to understand what a student is. How to think about student learning. How to approach what a course can be and do. How to structure a curriculum adequate to a 21st-century education. Where to locate expertise. What pedagogical goals to set. How to scale courses. In the next decades, faculty and doctoral students in the humanities will be immersed in, negotiating, and innovating in this new ecology of teaching and learning.

Disruption comes from without, from the economic and political forces already assayed in earlier sections of this book. Large forces: cost and debt, utility of degrees in the marketplace, political pressures. Disruption comes from technological advances, the platforms and affordances of social media, Big Data, and cyberinfrastructure. Disruption comes from the open-access movement. Disruption comes from new research and theorizing about learning itself. Disruption comes from pockets of innovation in the curriculum and in cocurricular initiatives that emerge from student needs. Disruption comes from the changing demography of students seeking higher education.

Oh my! I'm exhausted just registering all this disruption. But I can't stay exhausted. True, humanities faculty and doctoral students cannot become "experts" in, say, research on learning or on posttraditional online higher education; but they benefit from gaining some perspectives on the new ecology of teaching, as they do on the new ecology of scholarly communication.

Let's start by registering the shifting demography of the student populations coming into classrooms. Numbers of students continue to be what is commonly understood to be the typical college student, a young person between the ages of 18 and 22, living away from home for full-time study on a university or college campus, whose parents assume much of the obligation of tuition and room and board. But according to *The Condition of Education 2010*, a report by the National Center for Education Statistics, this situation is the case for something like 15% of undergraduates.[1] The majority of students pursuing coursework, certification, and postsecondary degrees in the 2010s are not of that traditional age group. They are older adults, many of them part-timers. They are veterans returning from war zones. They are employees seeking career advancement, or retraining for new kinds of jobs. They are people responding to their employment situation or to shifting life course learning needs. They are transfers from junior and community colleges who hone the habits of sustained study. They are urban students living at home and working two or three jobs to support themselves and their families. They are low-income students bringing with them anxieties about belonging, and confidence, and facility in code-switching to the language of privilege. They are international students from all over the world, living far from home. Some of the young people are homeless, orphaned, on their own entirely or coming from foster homes. Deterred by inconvenience, inaccessibility, or incomprehensible cost, many students seek a way to learn in the place they find themselves, at any pace, in flexible programs, at some level of reasonable cost. They seek "posttraditional" higher education through online opportunities.

Diverse cohorts of students thus enter classrooms. Privileged students enter, ready to go, with the requisite aptitudes and technologies. So too do students who are new kinds of learning subjects, in what are for them new kinds of learning environments. Students enter with differential depths of preparation for college due to increasing inequalities in secondary school systems. They enter struggling to find their place in institutions of higher education, a struggle intensified by the unrepresentative distribution of students from marginalized communities and first-generation students across the different higher education sectors. Many come without the common technological accouterments of daily life, the laptops or netbooks or iPads that enable multitasking, instant networking, and access to vast databases and millions of texts. And beyond classrooms, around the globe, there are vast numbers of people seeking educational opportunity in locations of educational scarcity. It's not just those who register for a seat that impact how humanists teach and think about learning now; it's also those out there seeking to get access to information, disciplinary knowledge, and certification.

I've registered the shifting demographics of student learners, of who they are. Let me register as well the changing subjectivity of student learners in a digital age. Cultural theorists such as Brian Rotman argue that the "alphabetic self" constituted through the written word, with attendant attributes of disembodiedness, interiority, and the boundedness of the singular, is giving way to an algorithmic subject that is increasingly distributed, networked, and plural.[2] Networking technologies may well be reorganizing desire as the desire to be "in the know" and increasingly the desire to be "locatable." Self-positioning technologies at once link subjects in networked sociality, intensify forms of social surveillance, and locate the subject as a concatenation of mineable data. The notion of privacy is recast as publicity in a world of instant dispersal through code. And the sense of embodiment itself may become technologized as so many digital circuitries calibrate and reroute synapses, hormones, and heartbeats.

The technologies and dynamic media environments through and in which people now live their lives and make their relationships evidence the restless mobility of hyperattention. N. Katherine Hayles has written extensively on the way in which the neurocircuitry of the brain is changing with the intensification of life lived with technological prostheses such as laptops, smartphones, and PDAs of all kinds. The students who are coming to courses now, and will be there in the next decade, are less adept in processes of deep attention (and deep reading) and more adept in processes of hyperattention (fragmented reading). The pleasures in deep reading will be joined in "synergistic interactions" of "hyper reading" and "machine reading" as students gain facility in combining interpretation with algorithmic analysis to seek patterns as well as exercise interpretation.[3] Further, according to Hayles, habits of deep reading will be tempered with the new pleasures of distributed readings across networks.[4] She enjoins faculty to address this shift in pedagogies, precisely because "critical interpretation is not above or outside the generational shift of cognitive modes but necessarily located within it, increasingly drawn into the matrix by engaging with works that instantiate the cognitive shift in their aesthetic strategies."[5] Naomi S. Baron, among others, enjoins humanities faculty to "think more carefully about students' mounting rejection of long-form reading, now intensified by digital technologies that further complicate our struggle to engage students in serious text-based inquiry."[6]

New kinds of students. New dynamics of subjectivity. And third, new relationships of students to delivery systems of higher education.

To suggest the complexities and conundrums of the capacities of cyberinfrastructure to shift the locus of learning and the relationship of learners to an institution and its bricks and mortar, and faculty to their students, let me consider the new rush to open in curriculum delivery. I explored in the previous section the open-access movement as it pertains to access to research, data, and scholarly publications. Within the arena of teaching, the open-access movement has given academics the discourse of open data, open-source software, open educational resources (OER), OpenCourseWare (OCW), open and distance learning (ODL), and a continuum of practices of open depending upon the kind of license attached to the content, the platform, and the software.[7]

Of course, it's not at all unusual for humanities faculty to adapt learning assets developed and digitized by other scholars, on their own campuses or across the world. Nor is it uncommon for humanities faculty to share their syllabi with others, in their department repositories, on listservs, on their personal websites, or through professional association "commons." Faculty in digital humanities collaborate with techies and librarians and project managers, all dependent on open-source software and open-source platforms. Faculty in all fields use shareware, such as Wordpress and Zotero, often incorporating such platforms into courses. They're already doing open teaching in modest ways. But in the last half decade, open has been scaling up.

As more and more databases become available, such as open government data and research data in the social and health sciences, for instance, humanities faculty will pursue opportunities to incorporate new kinds of projects into courses, though not without considerable support from IT professionals and librarians. They will also find themselves intrigued by new opportunities made available through the open-source software movement, which enables open access to computer programs and their code for use and modification under collaborative license provisions. One such program for use, reuse, and modification is the collaborative mapping program WorldMap, developed at Harvard, funded by the National Endowment for the Humanities, and dedicated to compiling a global service registry of maps.[8] For humanists, this open-source software has great potential for teaching as well as research; it promises humanities faculty the ability to draw upon, develop, and upload map data critical to the turn to the spatial humanities.

The discourse on and the resources available through OER will impact the pedagogical goals, strategies, and teaching practices humanities scholars will adapt in the coming decades. As defined by the 2012 Paris Declaration on Open Education Resources, under the auspices of UNESCO, OER encompasses teaching, learning and research materials in any medium, digital or otherwise, that reside in the public domain or have been released under an open license that permits no-cost access, use, adaptation, and redistribution by others with no or limited restrictions. Open licensing is built within the existing framework of intellectual property rights as defined by relevant international conventions and respects the authorship of the work.[9]

The ideal of OER is global access to open educational content, open-source software, and OCW, while preserving attribution of authorship. Anyone, including professors and students, can easily access open educational resources, as well as tools, training, and support systems through such sites as the OER Commons, created and curated by the Institute for the Study of Knowledge Management in Education, a nonprofit supported by the William and Flora Hewlett Foundation.

OpenCourseWare is a component of OER. The movement for OCW started at MIT when faculty voted to make syllabi and other course materials available to the public. As of 2014 some 1,000 institutions have some kind of OCW commitment "to distribute their own learning assets to the world."[10] "Digital Harvard" mounts on its website the video lectures of distinguished faculty as noncredit free courses sponsored by Harvard Extension School. Harvard's Berkman Center began experimenting with the Coursera platform, "freely shar[ing] software platforms for free online lectures and discussions."[11] These initiatives aimed in two directions: to address a general public with interest in lifelong learning and to develop and adapt credit-bearing online learning environments for on-campus students.

At the same time as MIT built OCW and blended learning environments took shape at Harvard, the two institutions joined together in launching edX, the online education platform that mounts open-access non-credit-bearing courses for people across the globe. Now edX has many institutional partners and offers a robust curriculum.[12] In excess of 100 institutions from around the globe have become partners in another venture, the public/private Coursera, described on its website as "a social entrepreneurship company." Coursera, announces the website, "offer[s] courses online for anyone to take, for free. We envision a future where everyone has access to a world-class education. We aim to empower people with education that will improve their lives, the lives of their families, and the communities they live in."[13] Enter the massive open online courses, the MOOCs.

Collaborations joining universities, venture capitalists, nonprofits, and corporations, xMOOCs represent a radical rescaling of the delivery system of higher education. They are products of the new knowledge economy, involving rapidly expanding cyberinfrastructure, distributed learning, networks of knowledge workers, Big Data analytics, resource pooling, and entrepreneurial savvy. In these collaborations, elite universities join venture capitalists, the big players edX and Coursera, and also Udacity and NovoEd. Entrepreneurs spin off a proliferating number of smaller start-ups—Udemy, Mooc2Degree, Thinkful, Accredible, Codecademy, Peer2Peer University, OpenStudy, UIU Link, to name a few. And now pop-up initiatives emerge to address the high costs of MOOCs themselves. One such initiative is "Mechanical MOOC," a mash-up of platforms from start-ups designed to provide the "building blocks" for delivering MOOCs and for credentialing students at bargain prices.[14]

Since the buzz generated when two computer scientists offered the first xMOOC out of Stanford in fall 2011 and drew 150,000 initial registrants for the course, debates about MOOCs as the new frontier of an affordable, scalable higher education have swirled around campuses and in the pages of the education journals and national press. When open teaching reaches for this kind of scale, the hype goes viral, captured in the *New York Times* article announcing 2012 as "the Year of the MOOC": "Nothing has more potential to lift people out of poverty—by providing them with a free education to get a job or improve the job they have."[15] A mere three years later, the buzz had subsided, and the reality set in as people sorted through the mix of utopian, opportunistic, and troubling aspects of MOOCs.

At this point in time, here's what the research reveals about MOOC offerings.[16] Nearly two-thirds of registrants come from countries other than the United States. For those who complete MOOCs, the satisfactions can be multiple. They deliver learning to anyone anywhere with an access device. They enable students to pace learning to meet their needs. They may locate individuals in a transnational network of peer tutors. For some entering new job markets and new conditions of employment or seeking to advance in their professions, MOOCs deliver certificates or "badges" for the completion of series of courses (as MITx now does).[17] For a few, they offer a route to admission to a prestigious U.S. university. While the platforms for delivering MOOCS originated in the United States, MOOC platforms have launched in Spain, Germany, Australia, Brazil, China, and Rwanda.[18] In these ways, the utopian impetus for higher learning without walls, for sharing learning assets around the world, seems to be partially satisfied.[19] On the upside, then, the MOOC delivery ensemble may turn out be, as Nina Augustsson observes, "the 'leapfrog' solution that allows countries full of undereducated youth to move into the middle classes."[20]

But the utopian and utilitarian hype about MOOCs remains hyperbolic. The vast majority of courses come from science, engineering, math, and computer science fields. Researchers report that while thousands register for courses, small percentages of registrants complete them. At the University of Pennsylvania, for instance, researchers from the Graduate School of Education in 2013 found the completion rate of Penn's online courses to be only 4%.[21] A 2014 article by Jonah Newman and Soo Oh, on data from the first 16 edX MOOCs offered by Harvard and MIT, reports that the majority of those who register for MOOCS already have a postsecondary degree of some kind, that some even have doctorates. Those data also reveal that "nearly half of registrants never engage with any of the content."[22]

Beyond the data, there are other troubling aspects of MOOCs. On the whole, they are not radically posttraditional projects. They are offered open and online for sure. But their format is fully traditional. The teacher often stands at the center of the video, radiating expertise. Thousands of students attend to that figure as the authority in the virtual classroom. Moreover, as Neil Butcher observes in "A Guide to Quality in Post-traditional Online Higher Education," "xMOOCS tend to follow traditional behaviorist approaches to learning and the structure of existing educational practices. They typically have traditional course structures, content, and methods, with videotaped lectures, online quizzes, and weekly assignments. Their primary innovation is scaling."[23] The disruption of traditional teaching is in scale, not in the pedagogy or in the power relationships of faculty to students.

Nor is the faculty delivering MOOCs a diverse one. The MOOC business thrives on star-quality performers, faculty who dazzle on the small screen. There's already a two-tiered professoriate made up of large numbers of non-tenure-track or contingent faculty and a shrinking percentage of tenure and tenure-track faculty. What happens when there's a third tier added to the mix: the online megastars, the rest of the tenure-track and tenured faculty, and the contingent faculty? Further, star professors come primarily from elite private and public universities; and those who deliver MOOCs are overwhelmingly male, as a spring 2013 survey by the *Chronicle of Higher Education* confirms.[24] As well, the Harvard and MIT data reveal that "the overwhelming majority of MOOC students are male."[25] So if the MOOC world functions as an extrainstitutional academy of learning, founded on the values of sharing and distributing learning assets around the globe, then it's a problematic world. Educators, humanists among them, would be hard-pressed to see it as a diverse community coming from and presenting diverse lived experiences and cultures of scholarly inquiry, on the faculty side or on the student side.

Then there are the corporate aspects of MOOCs. In the land of MOOCS, the brand is all. Like T-shirt franchises, the public-private ventures that are MOOCs bring a university's intellectual brand to "millions of people" around the world. Students and learners abroad seek the imprimatur of the best of U.S. universities—Stanford, the Ivys, Berkeley, Michigan, and so on. They seek prestige badges and certificates of completion. Further, the development of MOOCs has been accompanied by experiments in outsourcing the curriculum at small colleges and starved state universities to the star brands and the higher education entrepreneurs. And in developing nations, the concern for some critics is that the importation of platforms and curricula and expertise from the brands of the developed world has the potential to occlude local educational cultures and to create and sustain a "two-tier system of global higher education, with a small number of elites able to participate in traditional university educational environments . . . while the vast majority of students, especially those in developing countries, have to make do with participating in watered down education experience delivered through MOOCS."[26]

And there are issues related to the differential potential for scaling the curriculum delivered by xMOOCs. The MOOC agenda often directs resources to easily scaled curricula that are also priority curricula in a time of an instrumentalist educational ethos. The number of humanities courses offered has been modest, though with each year that number is increasing, and the courses offered diversifying.[27] Further, while humanities faculty in the virtual classroom of the MOOC may be able to model deep reading, archival serendipity, and the rhetorical styles of humanistic inquiry, the scaling of MOOCs precludes assigning significant reading and diverse writing exercises typical of humanities courses. The labor involved in grading, say, 2,000 or 20,000 five-page essays, in a for-credit course, is prohibitive: it would require exploiting graduate students and contingent faculty. The alternative to the use of human labor is to automate grading of written assignments; but machine grading, though a subject of ongoing study, is obviously controversial, and premature given the state of the programming. As my colleague Paul Conway observed to me, this is the dilemma in the state of play of MOOCs—exploited labor or machine grading. Equally concerning for humanists, the language of instruction is almost always English. And the occasions where translations are available may depend upon volunteer labor. Thus, many humanists, who consider learning to speak, live, and imagine in multiple languages central to a liberal arts education, find themselves enlisted to deliver an open-access opportunity that shores up the global currency of English and may well exploit volunteer translators for the profit of corporations in the education business.

Finally, there are the issues related to the practical aspects of MOOCs. The business model for MOOCs is not yet viable, as an answer to keeping tuition costs from escalating on campuses, to constituting new profit centers for universities, or to generating big profits for education entrepreneurs. The thorny challenges to operationalizing MOOCs at scale are mounting: accreditation, credentialing, badging, credit transfer, quality assessment, copyright, compensation, among them. The negative side-effects of the virtual classroom are scaled up—absenteeism, plagiarism, and cheating. Nor is the model for on-campus development adequately worked out. And the time and effort required of faculty to develop a MOOC are significant. Here's the message implicit in Michigan's guidelines for proposing a Coursera MOOC over the last couple of years: Design tightly. Record charismatically. And do so on your own "research" time. Some resources will be available to you for the development and piloting of the course; but course preparation will not be part of your course load. It will be approached, in evaluative contexts, as equivalent to preparing a textbook on your topic. Given the faculty labor, and the ensemble of people with different kinds of expertise required to develop and pilot a MOOC, the activity will be concentrated in the major research universities. And in the end, the degree of open is less than the ideal: courses and course contents remain licensed and as such cannot be reused without the payment of fees.

The short-lived rush to MOOCs can be thought of as part of the corporate strategies adapted by universities to address financial challenges. The people most enthusiastic about the potential of MOOCs to transform higher education have been Silicon Valley entrepreneurs and members of university boards. For the entrepreneurs, MOOCs promise access to Big Data on registrants, data that can be monetized and sold to college recruiters and to businesses seeking the best candidates for the new kinds of jobs in the knowledge economy. And boards of governors, such as the board that fired President Theresa Sullivan at the University of Virginia (and then was forced by intense pressure from multiple constituencies to rehire her), gravitate to the promise of online learning and MOOCs as a way to solve the problems related to the escalating costs of higher education; they seem the way to efficiency, branding, and profit centers within the university.

University presidents themselves have been and continue to be far more circumspect in their assessment of MOOC potential, as Sullivan was at Virginia.[28] And skeptical faculty have warned of the unintended consequences of going open on a large scale via this model. In a late 2013 commentary for *Liberal Education* Aaron Bady spins out the dystopian scenario, provocatively elaborating the insidious logic of equivalence that shadows the xMOOC. He writes:

> Once market equivalency has entered the equation, once the market recognizes an equivalence between a MOOC and an in-person class, pointing out the difference that is experienced by the student will be trumped by the equivalence of market logic, which will dictate paying for the cheaper of the two. An in-person education will become an unnecessary luxury, an ornamental marker of elite status.[29]

Bady applauds the vision behind the first MOOC (referred to as a cMOOC), developed at the University of Manitoba in 2008. It was an experiment in community-organized, student-centered learning, an open online opportunity for student learners to follow their own paths, collaborating in a social network as they remixed open course content aggregated from "experts, educators, and instructors."[30] By contrast, he observes, "Instead of building social information networks, the neoliberal MOOC is driven by a desire to liberate and empower the individual, breaking apart actually existing academic communities and refocusing on the individual's acquisition of knowledge."[31]

Hype. Jeremiad. Utopian fantasy. Dystopian scenario. The achievement of the MOOC movement is, at this moment, very modest.

But online ecologies of higher education are nonetheless important to understand, and established and emergent humanities scholars can find thoughtful approaches to the MOOC concept out there, as in Jonathan Haber's MOOC[32] and in the experiments of their colleagues. For one thing, humanities faculty have been developing MOOCs. In winter 2014, Cathy Davidson offered a Coursera-Duke MOOC titled The History and Future of Higher Education; and she blogged about MOOCs and the process of developing one on the HASTAC website in "Clearing Up Some Myths about MOOCs."[33] In her iteration of a MOOC, Davidson sought to realize the alternative legacy inherent in the promise of the earliest iteration of the cMOOC as networked, participatory, collaborative, student-centered.

Humanities faculty are also innovating anti-MOOC initiatives. One such initiative is that of FemTechNet, a collaborative of feminist technology scholars from multiple institutions of higher education.[34] They have designed what they term a DOCC, a distributed open collaborative course entitled Dialogues on Feminism and Technology.[35] Different institutions sponsor and record dialogues among feminist scholars on particular topics, such as "technology and the body." The open events are taped, and the tapes edited into usable 45-minute to one-hour units; then tapes are uploaded to the FemTechNet website; there they are open for reuse in anyone's course. Ultimately, the DOCC is an antibranding praxis that takes advantage of digital technology but for a different vision of higher learning. No one brand is attached to the conversations. There is no one source of expertise. Video conversations archived online are free for reuse and remixing in classrooms around the nation and the world. And feminist issues and analyses are inserted into the practices and intellectual core of online learning.

It may be that only a modest number of humanities faculty will develop a MOOC or a DOCC; but humanities faculty will be among those who adapt, remix, and incorporate open online content available to them without licensing fees for incorporation in hybrid on-campus courses.[36] And it is certain that many will be expected to deliver courses to online instruction at their institutions. Online courses and degrees are an expanding sector of the academic curriculum for enrolled students. ASUOnline offers a roster of undergraduate and graduate degree programs online, for which faculty are expected to adapt their courses. The University of Illinois, Urbana-Champaign (UIUC) offers students upwards of 100 online or hybrid general education courses, among them a good number of humanities courses.[37] Other universities, the University of Florida, Penn State University–World Campus, San Jose State, and Central Michigan University, to name a few, have robust online degree programs. The trend to posttraditional online educational opportunities for enrolled students will impact how humanities faculty approach teaching; it will put a premium on pedagogical innovation, media savvy, and instructional flexibility. It will immerse faculty in new teaching platforms, new teaching pedagogies, new operative discourses. It will encourage humanities faculty to think about the ensemble of actors and the repertoires of expertise necessary to make the transition to online learning environments successfully.

Ethically driven and thoughtfully conceptualized online learning can strengthen humanities education and contribute to the development of mobile transdisciplinary collaboratories of faculty, enrolled students, and even lay researchers. It can make the epistemic infrastructure available to those for whom an on-campus college education may be too costly to pursue; or those who cannot travel to centers of learning. It can enrich the curriculum in less-commonly-taught languages, through consortial arrangements for sharing language instruction across regions. Moreover, a 2013 *Chronicle of Higher Education* survey suggested that reorienting course design and pedagogical strategies for online teaching environments yields considerable benefits for on-campus teaching.[38] In preparing videos of lectures, sets of materials, and evaluation instruments, faculty discover ways to improve their on-campus teaching. Information gathered on how students interact with the site, the materials, the assignments, and the community of class members offers a fund of data for faculty keen on gaining knowledge about how students learn now.

And what of on-campus, in situ, learning, not on the scale of the MOOC or in the venue of online offerings? Derek Bok noted in *Our Underachieving Colleges*: "New courses and new knowledge regularly find their way into the curriculum, but teaching methods change very slowly."[39] Humanities faculty may be eager, or merely dutiful, or even reluctant curricular tinkerers; no matter the posture, they are constantly engaged in curricular revision. Successive generations of scholar-teachers remake standard courses into their own versions, design new ones that bend toward the horizon of disciplinary change, imagine new configurations for majors or minors or general education courses.

As an example, the undergraduate major in English has changed without necessarily changing formally, as colleagues introduced into their courses sexuality studies, hemispheric studies, global studies, transatlantic studies, comparative studies, material studies, visual studies, disability studies, and digital studies. Language departments have been reconceptualizing what a major is, what a minor might be, often focusing on cultural studies rather than literary studies approaches. And so on across humanities disciplines. Multitrack majors. Integrative majors. Interdisciplinary majors. Individually configured majors. The motivations are multiple. They are intellectual responses to changes in humanities fields. They are pragmatic—keeping up enrollments and attracting more majors, those consumers across the curriculum. They are also responsive to student needs in a changing economy and world of work, knowledge based, skills based, praxis based. They are cognizant of the technological devices, media, platforms, and affordances through which students live their lives and through which they themselves do their work.

And with respect to the curriculum writ large: In the last decade and a half, a succession of undergraduate initiatives have been incorporated into higher education, including the freshman seminar taught by tenure-track faculty, the sophomore experience, the capstone experience for graduating majors, the integrative experience of the general education program, and writing across the curriculum. Opportunities for study abroad have been expanded and alternative spring break experiences introduced. Undergraduate research opportunities have been implemented as well as engaged and community-based learning, and most recently the internship experience, the experience in entrepreneurship, and integrative courses that tie the classroom to the performing arts and exhibition cultures on campus. These initiatives are "high impact"—because research shows they are paradigm-shifting, mind-blowing, memorable, and personally transformative for students; in other words, they bear long affective and intellectual tails.

Increasingly, academic leaders are speaking passionately about reimagining institutions of higher education for the 21st century. Nancy Cantor, chancellor of Rutgers University–Newark and former chancellor of Syracuse University, calls for institutional transformation that would involve shifting from the ivory tower model of the university to a model of the engaged institution, from a meritocracy to a talent incubator, from a rigidly structured set of disciplinary silos to collaboratories of academics and nonacademics, from the cult of the expert to the common good of distributed expertise.[40] Randall Bass, vice provost for education at Georgetown University, speaks out about the "shift from the instructional paradigm to the learning paradigm" in what he terms the "post-course era."[41] The phrase references the way in which the formal curriculum through which higher education has been structured is being decentered as the locus of learning. Now learning is recognized to take place in non-traditional-course-based venues, in zones of informal learning, in the dynamics of participatory cultures, in the intensities and curiosities of high-impact practices, and in the experiential cocurriculum of internships, study abroad, and public projects. Courses won't go away; but the unifying and reifying concept of the course is no longer adequate to capture where and how learning occurs in higher education.

Recognizing this new environment of learning, Bass, Davidson, and Goldberg, among many others, advance the importance of cultures of participatory learning that aim to tutor students in how to speak from positions of authority, how to recognize disciplinary competence and interdisciplinary synergies. To focus on learning, writes Bass, is to recognize that "the connection between integrative thinking, or experiential learning, and the social network, or participatory culture, is no longer peripheral to our enterprise but is the nexus that should guide and reshape our curricula in the current disruptive moment in higher education learning."[42] To focus on participatory learning turns upon what happens with students as they engage new information, new models of inquiry and practice, new disciplinary imperatives, new applications of thinking, new venues for self-reflection. It is to shift from the teaching dyad to the learning ensemble. It is to shift from the subject positions of teachers "showing what we know" and acolytes absorbing that knowledge to fluid subject positions within exchange network and collaboratory. It is to shift from a singularity of purpose to a heterogeneity of worldviews. It is to shift from the ends of accumulating knowledge to the practices of producing and performing knowledge.

The affordances of technologies—among them social media, digital archives, platforms for online composing, multimedia open educational resources, and online and offline learning networks—have brought disruptions of the formal curriculum and enabled new possibilities for the dispersed, informal curriculum. Yet, this is learning and teaching derived from the goals of education rather than the affordances of technology—though technologies are central to achieving these goals. Bass's challenge to administrators and faculty alike becomes "how to reinvent a curriculum that lives in this new space," and in a "post-course era."

Humanities faculty are out there, in this new space, breaking through the routines of faculty exchanges with students around reading, writing, and testing. Bass foregrounds new student-centered assessment formats, such as e-portfolios. He talks about a new model for organizing courses and curriculum, one he adopts from John Seely Brown termed "reversing the flow": forgoing the model that begins with inculcation of expert knowledge and then follows with practice in applying that knowledge, in favor of a model that entwines learning and practice from the get-go.[43] Eric Rabkin talks, blogs, and writes about his concept of "real work not home work."[44] Homework he describes as the usual kind of assessment instruments faculty ask students to fulfill: formulaic, deadline-driven, inconsequential after submission. Effort, deadline, grade. Real work, by contrast, engages students in activities and writing projects that contribute to the shared classroom experience; it advances the conversation and enhances the learning environment. It links to the vision of participatory learning elaborated by Davidson and Goldberg with high-impact experiences Bass locates in the informal curriculum.

Humanities faculty are imagining the end point of their courses as something left behind or something spanning semesters: a link on the department website; databases upon which later researchers draw; a digital curation; an open-access journal. One of my colleagues, Anne Curzan, is a scholar of language change and an inspired classroom teacher. In a course on grammar, she had upwards of 100 students enter three of their past papers into a searchable database of student essays. That database, combined with historical databases, then became the evidentiary material through which students explored shifts in language usage. She had her students doing real work, developing hypotheses, searching for patterns across time, rethinking the constantly changing action of linguistic usage, recognizing it in their everyday exchanges. David Damrosch talks of the classroom as an island of wikis through which he asks students to do the real work of teasing out transnational interfaces in national literatures and leaving the knowledge gained behind as an archive for the next group of students.[45]

An increasing number of humanities faculty at big universities and small colleges are imagining new designs for blended classrooms, joining students on different campuses together for project-based learning, as William Pennapacker is doing with his "Digital Liberal Arts" initiative at Hope College and within the Great Lakes Colleges Association.[46] Some are designing courses attractive to the public, to autodidacts and lifelong learners. Some are trying experiments in slowing down, as Richard Miller does in his course "reading in slow motion." Here are his rules: one book read during the entire term; weekly three-hour sessions; no technology in the classroom; no reading ahead; a final paper based on anything except the assigned text. Miller calls this "teaching for resourcefulness."[47] Others are rethinking the notion of skills as forms of knowledge. Some are developing multicampus courses for delivery of less-commonly taught languages.

In the next decade, humanities faculty will be challenged to innovate in their courses in ways that introduce real work, reversed-flow, participatory learning. "In this new space," the urgent issues confronting humanities faculty multiply. How to understand the ways students study, research, process, and compose now? Where to find attention and how to mobilize it? How to model "reading" on multiple levels simultaneously? How to negotiate student participation and resistance to participation? How to "assess" learning within the context of new technological environments? How to insist on and demur from reinforcing faculty expertise? How to collaborate with the experts upon whom faculty depend to realize pedagogical visions? How to even know what needs to be known of this emergent environment?

How humanists teach now is a changing assemblage of software and platforms, politics and economics, student interest and institutional structures, infrastructure and generational competencies, people and objects, expertise and curiosity. How they teach now is a hybrid of traditional classroom practices and participatory or practice-based learning. It takes place in hybrid formats combining face-to-face and online environments. Learning is close and distant, course-based and postcourse, flexible and adaptive to meet student needs.[48] Classes are flipped. Expertise distributed. Sociality networked. Learning collaborative. And students become "open scholars," a subject position of the new posttraditional education and of the participatory ethos of online and offline hybrids. Here is Neil Butcher's parsing of the concept. "Open scholars" he writes, are

> able to create, use, and contribute OER, self-archive, apply their research, do open research, filter and share with others, support emerging open learning alternatives, publish in open access journals, comment openly on the works of others, and build networks. This can also improve research, as academics can focus on teaching research skills, and developing students as producers.[49]

In this world of traditional, flipped, and feral learning activities, concepts of expertise, authority, ownership, and the provenance of learning come unmoored from their traditional significations.[50] In these environments, learning joins teacher and student, peer to peer, and student to crowd and cloud. It unfolds through multiple modalities, involves all the senses, the powers of the textual, visual, oral, aural, and haptic. In these encounters, students gain critical intelligence about what it means to live in new environments of information, communication, ethical exchange, and social identities; and the interpretive skills to assess the impact of technologies on society, the environment, the global economy, and their own self-understanding.

It's a stressful time. It's an exhilarating time. Humanities faculty and graduate students will be overwhelmed by the work of preparing and uncomfortable with the sense of inadequacy before the tasks. They'll need to pressure institutions to provide adequate resources to support new kinds of courses, new collaboratories of inquiry. They'll be challenged by the new kinds of learners in classrooms and their needs, and disturbed by the inequality of access to those classrooms, the insufficient diversity, the off-putting climate for some.

And so this time must also be a creative time, a time to affirm and demonstrate how critical a humanities education is in this moment. In a world of information abundance and constantly shifting ecologies of labor, work, and profession, undergraduate students need the breadth of knowledge and practical competencies the humanities provide, for a capacious imagination, for deft interpretation, for sophisticated skills in myriad forms of writing, composing, and communicating, for a sense of pleasure in human creativity, for an ethical commitment to egalitarianism and the sustainability of the planet. The challenge is to adequately prepare doctoral students in the humanities to become the teachers undergraduates deserve, whoever they are, whatever needs and aspirations they bring, however they engage with their teachers and mentors.

The Possibly Posthuman
Humanities Scholar

My final observation about the shifting environment in which humanists will go about their everyday lives in the next decades is a brief one, offered in a speculative mode. It has to do with the agent of knowing, the scholar-teacher. What kind of scholarly subjects will humanists be? How might they think of themselves productively as "posthuman" scholar/teachers? In what sense and to what end? It is not the place here to parse the several strands of contemporary theorizing of the posthuman. That can be found elsewhere. But what I can do here is to offer an impressionistic portrait of the possibly posthuman humanities scholar.

For one take on the possibly posthuman humanist let me go to William J. Mitchell and his 2003 *Me++: The Cyborg Self and the Networked City*. I read Mitchell's *Me++* as a kind of autobiographical manifesto of "the electronomadic cyborg," and a riff on Donna Haraway's cyborg politics.[1] He writes: "I am plugged into other objects and subjects in such a way that I become myself in and through them, even as they become themselves in and through me."[2] No isolated singularity he; no autonomous individuality of the Enlightenment subject or humanist "Man." His maxim and motto for the Me++ is counter-Cartesian: "I link, therefore I am."[3] Mitchell's Me++ subject is at once custom-designed via enhanced embodied capabilities and radically extended via technological devices and digital networks. Or to put it in other words, that subject is a prosthetically extended conjunction of carbon and silicon.[4]

This is the technologized concept of the posthuman, outfitted in a kind of feminist ethic of relationality. I'm not quite going there with what I am trying to convey about the importance of attending to the kind of subjects academic humanists are becoming in this knowledge ecology. Riffing on Mitchell's subject as a composite of fleshware, hardware, and software strung along the electric currents of networks, I want to propose the new scholar subject as a performative of passionate singularity, hybrid materiality, and networked relationality. This is one sense in which the humanities scholar to be is possibly posthuman, and a posthumanist scholar.

But there is more to consider of this scholar subject presumed to be the locus of thinking. What, exactly, is doing thinking now? As successive generations of computer devices and their algorithmic codes are built, those devices come, as Daniel Atkins observes, to seem "natural." Some are integrated physically into human bodies. This hybrid materiality involves not only device and human; but device, human, and networked cyberinfrastructure. If Atkins writes on the sanguine side of technologized subjectivity, Siva Vaidhyananthan is less sanguine about the human-device interface that is becoming the embodied self. Writing on the occasion of the death of Steve Jobs, he observed: "We now view computers as prostheses to our bodies, albeit prostheses as dazzling as amulets. . . . We touch devices directly with our oily skin. We manipulate data and images as if there were no lens between them and us. We are embedded in a lattice of devices and digital radio signals. And those devices and signals are embedded in us."[5] Whether one is sanguine or not in assessing the naturalized, technologically hybrid subject, the implications of this state of being human for the humanist scholar whose coin is reading, interpretation, critique, and storytelling are profound.

The locus of thinking, for the prosthetically extendable scholar joined along the currents of networked relationality, is an ensemble affair. It involves the scholar, the device, the algorithm, the code. It involves the design architecture of platform and tool, the experiential architecture of networks, and the economy of energy. It involves the cloud, the crowd, and the "rooms," bricks and mortar and virtual, in which scholarly thinking moves forward. David Weinberger's witty title for his book on the emergent knowledge ecology captures the complexities and perplexities of the scholar's life that is becoming: *Too Big to Know: Rethinking Knowledge Now That the Facts Aren't the Facts, Experts Are Everywhere, and the Smartest Person in the Room is the Room.*[6]

Ultimately, thinking is a collaborative affair of multiple actors, human and nonhuman, virtual and material, elegantly orderly and unruly. Jane Bennett, in her project to "g[i]ve the force of things more due," would call this "distributive, composite notion of agency" an "agency of assemblages."[7] This concept of agency is posthuman in the sense that it dislodges the human subject as the entire site of rationality, autonomy, intentionality, and effectivity and joins the human subject to the "material agency of non- or not-quite things."[8]

Through this discussion of the possibly posthuman humanist, I am making the point that it's critical to complicate the understanding of how humanists do the work of the humanities. Yes, the mode of doing humanities scholarship in the academy has commonly been described as that of the isolated scholar producing a long-form argument in the shape of the book; and faculty needs have commonly been described as individual study, computer screen, archive, and time. In this time, however, possibly posthuman humanities scholars will accumulate new skills, including that of algorithmic literacy, "not only learning how to interpret results but to understand the whole 'cooking' process of algorithm development," as Dean Rehberger observes.[9] They will be at once multimediated self-presenters; self-archivers; bricoleurs of intellectual inquiry, individual and collective; anonymized databases; networked nodes of a knowledge collaboratory involving scholars, students, laypeople, smart objects, robots. Networked scholars will not only be connected to knowledge communities close at hand—in the room, so to speak—but also connected across the globe in an interlinked ecology of scholarly practices and knowledge economies.

The scholarly environment is thus an assemblage of human and nonhuman agents, ever mobile, forming and reforming, expanding in number and complexity and contracting, traveling along one itinerary and then another, purposeful and unpredictable. And the work of the humanities scholar becomes, perhaps, that of Haraway's "witness"—"an interpretative, engaged, contingent, fallible engagement . . . never a disengaged account."[10] Or it perhaps becomes that of Rosi Braidotti's "process ontology"—"a role for the intellectual which consists not in leading the opinions (doxa), legislating the truth (dogma) or administering the protocols of intellectual life, but rather in creating and disseminating new concepts and ideas."[11] The stakes here remain high, for, as Leela Fernandes cautions, "Knowledge does not simply represent reality, it also makes reality; in other words knowledge literally matters."[12]

But even as the ethics of scholarly inquiry are rethought along these posthumanist lines, it is necessary to recognize the less salutary aspects of the algorithmic transformation of the humanities scholar. For that is another dimension of the possibly posthumanist scholar/subject. That subject is already captured in the Big Quantification Engine of higher education. This data-ization of the humanities scholar is at once a given and troubling to contemplate, just as current trends in self-quantification are sometimes amusing and oftentimes disquieting. North American institutions have embraced the mantra of assessment and quality outcomes, a mantra extending across all the domains of higher education. Humanists are enjoined to use models of quantitative assessment of scholarly productivity, as colleagues in the sciences and social sciences have long done with their citation indexes.

Google Scholar has already become a kind of vanity mirror of citations for humanists, if, that is, the name is sufficiently unique and one has few googlegängers. But the mirror on the virtual wall is not just for vanity; it is for professional survival and advancement. The "quantified" scholar/subject is constantly asked to produce data on scholarly impact and to produce running commentary, or metadata, on how that data should be interpreted by colleagues and external evaluators. Just as the quantified self movement awaits the next device for self-monitoring, soon humanists might see a citation device embedded in the wrist of the humanities scholars with its own scrolling readout of real-time citations; a printout of intellectual passions distributed through reading publics. Indeed, technology might be found at fingertips—in the apps for smartphones, such as Evernote, Officedrop, Notebooks, Scrivener, and so on.

And now the scholar/subject is assuming another task: producing oneself as data on annual activities forms. These data-driven forms are the online forms colleges and universities are using to track faculty activities for the purposes of mining data regarding teaching, research, and service. Such data-driven forms are overwriting faculty and departmental understandings of value. They are turning faculty into form-fillers, with often frustrating results with regard to time and energy. And they are extensions of efficiency measures that allocate staff to shared services centers and transform scholar/subjects into accountants of activity. And for this, faculty have to once again critique that accountancy, and pressure administrators to ensure ease of use and flexibility.

Whether humanities faculty think of themselves as posthuman scholars, in utopian or dystopian mode, or as some kind of hybrid witness, avidly going about the work of the humanities in the world, or whether they understand themselves as humanists in a transition of uncertainties, they face daunting questions:

- What will their scholarly and teaching projects look like?
- How will they do their work?
- What energizing infrastructures will they depend on?
- What set of skills will they need to do work?
- How will their work be communicated?
- Who will their audiences be?
- How will it be funded?
- Who will own their work?
- What will its impact be?
- How will it be evaluated?
- How will ecologies and networks of knowledge be organized?
- How will they imagine a career in and/or outside the academy?
- What will their relations be to others in the humanities workforce, inside and outside the academy?
- How will they work for institutional change in this environment?

- How will they advocate for what they do to a larger public?
- How will they meet the needs of students they teach and mentor?
- What will be their ethical obligations—to students, colleagues, and the publics of which they are a part?
- How will they maintain their integrity and values in the midst of an increasingly bureaucratized, efficiency-chasing, corporate-speak sociality, economy, and academy?

To be sure, old habits of doing scholarship and old scholarly subjectivities will certainly persist. But new habits are now mobilized, and new scholarly subjectivities emergent. How those habits and subjectivities will evolve in the midst of future technologies and cultures of sociality can only be dimly glimpsed. That is the distinctive work of the humanities in the world. That is the lens scholars must turn on themselves—doctoral students, faculty, and administrators alike.

Manifesto for a Sustainable Humanities

Anxieties about the vitality of the humanities within higher education run high. So, too, do anxieties about the evolving conditions of working as academic humanists. For some, talk of change, with its rhetoric of urgency, becomes a trigger for holding fast to certain understandings of the life of the academic humanist. For others, it is a conundrum and a headache. I see it as an occasion to think purposefully about how to meet future challenges and how to calibrate the potential upsides of transformation.

So here is my manifesto for a sustainable humanities, one that can meet the Grand Challenges facing the university in the next decades.

- *Preserve the intimacy of the small*, and steward the distinctiveness of the local while recognizing the attraction of global networks and the new configurations of "thereness" in institutions of higher education.
- *Forge a new ethics and praxis of scholarly communication*, simultaneously sustaining commitment to the long-form argument, and recognizing and pursuing myriad alternative forms and media for communicating our work.
- *Reconceptualize the scholarly ecology as a flexible collaboratory*, one that positions the scholar as singular producer of knowledge, and also as a member of a collaborative assemblage involving students, colleagues, computer engineers and graphic designers, project managers, and strangers of the crowd as well as algorithm, code, platform, and protocol.
- *Rethink the relationship to scholarship*, loosening the hold of an ownership model of scholarly work and closed system of communication by appropriating the best that open-access promises.
- *Relish the commitment to teaching* through innovations in the classroom, among them explorations of participatory and project-based humanities inquiry, adaptation of interactive technologies, and mobilization of flipped classrooms, hybrid classrooms, and cross-institutional learning collaboratories.

- *Commit to being here, there, and everywhere* that policies are being made, new e-research initiatives placed on the drawing board, codes and architectures affecting humanities research discussed; or call attention, insistently, unabashedly, to the absence of humanists at the table.
- *Remain self-reflexive about* the complex dance of singularity, networked relationality, and adaptive technological extension that complicates the self-understanding of what it means to be a humanist now.
- *Encompass in discourse, project, and vision all members of the humanities communities*—graduate and undergraduate students, non-tenure-track faculty, humanists in our libraries and institutes, our digital labs and administration, tenure-track faculty, associate faculty, full professors, and humanists who are administrators[1] and seize opportunities to build networks with professional and lay humanists in local communities and around the globe.
- *Transform doctoral education to realize this 21st-century agenda.*

Reconceptualizing doctoral education is critical to meeting the grand challenge of sustaining the centrality of the humanities to a liberal arts and the centrality of the liberal arts to the university and society. Let me turn, then, to my vision for, and argument on behalf of, a posttraditional doctoral education in the humanities.

PART 3

Toward a 21st-Century Doctoral Education

Future humanities faculty need to be savvy about global influences on higher education and the evolving concept of the university. To be cognizant of institutional practices and their transformation in the new epistemic infrastructure. To be familiar with, even if not practitioners in, an expanding array of vehicles, forms, media, and platforms for scholarly communication. To be willing to go open. To be knowledgeable about new learning and thinking environments, and pedagogies for participatory classrooms. To be imaginative in self-understanding as an emergent, possibly posthuman, humanities scholar.

Given these rapidly unfolding macronarratives of everyday life in the academy just surveyed, it is beyond time to transform doctoral education. Doctoral programs cannot launch students into this knowledge ecology and political economy with a late 20th-century training. That training is one that too narrowly scaffolds the degree around the traditional triad of coursework, exams, and the singular form of the monograph dissertation as the testament of readiness to enter the professoriate. Preparing for a career as an academic humanist will involve recognizing what is enduring in the work and world of the humanities carried over from the last century and what is enabling in the environment of higher education that is becoming.

This is the intellectual argument for transforming doctoral education in the humanities. And I'm going to make the best case I can for this transformation. I emphasize this point here, at the beginning of Part III, because I don't want to give the impression that what I propose is only a response to the time-to-degree issue, or only a response to the state of job prospects for humanities doctorates. Nor do I want to give the impression that the transformation I am proposing (and I'm not alone here) is unrelated to those issues. I see the connection between insisting on an intellectually rigorous vision of a 21st-century doctoral education and making an intervention in the conditions on the ground with respect to time-to-degree and the job market, and to the larger issues of diversity of the professoriate and the casualization of academic labor force in the academy.

My itinerary through Part III proceeds along this route. I begin with the picture on the ground that data provide. I then make the case for a new concept of the dissertation as the capstone of the doctorate and respond to the kinds of challenges raised by those skeptical of this concept. I follow with suggestions for transformation of other components of doctoral education. And I conclude Part III by suggesting how new concepts of doctoral education can be responsive to the challenge of sustaining a vibrant humanities in good-enough times.

A Time of Troubles, a Time of Opportunity

Let's start then with what numbers reveal about the current state of humanities doctoral education. Data available on earned doctorates, as reported by individuals and by departments for national surveys, give context to the urgency of now. They provide information about numbers of humanities doctorates, time-to-degree, completion rates, the job market, debt, and demographics.[1] Those data can also give up stories to be imagined of students as they move through their studies or move out of them. That data has also driven over 15 years of initiatives and reports that have motivated administrators, faculty, and doctoral students to advocate for change.

Data Realities and Stories

Here are summary snapshots of the data, spiced with some observations.

Numbers of humanities doctoral degree recipients. The National Science Foundation issues data from its Survey of Earned Doctorates, with a lag time for reporting of approximately one and a half years. Data from the 2011–12 survey, the latest data available at this time, indicate that 5,503 people received their doctorates in humanities fields (including history), of which 48.3% were male, 51.6% female.[2] For my field of English, including language, literature, rhetoric and composition, and creative writing, the figure for 2012 was 1,286 earned doctorates, a figure that falls midway between the high of 1,680 earned doctorates reported for 1973 and the low of 705 reported for 1987. In other modern languages the figure for 2012 was 685, again about midway between the high of 917 reported in 1974 and the low of 430 reported in 1989.[3] The longitudinal data thus register a narrative of the robust expansion of doctoral education from the 1950s to the early 1970s; the precipitous downturn in doctorates from 1973 to the end of the 1980s as an effect of the oil crisis and the recessionary retrenchment in funding for public higher education; the renewed growth in the 1990s up to a new peak in 1998 at 80% of the 1973 peak; the gradual decline, perhaps due to some downsizing of doctoral cohorts from the late 1990s in response to inadequate funding packages for doctoral students; and then the gradual rise after 2003 that brought the 2013 numbers up over 4,000 graduates in core humanities disciplines.[4]

Time-to-degree. According to the SED, the average time-to-degree for humanities doctorates is significantly longer than for other sectors of doctoral education. In its 2011 survey the SED reported that the average time-to-degree in the humanities was 9.3 years from entering graduate school (and 11.0 years from the baccalaureate) and, in 2012, 9.0 years from entering graduate school (and 11.0 from the baccalaureate). The longitudinal data reveal that in 1970 the average time-to-degree in the humanities was 6.0 years from time of entrance into graduate school (and 9.0 years from graduation from college). By the end of the 1980s, data reported by Thomas B. Hoffer and Vincent Welch Jr. revealed that time-to-degree had risen to 12.6 years (1989).[5] The figures for 2011 and 2012 continue to register a steady decrease since that high of 12.6.

Such reported data help paint the picture of a continuing time-to-degree problem in doctoral education. More recently, however, the Humanities Indicators project of the National Academy of Arts and Sciences, using SED data but shifting methodology, issued its report "Years to Attainment of a Humanities Doctorate." In late 2014, HI reported the following: "For each of the graduation years 2003 to 2012, the median time humanities Ph.D. recipients spent in their doctoral programs (measured as the difference between the month and year the doctorate was granted and the month and year the student started in the program) was 6.9 years or longer. . . . The median fell from 7.5 years for 2003 graduates to 6.9 years for students graduating in 2011 and 2012." This report offers a less dire story of time-to-degree and suggests that initiatives to address time-to-degree over the last decade, such as continuous enrollment policies, have borne results. But the fact remains that 6.9 is a median, that half of the graduates took longer to complete their degree. (As an aside: The data from 2010 indicate that the average age at time-of-graduation was between 34 and 35 years across all humanities fields.)[6]

Let me add an observation here. It used to be that faculty rarely worried about time-to-degree or the level of debt students accumulated. They knew they admitted more applicants than would finish; that graduate study weeded out the intellectually immature, the unready and unsteady. But that was then, when the cost of higher education was modest at most and when programs such as the National Defense Education Act supported students who were forgiven a certain percentage of the debt for every year they taught after graduation. For a decade now, time-to-degree has been a concern of every graduate college in the country and of most doctoral programs.

Completion rates in the humanities. The Humanities Indicators project analyzed data on completion rates provided by doctoral programs to the National

Research Council for its 2010 report rating doctoral programs across the country. These data revealed that the humanities and mathematical and physical science sectors registered the same median rate of completion at 42%. It is important to note, however, that expected completion for humanities doctorates was set at eight years out from the date of entry into the doctoral program, while for all other sectors it was set at six years out. Across humanities disciplines the rates varied: languages, societies, and cultures programs showed a 33% rate of completion after eight years; history 42% and English 46% after eight years.[7]

Periodically, the Council of Graduate Schools produces the PhD Completion Project figures for completion rates seven years out and 10 years out across humanities fields. In 2008, the CGS released its latest report on completion rates of those who began doctoral education in 1992–1993 through 1994–1995, showing that completion rates after seven years ranged from 17.1% for art history, theory and criticism to 34.2% in philosophy, and across all disciplines averaged 29.4%. Completion rates after 10 years ranged from 40.0% in religion and theology to 50.0% in philosophy (and 62.5% in performance and studio arts). For the humanities as a sector, the 10-year completion rate for these cohorts stood at 48.9%, one of the lowest rates after 10 years in the sectors of higher education measured for this metric.[8]

Some percentage of humanities doctoral students finish their dissertation and degree after the 10-year window set for this report. And, to be sure, other data moderate this picture somewhat. Data from the Mellon Graduate Education Initiative, analyzed in *Educating Scholars: Doctoral Education in the Humanities*, complicate the 10-year cutoff as definitive of an attrition rate. Research on the subject pool of humanities doctoral students in participating programs reveals that "about 25 percent . . . completed their degrees after remaining for 10 years or even longer." Furthermore, of the pool, "Almost 12 percent of the students who left graduate school at one point ultimately received their doctoral degrees—either in the same field at other institutions or in other fields. An additional 18 percent earned professional degrees in fields like law and business."[9] Another finding, important to this topic, is embedded in the data from this initiative. The authors of *Educating Scholars* reported of the cohorts in the project that they "found no indication that protracted degrees make better scholars"; indeed, they found, "Beyond seven years, the probability of getting a tenure-track position declined as degree times lengthened."[10]

More extensive and granular data are needed to get a clearer picture of the attrition rate across the humanities, and not just in certain programs at certain universities reported in *Educating Scholars*. But the percentage of students not completing degrees by 10 years out indicates that at some point in their doctoral studies, a number of students decide not to finish, or to change institutions, or to change careers, for a myriad of reasons. While the noncompletion rate may not be as dramatic as 50%, a time-to-degree extending to eight years and beyond remains concerning. In the words of the MLA Task Force on Doctoral Study in Modern Language and Literature, the average time-to-degree is "unacceptable."[11]

Job openings across the humanities. Statistics from professional associations in humanities disciplines continue to show that doctoral programs graduate more students than there are job openings in humanities fields. This mismatch has long been the case, as longitudinal data indicate, and as reports from professional organizations reveal. Back in 1970, the MLA Commission to Study the Job Market issued a report, authored by David Orr, that lamented the mismatch between graduates and job openings. The report concluded: "Should present trends continue, life in the professions, particularly in the humanities, could turn grim indeed."[12] Since then, there have been two periods in which the mismatch expanded, the early 1990s and the period following the economic meltdown after 2008. But there is another trend in higher education to factor into the overall job prospects for humanities doctorates; and that is the expansion of higher education and the reconfiguration of the professoriate as disproportionately non-tenure-track and contingent.

Let me take the field I know best and use the most recent data produced by the Modern Language Association as it studies the number of jobs posted in the Job Information Lists produced on a rolling basis through each academic year. Annually in December, a summary report analyzing the data of the Job Information List is released before the annual convention. MLA staff are careful to note that the JIL is a snapshot of job openings in English and foreign languages at a particular moment in the academic year; but they also note that over the last decades it has been "a reliable indicator of the job market in the current hiring season."[13] The 2013–14 report registers the precipitous drop in positions advertised in 2008–2009 and observes that "this past year marks the fifth consecutive year the number of jobs advertised in the JIL has remained at a trough level just above 1,000 jobs in each edition, matching the trough of the mid-1990s in both depth and duration."[14] While the JIL report cannot observe trends in part-time positions (since the jobs advertised are almost all full-time), it does register the ratio of full-time tenure/tenure-tracks positions and non-tenure-track positions. Here the evidence confirms that "the downturn in the number of ads since 2008 has been accompanied by a consistently lower percentage of each year's total tagged as tenure-track" (2), a cumulative 10-percentage-point drop in that time. As Laurence observed of the 2014 JIL data, the shift from tenure-track positions to non-tenure-tracks positions can be observed in the stark figure of the ratio.

The Survey of Earned Doctorates from 2011 and 2012 indicates that of the major sectors in the survey, the humanities had the lowest percentage of graduates with "definite employment or study commitments at doctorate award," somewhere around 58%–59%. The MLA's Laurence, reviewing the longitudinal data from the association's survey of student placement, observed that "the placement rate to a tenure-track position for new PhD recipients directly after graduation has barely, and only rarely exceeded 50%. . . . In the most recent, covering graduates who received degrees in 2009–10, only 37.1% had found a tenure-track position."[15] Figures Laurence cited from the same placement data indicate that for 2009–2010 "just over three-quarters (75.8%) had found faculty positions, full- or part-time, by the November following program completion. When positions in academic administration and placements in postdoctoral fellowships are included, 73.1% reported having found full-time employment in a postsecondary institution, and 79.0% reported having full-time employment of any type, in academia or other settings."[16] But to reiterate: of graduates, only 37.1% of graduates who reported their career trajectory took up tenure-track positions.

Since 2008, there might be observable a slight uptick here or there, but even with the upticks, the job market is likely to remain constrained for some time to come. And, according to many analysts of the academic marketplace, job prospects may never return to the level of job opportunities at the end of the 1990s. The over 25-year trend to a majority contingent and non-tenure-track academic workforce continues apace.

Debt. Humanities doctoral students currently support their studies through combinations of teaching assistantships, fellowships and other grants, personal resources, employment, and, very rarely, research assistantships. SED data show that from 1998 through 2012 the percentage of students relying primarily on teaching assistantships rose from around 33% to 40.2%. The data show that a far higher percentage of humanities doctoral students support themselves through teaching; indeed, 42% higher than in all other fields. During those same years the percentage of students accessing personal funds declined from 36.7% to 20.9%. As doctoral students spend a median time of seven plus years in preparation, they accumulate high levels of debt. According to the SED, approximately 60% of humanities doctorates completing their degrees in 2012 had accumulated a record-high level of debt: 28% graduated without education debt, 60% had accumulated some debt, and nearly 34% had debt of $30,000 or more.[17] Student debt for humanities doctorates was higher than student debt in all other fields. Data also reveal that students of color accumulate levels of debt far above the mean.[18] According to 2008 data from the National Postsecondary Student Aid Study and reported by the Council of Graduate Schools (the latest report), 85% of African American doctorate recipients across all fields had accumulated debt, averaging $68,000.[19] As the Humanities Indicators report on paying for doctoral study observes, "The average indebtedness figure for the humanities masks a 'feast or famine' situation with respect to the ability of doctorate recipients to secure funding for their studies."[20]

Time in this context, as in so many contexts, is money. It is the high cost of debt for many, though not for those with robust fellowship funding or personal resources. And it is the opportunity cost of delaying entering the job market. It is also a gamble on return, since the job market situation remains bleak and the first years out for many will be spent in part-time or non-tenure-track positions at woeful or modest levels of remuneration. As one of my research assistants observed: "The return on the investment of getting a college degree is often very low. Especially at first when the student loan bills start coming in and the student is still unemployed, underemployed, or working for barely a 'livable' wage. Extremely stressful, and definitely gives one the feeling of buyer's remorse."[21]

Demographics. Data reveal what has become common knowledge across humanities disciplines. The fields of the humanities are shifting toward a 45/55 split of men to women. And data and the lived experience of graduate directors in humanities disciplines reaffirm that the fields of the humanities continue to struggle to recruit applicants from underrepresented groups within the United States and first-generation students from working-class backgrounds. In 2012, the SED revealed that only 4.7% of doctorates reported their ethnicity as Asian, 4.3% black, 7.7% Hispanic, and 0.3% American Indian / Alaska Native, across humanities disciplines.[22]

Of course, more recent data will be available by the time this book is out. That's a given in the life and afterlife of data. And of course, the data one draws on, the statistics one foregrounds, are influenced by what data are collected and how information is organized, and who's telling stories about it. That said, the current available data offer a snapshot of the state of play in humanities doctoral education at this moment. This snapshot also captures trends; it charts differences among fields and among different demographic groups. It does not tell a story by itself, however. So let me give the numbers a narrative.

So, Now for Narratives to Put with the Numbers

Doctoral students pursue graduate education in the humanities because they imagine themselves doing the work of the humanities over the course of a lifetime. They come to graduate school with a long-nurtured passion for a book, an historical epoch, a twist of linguistic usage, a theory of identity, a question of deeply felt urgency. They come motivated by the models of revered professors or by the narratives people tell of themselves, their communities, their struggles, their traumas. They come driven by the desire to launch journeys beckoning from all around, amid the dust or digital affordances of the archive, in lines of poetry, in the logic of an assertion, in the dirt of the dig. They come with a fascination for ethnographic fieldwork, with a keen sense of the unsettling question, with perverse pleasure in thinking big—about society, culture, knowledge, politics, about gender and sexuality, racialization and ethnicity.

They come with diligent scholarly habits, with their trained disposition of mind, and, quite likely, with a reverence for solitude. They come with their brilliance in coining a phrase, tracking an argument, targeting gaps in logic. They come with their pasts, their relationships, their histories of success and disappointment, their politics and their nonacademic interests. They come with entangled forms of online and offline lives. They come driven and dedicated, gifted and versatile.

Some come savvy about trends large and small, in the academy, in the humanities, and in their fields. Some have already worked in academic institutions, some in libraries. Others have worked overseas or in the private sector or in an NGO or in government. Many have already published novels or books of poetry or written newspaper columns. Some have an ongoing blog presence.

They arrive and settle in. Here they begin to ask pressing, often disorienting, questions. What will my scholarly work look like? How will I do that work? How will it be communicated? To whom will it be addressed? How will it be funded? Who will own it? Who will have access to it? How will I teach? What will my students be like? What different roles will I play? How will I respond to the pace of change ahead? How will I make my case for this field of study I love—to peers and mentors, to hiring committees and decision makers, to alumni and the public at large? How will my career in the academy unfold? Everything about the life of an academic humanist, it seems, is shifting around them.

As one year passes into another, this doctoral study turns out to be not only an intellectual journey, but also a trial, a cacophony of unpredictable pleasures, a social network, a long slog, a disenchantment, a psychic landscape, a familial sacrifice, a demanding job, an initiation, a shifting terrain of tradition and change, and a cauldron of anxiety, about adequacy, performance, and future prospects.

For me, the numbers intersect with the stories of this lived experience of graduate training. The inflationary rise in the cost of higher education has led to the rise in debt level of students upon graduation. These financial costs to students will undoubtedly continue to rise as budget pressures prompt ongoing or periodic cuts in fellowship funding, travel funding, and summer stipends. Many students stay on track, even some of those who develop a deep skepticism about the project of doctoral education and the prospects ahead. Many find a workable balance between their personal and professional commitments. Many immerse themselves in the diverse opportunities for leadership and professional development available to them. Many bring brilliant dissertations to their defense. Many find tenure-track positions the first or second year on the market, or the third or fourth years.

Others lose momentum after completing exams, finding themselves suddenly adrift without the incessant and somehow soothing pressure of imminent deadlines. They watch debt accumulate, lose steam, dissociate from peers, avoid mentors and advisors, suffer disenchantment with their topic, stall out. They find themselves overwhelmed with teaching responsibilities, anxious at the stack of papers to grade, exhausted with responding to initiatives to improve one's pedagogy. They find themselves about out of funding, and with little progress made on the dissertation. One term passes with little progress, then a year. After fellowships and teaching positions dry up, some slip away entirely. Others enter an exploited labor pool of contingent faculty earning as little as $2,500 for each course they teach, becoming "freeway flyers" teaching multiple courses at multiple institutions. Some come to the defense after several years away with a less-than-promising dissertation.

And the future? Unpredictable for any individual graduate, it is distressingly predictable in terms of the academic job prospects. Students learn that openings for tenure-track positions track the economy, that the economic meltdown of 2008 brought a precipitous decline in full-time tenure-track academic positions. They find themselves in an academy with a growing imbalance in the percentage of tenure and tenure-track faculty and part- and full-time non-tenure-track faculty. They hear about doctoral students who enter contingent positions that may or may not lead to satisfying careers in the academy. They learn of the new job search in which advanced doctoral students and recently minted PhDs confront a protracted search process. They hear about graduates spending two, three, four, even five years in search mode, seeking postdoctoral positions or non-tenure-track positions, full- or part-time, along the way. They are pushed to become early and ready professionals, giving papers, writing essays, assembling lists of achievements so their dossiers grab the attention of search committees. They watch the details of the year's searches on the wikis that both compel them to look for news and to resist the call to look. As these realities sink in, doctoral students become even more anxious, and cynical. Many struggle to remain resiliently hopeful. An increasing number of them begin to think about, and plan for, alternative careers.

The numbers thus speak of isolation, of a sense of drift, of the pressure to maintain persistent self-motivation. They speak of anxiety, inertia, a sense of confusion, embarrassment, shame, a sense of failure. They speak of "languishing," the term the authors of *Educating Scholars* use to describe the condition of neither finishing nor dropping out.[23] They speak of a daunting overload of obligations to family, to community, to mentors, to peers. They speak of relationships under stress and parenting postponed, a major issue for women in the academy.[24] They speak of high levels of economic anxiety. They intimate high levels of stress, and mental distress. In the words of the "White Paper on the Future of the PhD in the Humanities," issued through the Social Science and Humanities Research Council of Canada, "As time passes, graduate study can become an increasingly unsustainable financial and personal sacrifice for students."[25]

The data also tell stories of graduate programs. They tell of the inability of some programs to adequately support students on teaching assistantships, but more importantly on fellowships. They tell of the increasing gap between resources and support available to those at the elite privates and public flagships and those at less well-funded universities. They tell of difficulties in recruiting diverse cohorts of doctoral students and the consequent lack of demographic diversity around the seminar table, and of the underproduction of doctorates of color. They tell of curricular straitjackets. They tell of sporadic mentoring. They tell of laissez-faire values of scholarly inquiry. They tell of a one-model-fits-all trajectory. They tell of the intensification of professional norms and the difficulties of breaking through normative expectations of an academic humanist.

The Time Is Now

Given these realities—of a higher than desirable average time-to-degree and dismal job prospects into the future—the call for the transformation of doctoral education has now become a broad one. Across North America, deans of graduate schools, foundation officers, faculty, and doctoral students are contributing to a national conversation about the humanities in higher education and about doctoral education for the next generations.

That sense of urgency follows a succession of efforts to address the stark realities of doctoral education in the humanities. Let me briefly, and only selectively, survey these efforts. In the late 1990s and early 2000s, foundations and professional organizations sought to stimulate improvements in the curricular shape and experience of graduate education in ways that would decrease time-to-degree and improve graduation rates. The 10-year Mellon Graduate Education Initiative, the Carnegie Initiative on the Doctorate, and the Council of Graduate Schools' PhD Completion Project all tackled time-to-degree and attrition by various means: enhanced funding packages, clearer goals and regularized feedback on advancement to completion, more rational curricular models, better mentoring, and a more supportive climate.[26]

A bolder initiative tackling time-to-degree gained attention in late 2012 when the national education press reported on the Stanford initiative on doctoral education in the humanities. At Stanford, a group of faculty leaders in humanities disciplines, among them Russell Berman, 2011 president of the Modern Language Association, wrote the dean of Arts and Sciences requesting 12-month funding for students to decrease time-to-degree to an optimal five years. In order to secure commitment to enhanced funding, the humanities departments agreed to revise coursework, timing of exams, and mentoring.[27] In 2015, the University of California–Irvine announced its Mellon-supported 5+2 initiative in doctoral education in the humanities. With two departments (philosophy and visual studies) leading the way, the 5+2 program guarantees five years of fellowship and teaching funding plus an additional two years of intensive teaching in a postdoctoral position for those students finishing their PhD in five years.[28] With prestigious private and public universities such as Stanford and Irvine boldly addressing time-to-degree, administrators, faculty, and students have joined in debate, registering enthusiasm or critiquing what they descry as a speeded-up degree concept.

In response to constrained job prospects, activism has shifted to preparing doctoral students for new career paths. In 2010, *The Path Forward: The Future of Graduate Education in the United States*, issued by the Commission on the Future of Graduate Education, called for increased emphasis on professional development and "nonacademic career pathways" in doctoral programs.[29] And in 2011, Anthony T. Grafton and Jim Grossman, president and executive director of the American Historical Association respectively, published a provocative statement entitled "No More Plan B," arguing that the job market in humanities disciplines, realistically confronted, would not come roaring back in the near future, even when the economy shifts from sputtering forward to a more robust mode. "As public contributions to higher education shrink, state budgets contract, and a lagging economy takes its toll on endowments and family incomes," they argued, "there is little reason to expect the demand for tenure-track faculty to expand."[30] What Grafton and Grossman observed of history doctoral students educated to become academic historians is generalizable across the humanities: this emphasis on plan A—academic employment as a tenure-track professor—"pushes talented scholars into narrow channels, and makes it less likely that they will take schooled historical thinking with them into a wide range of employment sectors," the sectors a large proportion of humanities graduates will enter.[31] Time to change the discourse of success; time to plan for multiple futures.

The Woodrow Wilson Foundation had already funded a five-year Responsive Ph.D. initiative designed in part to "illuminate paths to alternative careers outside the research university."[32] And the American Council of Learned Societies had begun its Public Fellows Program, placing recent PhDs from the humanities and humanistic social sciences in two-year positions in nonprofit and public service positions.[33] But after the "No More Plan B" mantra got legs, more and more sessions at annual conventions of the major professional organizations began to focus on multiple careers in and out of the academy. Humanities departments and graduate schools across the country now organize panels and workshops on alternative careers for humanities PhDs, inviting to campus graduates working in nonacademic sectors or in alternative academic jobs in higher education. And major intellectual leaders who hold professional jobs inside the academy in libraries, digital humanities labs, and museums and institutes blog, talk, and make the case for the new realities of this expanding sector of humanities professionals.

In addition to tackling time-to-degree and addressing preparation for alternative careers, there are two other strands of transformation on the radar. In the last decade, funding agencies and national organizations have shifted foci in recognition of the changing environment of humanities scholarship addressed in Part II. The Mellon-funded Scholarly Communication Institute, located at the University of Virginia from 2003 to 2013, for instance, held meetings and issued invaluable reports on new media and modes of scholarly communication, and the impact of this new intellectual ecology on doctoral training and its importance to new career paths for professionally trained humanists.

Another strand of program activism has focused on public scholarship. Across North America, initiatives in public or engaged scholarship gained momentum in the humanities with the launch of the Imagining America project at a 1999 White House Conference sponsored by the White House Millennium Council, the University of Michigan, and the Woodrow Wilson National Fellowship Foundation. Under the founding leadership of Julie Ellison and now Timothy K. Eatman, Imagining America has, over some 15 years, built a network of more than 100 colleges and universities and other partners, to "push the boundaries of civic engagement in higher education"; issued *Scholarship in Public: Knowledge Creation and Tenure Policy in the Engaged University*; held annual conferences; and now launched the journal *Public*.[34] Now there are programs in engaged scholarship involving doctoral students at many universities, including the robust program at the Walter Chapin Simpson Center for the Humanities at the University of Washington, under the leadership of Kathleen Woodward. The Center offers a graduate certificate in public scholarship and the Public Scholarship award program.[35] Ellison, Eatman, Woodward, and Gregory Jay advocate that opportunities for engaged scholarship expand the concept of humanities scholarship and its arenas; decenter academic knowledge production through collaborative cultures of inquiry; provide important models for doctoral training through project-based collaboratories; and contribute to community-based efforts to advance social justice and public goods benefits.

Two major reports issued within six months of one another captured the range of intersecting issues relevant to transforming doctoral education for the 21st century. They both acknowledge the troubling realities of the academic humanities and the changing conditions of the scholarly and teaching life of faculty; they both make recommendations for change. In Canada, the "White Paper on the Future of the PhD in the Humanities" appeared in December 2013, a product of the Knowledge Synthesis Project on the future of graduate education across the disciplines funded by SSHRC.[36] Held at the Institute for the Public Life of Arts and Ideas at McGill University, under the leadership of Paul Yachnin, the humanities meeting brought together faculty across the arts and humanities, professional humanists in arts institutions across Canada, and humanities doctoral students at McGill to think proactively about new directions, new partnerships, and new concepts of the degree.[37] And in May 2014, the MLA Task Force on Doctoral Study in Modern Language and Literature, chaired by Berman, issued its report and its extensive list of recommendations.[38] I was fortunate to have served on both committees and have benefited from extended conversations unfolding over the course of the year of meetings and consultations. Traces of those conversations and references to the recommendations will emerge in my arguments for change in the next sections of this book.

And finally, two 2015 books engage, directly and in depth, the troubles with graduate education in the United States: Leonard Cassuto's *The Graduate School Mess: What Caused It and How We Can Fix It* and Julie R. Posselt's *Inside Graduate Admissions: Merit, Diversity, and Faculty Gatekeeping*.[39] Cassuto's *Mess* tracks the history of graduate admissions across a century and a half of U.S. higher education; elaborates the ways in which graduate education enforces conformity to constraining norms of professionalism, devalues teaching, and reifies research training; offers a critique of the ethos of prestige; and calls for greater transparency in presenting future prospects to prospective students. Posselt's probing study gets granular with the actual work of admissions committees and the values that circulate through discussions of students who "fit" the program and those who don't. In their deliberations and their iterations of criteria for acceptance, Posselt observed the enactment of what she terms "homophily," the love of like kind, a disposition that is risk averse. As the abstract for her book suggests: "Good intentions notwithstanding, what counts in practice as merit often serves to institutionalize inequalities." Both scholars provide hands-on suggestions for transforming graduate education,

Cassuto by reordering the ethos of graduate education toward an expanded repertoire of values, most particularly the importance of pedagogical training and engaged scholarship, and Posselt by making admissions processes less constrained by reproductive norms that value prestige applicants perceived as having the right stuff.

What Is to Be Done?

Here's what the foundation initiatives, white papers, task force reports, and scholarly books do not call for in this disruptive, challenging, and daunting time. They do not call for the elimination of doctoral programs in the humanities. They do not call for some rationing system for doctoral education that would determine which programs survive, which grow, and which close down. They do not caution against developing and launching new kinds of doctoral programs in the humanities. They do not claim that graduate programs are educating too many humanists at the doctoral level. Others do make these arguments, as is evidenced in the media and in responses to the reports. They call for decreasing the number of programs and the size of cohorts. But not here, in the activities, statements, and aspirations of all those foundations, institutions, administrators, faculty, and students who are taking a stand, making a case, calling for change.

The SSHRC white paper affirmed the value to the nation of robust doctoral education in the humanities: "We argue that the world of the 21st century needs high quality humanities research and teaching now more than ever. The need has to do with the undergraduate education of tens of thousands of young Canadians each year. It also has to do with how the kinds of knowledge borne of [sic] the humanities can contribute to clearer, more historically informed, and more ethical understandings of problems that face modern Canada."[40] Of course, humanists make the case for humanities doctoral education before a skeptical and sometimes downright dismissive public; but that doesn't mean the investment in that case is only self-serving. I believe in the case that's made. There will never be too many doctorally trained professionals and lifelong learners in this country, this hemisphere, and around the globe.

For me, it's misguided to advocate for major cuts to doctoral programs in the humanities or for closure of some number of them. Critics who call for drastic cuts in admissions might recollect that many programs made significant cuts throughout the late 1990s and 2000s, after tenure-track positions did not materialize in the early 1990s when institutions experienced a robust number of retirements. In the wake of the 2008 financial collapse, *Inside Higher Education* reported in May 2009 on "Top Ph.D. Programs, Shrinking"; and three years later the *Chronicle of Higher Education* noted that "Grad Programs in

Humanities Are Shrinking," in reporting on several large flagship universities.[41] Those critics who call for the closure of programs never put on the table a realistic plan on how such an initiative for selective closure might advance.

And they might recall administrators who acted to close down humanities departments and doctoral programs in the wake of the 2008 financial meltdown usually made the argument for closure on similar grounds. Russell Berman made this point in his "Essay Defending the MLA Report on Doctoral Education," published in *Inside Higher Education* in July 2014: "The scope of the humanities in higher education in the United States already faces significant reduction. We should be fighting for the humanities rather than closing off advanced study, the key to sustained presence in colleges and universities."[42] Critics who call for the closure of programs should offer up their plan on how such an initiative might advance; should talk from the position of having acted on their argumentative principles. Let them say how. Let them say where. Let them say by what criteria. Let them say to what end.

I refuse arguments calling for fewer doctoral programs for several reasons. The strength of doctoral education in the humanities in the United States is the diversity of schools offering doctoral training: public, private, religious, secular, urban, regional, gigantic, small. The strength is in the diversity of emphases, constellations of faculty, and cross-disciplinary filiations. The more the diversity, from my point of view, the more energy and impetus for innovation, for risk-taking, for experimentation, for recognizing and achieving excellence. And here's a second reason, about another kind of diversity. It comes via Dolan Hubbard, who argues that "the national debate about the overproduction of PhDs dangerously ignores the underproduction of African American PhDs within the academy. . . . The quiet consensus to limit access to graduate programs is an ethnically and socially irresponsible position when viewed from the perspective of the underproduction of African American PhDs."[43] Humanities departments also underproduce doctorates who come from Hispanic communities, from indigenous communities, who are the first in their families to go to university.

My reasons are personal as well. I am the product of a second-tier, and some might say third-tier, doctoral program at Case Western Reserve University in Cleveland. I grew up in Cleveland and returned there after I got a BA and MA at the University of Michigan. I had trained for high school teaching but knew after one semester it was not the career I wanted. So I applied to Case because it was a university I knew. My brother got a PhD in physics there in the early 1960s. That university and the faculty in that department gave me my career. I was the beneficiary of the program's modest size, its small doctoral cohort, and its openness to women graduate students. I was the beneficiary of faculty who maintained high expectations of their female students at a time when larger, flagship state universities and the elite privates tolerated a woman or two but failed to mentor them adequately or with grace and generosity. I knew I would never have the bona fides of my many colleagues with PhDs from the Ivys. But I have always taken pride in my pedigree from Case. This is exactly the kind of doctoral program that could be seen as expendable when those trained at the elite privates and publics make the case for downsizing doctoral education in the United States.

I have also served on review teams for doctoral programs at large and small universities. I was bowled over, when on a review team at Duquesne University in Pittsburgh, at the quality of the faculty, the dedication of the doctoral students, and the sense of teaching mission absorbed and reflected. There are far more gifted, imaginative, and passionate candidates for doctoral education than can be served by the elites. Think of what would happen to diversity of vision, heritage, background, life circumstances, intellectual style, learning dispositions, if admissions filters were homogenized in certain metrics of preparation. That, for me, is that.

The overarching theme of the reports and white papers and initiatives, taken collectively, is that the times require the transformation of doctoral education, to prepare students for the new everyday life of the academic humanist, to energize them to complete their degrees and in a reasonable time, to design degrees that can be completed in five or six years, and to help students imagine many possible careers. That's what the MLA and SSHRC reports map out in their different ways. They call for new kinds of courses, new kinds of programs, new kinds of dissertations, new modes of skills training.

And doctoral students are partners in this call for transformation. They serve on task forces, sit on committees and staff meetings, organize panels, give papers. They seek out new sets of skills. They talk with advisors about new dissertation platforms and authoring tools. They press the norms of their discipline, if tentatively and with concern for the consequences to their careers. They conceptualize new kinds of dissertations. They push against the normative discourse of humanities doctoral training. They advocate for a more inclusive climate, and curriculum. They carve out new positions in the academy when they graduate. They are on the front line of change.

What is needed, then, is a posttraditional doctoral education, for students and for a sustainable humanities. What I am calling a posttraditional doctoral education involves several strands of transformation: conceptualizing flexible programs, expanding forms of the dissertation, and enhancing preparation responsive to conditions on the ground. Let's reimagine doctoral programs that will support and energize students to stay on track, hold fast to peer networks, find multiple kinds of mentors, minimize debt and anxiety, and maintain a sense of possibility, if not certainty, about the future, whatever career path unfolds. To meet these goals, and to prepare a generation of humanists to be change agents for the humanities, the academy needs flexible, imaginative, and rigorous doctoral programs, ones that encompass all kinds of experiences in and out of the classroom, that provide opportunities to develop expanded repertoires of skills and competencies, that prepare future faculty for the new scholarly and teaching life, that nurture the pleasures of long attention, that foster openness to new possibilities for scholarly communication to multiple audiences and via multiple forms and vehicles, that prepare the way for success in as-yet-unimagined professions inside and outside the academy. A 20th-century doctoral education will not meet these goals. A 21st-century doctoral education will.

Breathing Life into the Dissertation

What is fast becoming the "new normal" in the everyday life of academic humanists will require people to be intellectually nimble; conversant in digital media, networks, archives, and identities; energized by collaboration; flexible in their modes of address; imaginative in their pedagogical practice; and adept at telling the story about what they do. The challenge is to reorganize doctoral education to meet the imperatives and the opportunities of the 21st-century academy.

I'm going to start at the end, with the big kahuna, and work from there. Since 2010, I have been arguing that expanding the forms of the dissertation must be a cornerstone for responding to these conditions—precisely because it is the hardest nut to crack on the way to transforming the humanities doctorate. Both the SSHRC white paper and MLA task force report recognized this need for more flexibility in definition, form, and project of the dissertation.[1]

For me, the argument for embracing more flexible dissertation options proceeds from recognition that, in these good-enough times, it's imperative to affirm the *intellectual mission* of the PhD as a project and redefine its paths of achievement. The current model is no longer adequate to the state of higher education, the state of the disciplines, and the nature of future jobs in the profession. The quality, extension, and liveliness of scholarly conversations across humanities fields in the next decades depend on this redefinition as well as the vitality of the liberal arts in an academy pressured to pursue an instrumentalist vision of higher education. If doctoral study is to launch the careers of future academic humanists and contribute to a robust humanities, then more flexible road maps through the degree, and a more flexible set of models for its capstone, are required.

In earlier initiatives, cited in the previous section, what remained an unquestioned given in responses to the problem of the humanities doctorate was the dissertation monograph. The summary finding of the Mellon project reported in the October 12, 2009, *Chronicle of Higher Education* makes recommendations on the relationship of funding to attrition in humanities doctoral programs; it says nothing about rethinking the dissertation itself. No "thinking outside the box" with regard to the dissertation took place at meetings of English department faculty and students sponsored by the Carnegie Initiative on the Doctorate, in which I participated as chair of the English department at Michigan. And the seven-year project undertaken by the Council of Graduate Studies, and funded by the Ford Foundation and Pfizer, nowhere raises central issues about the dissertation as a genre of scholarly production in its recent, fourth monograph out of the project, entitled *Ph.D. Completion and Attrition: Policies and Practices to Promote Student Success.*[2]

There are reasons for the continuing investment in the dissertation monograph. It is the presumed measure of "promise" in most humanities fields, a demonstration that doctoral students can accomplish the arduous work of imagining, researching, digesting, organizing, and arguing in fluid prose important interventions in their fields. Here is the discourse that constellates around the proto-monograph as dissertation. It is performative, a sustained set of acts through which certain habits of mind are practiced and internalized, the pleasures of solitary inquiry, for instance. Encouraging these habits, faculty prepare the next generation of scholars for the extended intellectual inquiry requisite to producing an important first book and entering, enlivening, and influencing scholarly conversations. It is a ticket to a career in the academy. It leads to the tenure book. Without it, the probability of tenure for the individual diminishes and the institution of tenure itself becomes vulnerable to attack. No wonder it is difficult to unthink the proto-monograph as signature to the humanities doctorate. Skeptics, and there are and will be many, will thus decry what they perceive to be an assault on standards in humanities education with the introduction of options to the dissertation monograph. They will declare it reckless to launch candidates on the troubled job market without the security of a traditional dissertation.

Let's disentangle some of the assumptions behind the investment in the proto-monograph dissertation. The assumption is that in the humanities the terms *originality, expertise, mastery,* and *substantive contribution* are associated exclusively with the book as codex. The assumption is that writing a proto-monograph is the only form of preparation for writing a long-form book. The assumption is that a monograph dissertation needs only a modest amount of revision to become a book. The assumption is that the monograph dissertation is the only predictor of future success as a humanities scholar. The assumption is that all this is understood by doctoral students and doesn't require articulating. I am challenging these assumptions, as have many colleagues, dating back to 1995 and David Damrosch's *We Scholars*; or, as historians of higher education have observed, dating far back to a 1903 piece written by William James and entitled "The PhD Octopus."³

I would argue that insistence on only the traditional form of the dissertation as capstone will disadvantage doctoral students and adversely affect the quality of doctoral education in the humanities. Make no mistake. The hold of the traditional concept of the book as the sole criterion for tenure and promotion in humanities disciplines is loosening as I write. In the spirit of Recommendation 19 of the 2006 MLA "Report of the MLA Task Force on Evaluating Scholarship for Tenure and Promotion," it is beyond time to rethink the fetishization of the dissertation monograph as the culmination of doctoral education in the humanities.⁴ The current dissertation monograph remains inflexibly wedded to the traditional book culture format; and the habits of inquiry and production it reinforces may not train doctoral students in the many scholarly skills and the new kinds of dispositions necessary to navigate the emergent environment of scholarly communication, which I explored in Part II. Reaffirming that there is only one way of doing the dissertation—and that is as a proto-monograph—trains and constrains students in a one-model-fits-all version of doctoral education that is no longer adequate to the times. The need is great to ask questions anew, to energize inquiry into the implications of current practices. What is it to be "a scholar" and to be "scholarly" now?

A Short History

Of course, the concept of the dissertation has itself changed over time, as well as the conventions of producing it. Ku-ming (Kevin) Chang has observed of the early modern dissertation in scientific fields that it involved "the collaboration of two actors: the supervisor, who prepared the textual thesis, and the degree candidate who performed an oral defense. Neither of them had exclusive rights to, or claimed exclusive authorship of the thesis."⁵ In German practice (for which the historical archive is most robust), the student defended the disputation written by the supervisor; paid for the disputation to be written down; and, if successful, paid for its printing and the free copies submitted to the university.⁶ This arrangement of collaborative production through a differentiated hierarchy of authority had two effects: it furthered the supervisor's reputation and intellectual authority and trained the new generation of scholars in the skills of disputation. In such an environment of knowledge reproduction, Barbara Crossouard notes, "University education developed appropriate performances that reflected 'given' arguments. . . . It was therefore about internalizing and reproducing authoritative forms of expression and conduct in rehearsals of established canons of knowledge."⁷ This arrangement of practice derives from the medieval and early modern knowledge economy in which "truth" was already there to be found in Holy Scripture and in classical philosophy.

By the 18th century, an alternative model of the dissertation had emerged with the rise of the experimental method in the sciences, the inductive method for finding a truth that hadn't already been established. The new model dissertation, presenting the results of original experimental work in the field of the advisor's expertise, took shape in the labs of the medical scientist Albrecht von Haller at Göttingen, Germany. Haller introduced experimental labor as a key component of the dissertation, labor that eventuated in what Chang describes as "solitary or exclusive authorship . . . made possible by the supervisor's relinquishment of his share" of the credit; and this exclusive authorship, observes Chang, "was used to reward the students' experimental work and monetary investment."[8] This model of research became institutionalized in German universities by the beginning of the 19th century; and toward the end of the century it was the model adopted in the United States when Johns Hopkins established the first graduate programs in advanced study.

In the late 19th and early decades of the 20th century in the United States, the printing/publication of the dissertation, an original work by an independent scholar, remained a compulsory requirement for graduation, as it had been in earlier centuries.[9] Completion of the doctoral degree, what Cassuto references as the "researcher-in-training" degree,[10] thus ensured the publication of an "unvetted" monograph by a university press or publication office.[11] This publishing practice, Gary A. Olson and Julie Drew note in their brief history of the doctoral dissertation, "was premised on the notion that the dissertation is in fact a scholar's first full-length scholarly book," as it had been and continues to be in Europe.[12] With publication, the successful graduate could expect to find a position in a college or university through access to the director's professional network.

The number of doctorates increased substantially by the 1930s, and university presses no longer commandeered the resources to publish all dissertations produced. To fill the vacuum, University Microfilms launched in 1938, ensuring the preservation and cataloging of every dissertation produced in North America. This shift in responsibility from university presses to UMI eventuated in a change of role for university presses; according to Olson and Drew, presses focused on publishing books by seasoned scholars, thereby enhancing academic press profiles in the publishing world. This shift marked as well changes in the doctoral dissertation. "Rather than the first major project that a scholar completes as a 'professional,'" they observe,

> it became the last major project a scholar completes as a "student." This perception seems to have resulted in changes in the actual form of the dissertation, so much so that the dissertation became a different genre from

the scholarly monograph. As an academic exercise, the dissertation became primarily the instrument by which students demonstrated to their professors that they had a thorough grasp of research in the field.[13]

The humanities dissertation turned into proto-monograph.

The 1970s brought shifts in the relationship of dissertation to first job, first monograph, and tenure. These changes came with the consolidation of practices of peer review at presses and journals. Phil Pochoda elaborates several factors affecting the shifting ethos and practice of academic publishing with the introduction of peer review of manuscripts:

> While the scholarly disciplines had previously weighed in formally but erratically post-publication on the merits of monographs through reviews in prestigious professional journals, and informally in many other ways, by building in the review hurdle or authorization within the publishing process itself, it [sic] attempted to ensure that every published monograph, all published content, attained at least a minimal professional level.[14]

This shift was one of professionalization—from unvetted processes of publishing work by those from the press's institution to vetted review processes at all levels of acquisition, editing, and production.[15] The first book, peer reviewed and published by an academic press, would now be the gold standard for earning tenure; and the dissertation as proto-monograph would now be the predictor of success in that arduous realization of promise.

The 2006 MLA report on criteria for tenure and promotion delineated several contributing factors related to heightened expectations for successful tenure.[16] The 1970s was a buyer's market for untenured faculty in literatures and languages and other humanities fields. That's when the annual conventions of professional organizations, such as the MLA, became marketplaces in which multiple candidates competed for scarce positions, displayed their wares and their promise. The quality of the dissertation monograph, its sophistication, boldness, and demonstrable scholarliness became the major filter for distinguishing candidates in the new search process, now itself a vetting process. During this decade as well, the demographics of humanities doctoral students changed as more and more white women and men and women of color completed doctoral studies, diversifying the pool of potential candidates and testing the terms of candidate assessment. No longer could a newly minted PhD assume that he would find a job through the old-boys network. Additionally, the democratization of departmental governance eroded the formerly authoritarian power of the chair acting unilaterally and without accountability.[17] In the words of the task force *Report*:

The new emphasis on publication and other criteria for tenure was an expression, then, not only of the higher demands created by a buyers' market but also of the search for safeguards against the possible arbitrariness or bias of chairs and of department factions unsympathetic to the new demographics of the profession and to new developments in literary study.[18]

The shift to less personally based and autocratically guided hiring practices benefited many graduates entering their first jobs in the 1970s and 1980s. It did me.

These are changes that promised to serve the project of diversifying the profession by gender and race, and by intellectual and theoretical projects. Completion of the degree and its pedigree, publication of first articles, contracts for first books: these criteria were not only about the "fit" of a person for a department; they were demonstrable. But the expectation of measurable achievement could be, and indeed was, ratcheted up. In this intellectual economy, the entire edifice of evaluation for tenure and promotion depended upon the stability of academic presses and their economic models for finding and circulating scholarly work.

Critiques of the system tended to focus on the intensification of specialization and the calcification of the apparatus and the discourse of the dissertation. Olson and Drew, for instance, decried the fate of the proto-monograph:

> It became overburdened with exhaustive reviews of the scholarly literature, intended less to establish the context for a discussion (as a good scholarly monograph would do succinctly) than to demonstrate knowledge and competence. It also became bogged down in a superfluity of discursive footnotes, and even the language changed to the defensive, obfuscatory, stilted prose now referred to as dissertationese.[19]

Appropriate obeisance to scholarly conventions; acknowledgment of others' work; citations as recognition of intellectual property; careful, nuanced analyses; performance of disciplinary practice. Yes, all that. But also the navel gazing of intimate circles of interlocutors; the repetition of close readings without much difference; the easy recourse to insider's language; the freight of lethargic prose. I am purposefully overstating the case here—in part to counter the assumption of the proto-monograph dissertation as almost a book.

Fifteen years ago, Olson and Drew called for the "rehabilitation" of the dissertation from its capture in "dissertationese." Theirs was a call to make the dissertation more truly like a monograph. Then came the 21st century. In the 2000s, the crisis in scholarly publishing and the proliferation of digital affordances for new modes of scholarly communication unsettled the environment of publication and the relationship of dissertation as proto-monograph to first book and potential tenure. Presses under severe budget constraints eliminated series and contracted their fields of focus. Chairs and deans worried about the likelihood of probationary faculty getting contracts for first books as presses saw print runs dwindle. University press editors protested the way that tenure committees ceded responsibility for the assessment of scholarly work to anonymous readers whose reports were not written as tenure documents.

As the troubles in academic publishing intensified, colleagues, questioning the monograph dissertation as the culmination of doctoral study, issued calls for change in the publishing system and its impact on faculty careers, often invoking Lindsay Waters's pithy phrase "the tyranny of the monograph."[20] In 2006, Leslie Monkman wrote:

> The tyranny of the dissertation as larval monograph remains the key source of "the tyranny of the monograph" (the phrase is Lindsay Waters's, currently Executive Editor for the Humanities of Harvard University Press). In complex mutations, that tyranny emerges in the appointment, tenure, and promotion decisions determining not only our own careers but also our decisions on the careers of others, and it drives the current valuation of teaching, research, and service.[21]

That same year, the MLA *Report* cautioned about the fetishization of "the book" for tenure and recommended greater flexibility in the criteria committees, departments, and deans apply in making tenure decisions: "The profession as a whole should develop a more capacious conception of scholarship by rethinking the dominance of the monograph, promoting the scholarly essay, establishing multiple pathways to tenure, and using scholarly portfolios."[22] Reminding readers that "the monograph as the gold standard for tenure dossiers is a relatively recent development," the *Report* argued that "rigorous quality standards for scholarship are not tied directly to monograph production."[23]

In 2010, as noted earlier, I dedicated two MLA *Newsletter* columns to making the case for an expanded repertoire of forms for the dissertation. Then in late 2013 and early 2014 the SSHRC white paper and the *Report of the MLA Task Force on Doctoral Study in Modern Language and Literature* both called for more flexibility in the form the dissertation can take. Additionally, over the last half decade the appearance of dissertations in multimedia formats and new authoring platforms, even in comics form, has begun to register the diverse repertoire of models for innovative dissertations.

Making the Case

Here are five interlocking arguments for expanding the repertoire of models for the humanities dissertation. These arguments speak to the changing ecology of humanistic scholarship and teaching in the 21st century, reprising traces of earlier discussions.

1. The digital revolution requires doctoral programs to prepare students for new knowledge ecologies, new resource economies, new research practices and methodologies, and new modes of scholarly communication. Doctoral students need to know about the state of scholarly publishing, the shifts in scholarly practices, the new kinds of relationships scholars will have toward their work, and the opportunities and challenges of an open-access ethos. Students will increasingly use and create digital archives and innovate digital modes of scholarly presentation and communication in the next decade. They will have access to new funding opportunities, made available through foundations and the NEH, and through corporations such as Google. They will participate in open peer-to-peer review. Some will develop the persona of the scholarly blogger. Others may get involved in the work of new e-journals. Yet the current dissertation monograph remains inflexibly wedded to the traditional book culture format; and the habits of inquiry and production its conventional demands reinforce may not train doctoral students in methodologies enabled by, and skills necessary to navigate, this emergent environment.

2. The singular and solitary model of the scholarly career in the humanities, a model inaugurated in graduate school in the student's struggle to write a proto-monograph, can no longer be the only model of the humanist's life. Future faculty in humanities disciplines will require flexible and improvisational habits of mind and collaborative skills to bring their scholarship to fruition. Scholarly inquiry will move forward through the mobilization of scholarly networks, networks that include not only scholar-peers but graduate and undergraduate students.

Remaining wedded to the dissertation monograph as an isolated venture will limit students' preparation for this increasingly collaborative scholarly world. Opening opportunities for diverse models of the dissertation and diverse ensembles of scholarly inquiry will signal the importance of preparation for new cultures of collegiality, what Damrosch, in We Scholars, terms "intellectual sociability":

> When people acculturate themselves to academic life by enhancing their tolerance for solitary work and diminishing their intellectual sociability, they reduce their ability to address problems that require collaborative solutions, or even that require close attention to the perspectives offered by

approaches or disciplines other than one's own. The structuring of graduate education quietly but pervasively discourages such close attention, fostering instead a culture in which people work alone or within the perspectives and expectations of a small group of like-minded peers.[24]

Recognizing and playing to different scholarly dispositions, learning trajectories, intellectual passions, and expertise, a 21st-century doctoral education encourages students to engage their peers as co-inquirers rather than competitors; to engage their faculty advisors and mentors as partners; and to engage an ensemble of colleagues whose expertise animates their imagination, sense of opportunity, and purpose.

3. The primary message currently conveyed is one about final product, the proto-monograph. There's a long history to that message, as Cassuto observes: "Early practices laid the ground for the researcher bias that endures today—with teachers barely allowed on the island and then only because their tuition supports researchers. And most important, teaching is explicitly disrespected as a constituent part of the research enterprise."[25] The message is not one about preparing for a career as a scholar-teacher in the next decades. The time and stress involved in completing the dissertation monograph now absorb the psychic, affective, and intellectual energies of doctoral students, often overwhelming what attention they might want to direct toward preparation for and intellectual inquiry into the future of learning.

Doctoral students will be shortchanged if they do not graduate as skilled teachers, excited to be in the classroom and adept at engaging classes of various sizes, of diverse student literacies, and diverse demographics; and familiar with and innovative in digital teaching environments. They will benefit from knowledge of new modes and methods of organizing classroom dynamics, activities, and relationships. They will benefit from knowledge of hybrid course formats, and from some familiarity with trends in online teaching and open educational resource development and adaptation. They will benefit from articulating an elegant story of the relationship between their teaching and their scholarship. They will benefit from having written, and perhaps even published, an article analyzing pedagogical practice, or from having created innovative open educational resources. And all these benefits will position them to tell the story of their future plans in the classroom in letters of application and in interviews. For as various commentators note, not all graduates will go on to elite research institutions; and even those institutions have recalibrated the balance between attention to the quality of teaching and the quality of research in their personnel decisions.

4. With so much riding on the production of the proto-monograph, doctoral students invest years in developing a careful scholarly voice. That voice

is one that takes care, demonstrates due diligence, catches brilliance, digs for persistence, rehearses discursive knowledge, and aims for scholarly credibility. Yes, the honing of a scholarly voice is part of graduate education in the humanities. But so much is invested in one form of scholarly voice that aspiring humanists do not experiment with speaking through multiple voices to multiple audiences. Future faculty will want to communicate their work in different modes and write for different audiences.

They will write for specialists in their fields, of course, but there are other audiences to address: academics outside the humanities, collaborators from multiple disciplines, public policy professionals, nonacademic advocates for the humanities, donors, the savvy crowd, and a range of what Virginia Woolf termed "common readers." These are the people who attend events sponsored by state humanities councils, who read broadly, who support cultural institutions. These are people in communities with whom public scholarship engages. These are people who exist in publics that are radically reconfiguring as online and offline, communally located and born digital.

The era of overspecialization and the insider's language and rhetorical mode is on the wane. As access to knowledge and knowledge production, to archives and databases, expands, those with facility in a repertoire of voices will be able to imagine, inspire, and organize colleagues, undergraduate and graduate students, and nonacademics to contribute to the intellectual enterprise of humanities scholarship, at once traditional in the best sense and engaged with publics. In 2009, Bulbul Tiwari, whose born-digital dissertation on performances of the Mahabharata received an honorable mention in the Emerging Scholars Prize awarded by the University of Michigan's Institute for the Humanities, talked of reaching new audiences through new modes of scholarly communication and of "creating new kinds of readers."[26]

Let me bring in William Germano's reflection on academic writing here. In 2013, Germano, dean and professor at the Cooper Union and former editor of Columbia University Press and publishing director at Routledge, announced the "Age of the Reader," opining that "the conditions of scholarly writing depend in new ways on the reader as arbiter and recipient."[27] In "Do We Dare Write for Readers?" he wrote pithily of academic monographs as "snow globes": "Academe has been in the snow-globe business for years. The problem here is not the specificity of research but the intention of the finished product. Inward-looking, careful to a fault, our monographs have been content to speak to other monographs rather than to real, human readers."[28] Germano called for the shift from the snow-globe, the isolated, small, careful world of modest consequence, to the monograph as "machine," a thing that "waits to be deployed" and thus has "consequence." Thinking of the monograph as machine, for Germano, puts the emphasis on acts of doing, moving, and inviting active reading. He termed this "writing as activism": "The book-as-machine requires that the scholarly writer imagine a problem or concern that will engage the reader, making the investment of reading time worthwhile."[29] In other words, the scholarly voice in the academic monograph can take more risks, display more zing, and open up to broader readerships.

To be sure, facility in shifting from a scholarly mode of voice to a voice directed to people outside one's discipline and beyond is hard-earned skill. Public intellectuals hone their distinctive voice over years. And faculty who imagine themselves writing a "crossover" book know only too well how daunting and frustrating that project can be. But there are ways in which that transition can become more conceivable, more energizing, and more successful. What I am suggesting here is that to the extent that doctoral students begin early to experiment with aspects of code-switching, they will be well served for opportunities to address multiple publics as well as scholarly interlocutors as they move through their careers.

5. The model of success narrowly focused on one outcome—completion of the long-form proto-monograph and then a tenure-track position at an R1 institution—has run its course. It is exhausted; it is exhausting; it is no longer tenable in terms of student interests and prospects. As Megan Pincus Kajitani and Rebecca A. Bryant advised in 2010, the "one model" of success instilled in students has to be displaced by an ethos of flexible success.[30] Or, as Grafton and Grossman write in "No More Plan B," it is time to reorient doctoral education away from a professional ethos that projects the message that "the life of scholarship [is] somehow exempt from impure motives and bitter competition" and that those who move into jobs outside the academy are understood to be leaving the virtuous life.[31] It is past time to reimagine success away from its equation with isolated research and long-form publication only, away from the replicative model that equates brilliance and "bestness" with entry into a tenure-track position at an R1 university and a long career in the academy. Projecting a one-size-fits-all model of success and expecting a one-model-fits-all form of the dissertation will not serve well the interests of humanities doctoral students who benefit from preparation for diverse professional environments and diverse career trajectories.

Doctoral students will enter many different kinds of institutions. Yes, a number of graduates will take up positions in R1 universities; they are collectively one of the largest sectors employing humanities doctorates. But many (about a third) will find academic teaching positions in regional universities, liberal arts colleges, and community colleges. And the latter, as noted earlier, educate around 44% of undergraduates across the United States. Others will pursue and find academic positions in libraries, institutes, administrative offices, student services, development, and outreach. Some will move to the nonprofit world of the humanities workforce; some to the world of government and public policy. Practically, graduate students need to optimize the range of opportunities they can pursue by recognizing the transferability of skills they already have and finding opportunities to gain skills they do not already command. If, as Alexandra Rausing argues, the new Alexandria of the future is an expanded network of knowledge producers inside and outside the academy, if the production of knowledge is an effect of the cloud and the crowd as well as professionally trained researchers and scholars, then preparing doctoral students for the larger humanities workforce will enhance opportunities for collaboration among intellectuals and researchers within and without the academy.

These are my five good reasons.

Multiple Forms

So let's design a dissertation of expansive possibilities, of which the monograph form will be one among several options. Some students will pursue the traditional dissertation; but they will also recognize that there are other options and thus other kinds of preparation important for their future careers. Some will opt for alternative models if that option is available to them, and they will surprise advisors and graduate directors with their conceptualization of this capstone to their studies.

What are these alternatives?

The most common alternative to the long-form dissertation is the "suite" of three or four essays, a concept of the dissertation advanced 20 years ago by Damrosch.[32] A suite might involve a theme and its variations; or a set of distinct essays, probing different topics, using different methods, elaborating different theoretical frameworks and approaches. The emphasis here would be on honing skills in the short-form essay (of 25–35 pages), precisely structured, persuasively argued, elegantly written, at once lean in purpose, compelling in the story it tells, and provocative in the intervention it proposes. Students might be expected to submit the essays to different kinds of journals, a project in researching the world of scholarly communication in the short form.[33] Philosophy often requires this form of the dissertation, with this expectation of publication. "Form" in this context has two aspects: form as discourse and form as material vehicle. The essay ensemble might be conceptualized in such a way as to ask the student to experiment with different scholarly voices and discursive contexts; or to experiment with a variety of material forms, such as scholarly print, public print, born-digital essay.[34]

The suite of essays constitutes one form of an ensemble dissertation. And there are other projects that could be combined into an ensemble dissertation involving multiple components. Here are several possibilities: Preparing a teaching portfolio, including an extended essay on pedagogy and a design for sequenced courses geared to different levels, class sizes, and audiences. Writing a metacritical essay on the intersection of scholarship and teaching in the classroom. Pursuing a project of "public scholarship," of "making knowledge 'about, for, and with' diverse publics and communities," as sketched by Julie Ellison and Timothy K. Eatman in "Scholarship in Public."[35] Addressing issues of the humanities and public policy. This latter possibility would involve learning how to translate in acts that, in the eloquent words of Kathleen Woodward, "embrace our knowledge and [do] not dilute it; translate it, yes, but not water it down completely."[36] An ensemble dissertation might combine a scholarly essay of original research of 80 pages; a metacritical essay on teaching in the field; an essay on theorizing digital curation; and an essay on the experience of community-based scholarship; all of which would evidence flexibility in communicating scholarship in different voices, media, and venues. Or, given the affordances of new platforms for scholarly communication, the dissertation project might involve an edition of some text or corpus of texts with multiple components to it. The expectation of research "scope" of a capstone project would derive from the depth of thought, sophistication of methods, and intellectual ambition arrayed across multiple modes and media assembled in the ensemble dissertation.

For students in language and comparative literature units, a dissertation project might include a translation of a formerly untranslated scholarly or literary work or a new kind of translation of an already-translated work. The translation could be accompanied by a robust introduction that situates the work historically, or generically, or theoretically, or geographically, and an essay critically engaging theories of translation as a practice. As a colleague of mine recently observed, only a small amount of the world's literatures is available in English translations with introductions and commentary. How much the public, students, and colleagues would benefit from broader access to the world's heritage!

Then there are the new opportunities for born-digital dissertations. This mode of dissertation involves conceptualizing, mapping, composing, displaying, and offering metacommentary on a digitally environed scholarly project, often of significant value to other scholars, teachers, and students. As Kathleen Woodward suggests, such projects might be conceived under multiple rubrics, one of which would be "curation"[37]; others might be ideation, multiple pathway argumentation, visual mapping, multimodal syncopation, interactive reading, and tool building. Here is McPherson's bookishness of another kind.

There are a growing number of examples out there. For his doctorate at

Teachers College of Columbia University, Nick Sousanis composed a dissertation in comics form that is about the centrality of visual thinking to teaching and learning.[38] This is the long-form dissertation in new media of presentation. Or there is the project Amanda Visconti is completing at the University of Maryland's Maryland Institute for Technology in the Humanities. *Infinite Ulysses* is "a participatory digital edition of James Joyce's difficult but rewarding novel *Ulysses*." An ambitious project, *Infinite Ulysses*, Visconti tells visitors to her website, "takes a unique non-monograph form, consisting of the *Infinite Ulysses* participatory digital edition (plus a code repository and documentation on using my code to create your own participatory digital edition); user testing, site analytics and analysis; and regular research blogging culminating in a scholarly article final draft."[39] Other innovative, hybrid dissertation projects were highlighted at a session entitled "Transforming the Dissertation: Models, Questions, Next Steps," organized by Cathy Davidson at the 2015 HASTAC conference at Michigan State University, and available for viewing on the HASTAC 2015 website.[40] They are also supported in the work and events sponsored by the Futures Initiative at the CUNY Graduate Center, under the leadership of Cathy Davidson and Katina Rogers.[41] As graduate students pursue more and more born-digital, multimedia, and hybrid modes of the dissertation, departments and graduate schools will be pressed to develop adequate policies and mechanisms for filing and preserving these innovative forms.[42]

A radically reimagined doctoral dissertation might involve a multiyear collaboration of doctoral students and faculty in a large project. Todd Presner at UCLA and Andrea Abernethy Lunsford at Stanford talk persuasively about large-scale collaborative research projects and even collaborative dissertations.[43] The idea here is that admitted students enter into a long-term project as a cohort, gaining experience in collaboration, benefiting from the expertise of the collective, working with multiple faculty, and elaborating for themselves as they go what kinds of scholarly communication make sense at what stages of the research. Such projects might eventuate in a traditionally published or born-digital initiative, such as a scholarly edition, or publishable essays for all students involved or a book-length set of essays, or all together.

And there are other possibilities imaginable, such as documentary film or the creative dissertation of mixed modes. The SSHRC white paper presents two possible models, as it calls for "a diversified, outward-looking program of study" that "will afford doctoral candidates a much fuller sense of the implications of their own work and of their field generally, and will help them establish a more vigorous and usefully active network of colleagues beyond the formal academy."[44] The models are the Workshop PhD and the PhD in the Applied Humanities. The Workshop model eschews the rigidity of the coursework, exams, dissertation triad in favor of a four- to five-year apprenticeship in "an interdisciplinary research workshop led by a small group of faculty who have agreed to take a leadership role in the workshop for five years."[45] During the apprenticeship students would undertake four linked projects building expertise in a field; one involving collaboration; one negotiating the complexities of interdisciplinary practice; one directed to a nonacademic constituency; and all culminating in a singly produced/authored "masterpiece." The PhD in the Applied Humanities would involve coursework in policy and management studies and specialist field courses; put students in an internship; and require them to "integrate management/policy with humanities research on their chosen subject."[46]

However the dissertation is configured, whether as the long-form proto-monograph or some alternative ensemble of modes, projects, and vehicles, the prospectus stage of the doctoral study will take on a more dynamic, rather than formulaic, dimension. No longer a formality to get through, with a nod to the recognition that the proto-monograph will be very different in the end so the prospectus doesn't much matter, the prospectus in a time of choice could become the occasion to think about the content of the project and the vehicle together. As a graduate fellow at the Institute for the Humanities here at Michigan recently observed to me, "How beneficial it would have been to think through why I was writing a monograph for the form of my own dissertation— what specific skills I wanted to gain from writing a monograph, the rationale behind presenting my work in monograph form, etc. If doctoral students, with their advisers, were invited to think about and then make a case for the form they wanted their dissertation to take, I think this could be quite helpful."[47]

There is so much to be gained by expanding the repertoire of possible kinds of dissertation. I am convinced that the availability of more flexibility in programs, projects, and pathways through the doctorate will attract more diverse cohorts of students. I am convinced that humanities departments and doctoral programs will gain in creativity, cross-fertilization of ideas and practices, energized learning communities, and more satisfied students. With Damrosch, I am convinced that, with an ensemble dissertation project, students will expand their critical, theoretical, and methodological perspectives and their collaborative sociability as they work with multiple mentors instead of "the single parental figure."[48] I am convinced that the dissertations produced will be of higher quality than many of the proto-monographs delivered to faculty after long years of forcing five chapters to their less-than-compelling conclusion. I am convinced that doctoral programs will become more innovative, inclusive, and vibrant.

Responding to Counterarguments

Of course, talk of dislodging the pride of place of the monograph dissertation raises all kinds of anxieties. While faculty may be intrigued by the idea of expanding forms of the dissertation, they understandably express concern about the potential downsides of allowing doctoral students to pursue alternative forms and experiment with alternative media and modes of scholarly communication. So let me take on the four major concerns, even if it seems counterproductive to introduce powerful arguments against the change I am advocating.

What's "Scholarly" about It?

One argument against expanding options for the dissertation constellates around the question of whether the long form is necessary for a dissertation to be "scholarly," and for the scholar to be credentialed in the humanities, which is what the PhD confers. Will introducing options erode the standard of excellence associated with doctoral training, substituting instead a PhD Lite?

Implied in this question about the PhD Lite is an abiding concern about the disadvantaged status of the humanities in the academy. The way to save the humanities from the assaults of deans and provosts, this argument goes, is to maintain traditional standards; and the proto-monograph dissertation is the thing that humanists do that distinguishes them from social scientists, scientists, and professional-school faculty. Humanists study books, they need to keep book culture alive, and they should put their money where their mouths are by writing them. To write them they need to have trained by writing the proto-monograph dissertation. Thus, to do away with the proto-monograph is to undermine the self-understanding of humanists, the intellectual preparedness of graduate students, and the value to the academy and to the public of the humanities. It is to concede the eroding importance of deep reading before a culture immersed in multitasking, networking, and distributed attention.

Scholarly inquiry in this argument is associated with the long-form book and its depth of thought, or what is termed a coherent intellectual project of long duration. The coherent intellectual project of the proto-monograph, requiring depth of research and scope of argument, trains students in the formidable habits of humanistic inquiry. Even as they call for greater recognition that doctoral students would benefit from preparation for multiple possible careers, then, Grafton and Grossman succinctly insist on maintaining the form of the proto-monograph dissertation: "We leave the feasibility of shorter dissertations in other humanities disciplines for our colleagues to assess," they argue: "It's in the course of research that historians firm up their mastery of languages and research methods, archives and arguments; and it's while writing that they learn how to corral a vast amount of information, give it a coherent form, and write it up in a way accessible to non-specialists."[1] Many of my colleagues across the humanities disciplines would add "amen" to that.

I want to put pressure on this notion of the equation of humanistic scholarship and long-form dissertation. Some may think they have a quick answer to the question of what is scholarly about a dissertation, and what is distinctive about the humanities dissertation, as Grafton and Grossman suggest above for the discipline of history: the long arc of a sustained argument; the deep engagement with the archive or fieldwork; the apparatus of citation of archival material and the scholarship of others; the rehearsal of familiarity with the history of the field; the sophistication of the method or theoretical approach; the elegance of the interpretation, that is, the deep reading; the independence of thought; the intellectual flair; the originality. But are these criteria of excellence only achievable and measurable in the long form?

Of these aspects of the scholarly, only the "long arc" seems to be realized only in the long-form proto-monograph. But wouldn't the long-arc feature also be realized in, say, the composition of three or four 40-page essays or two 80-page pieces, all of which reach that stage of development where they are ready for submission to a scholarly journal for print or online publication? Wouldn't the long-arc feature be realized in a translation project that combines theory and practice? Wouldn't it be realized in a born-digital project that creates multiple pathways through a topic?

Length doesn't ensure quality. So many pages, so much excellence. This default to quantification is an unintended consequence of fetishizing the proto-monograph. Often I've observed over the years that faculty, and I include myself here, are willing to pass a less-than-completely-realized and less-than-excellent-in-all-its-parts dissertation because of the desire to help a student who has lingered long beyond seven years, or faces loss of funding, or because enough of the dissertation shows enough promise of excellence down the line. I've observed that they, and I include myself here, are willing to pass a dissertation that is rangy in parts, or repetitive throughout, or too rigidly theorized, or too slavish to certain interlocutors.

The scholarly boldness and imagination needed for a coherent intellectual project can be stimulated, modeled, and intensified by gaining invaluable expertise in a range of forms, short, or middle state, or long; multimedia, born digital. To bring an ensemble of essays to publishable quality, students must find compelling topics, command the archive, survey work in the field, define the argument and its stakes, refine the methodology, establish the generative theoretical terms of reference, project possible structures of development, and deploy evidence and nuanced analysis. Then, too, there are depths of many kinds. Other kinds of depth are evidenced in experimenting with different scholarly voices, trying different modes of dissemination, working not only alone but collaboratively. And the deep attention required of a humanist in the academy and necessary to turn ideas into books, however performed or distributed, can be reinforced through rigorous conceptualization, research, and ideation that is required by whatever form may be appropriate to the topic and the project. There need not be only one way—the monograph dissertation—to gain scope, depth, and credential. The issue is the expectation and achievement of excellence of and in all forms and modes.

Moreover, the overvaluation of the proto-monograph as the most excellent form of a dissertation, as the real thing, can create problems down the line for those who enter tenure-track positions. And here I take recourse to my experiences as a dissertation chair, committee member, and department chair. Graduates often imagine that the dissertation they take away with them is just about a book. A little tweaking here. A little tweaking there. I've seen many assistant professors begin their probationary period with the weight of the monograph dissertation hanging around their necks as an albatross, in print form. They have brought with them a demonstration of tutelage and the promise of field expertise, not the draft of a publishable long-form book, however bold or sophisticated or deftly written. They have brought with them a long-form project that shaped itself around dialogues with faculty mentors, with major theorists in the field, with a powerful set of theoretical insights. They have brought with them a partially digested set of chapters, some of which are promising, others of which remain thin. They have brought with them a particular scholarly discourse and scholarly voice that is often, as William Germano observes, too careful, or too protectively opaque.[2] They have brought with them a compendium of reviews of the work of others. They have brought with them something that weighs as much as a book but leads to a modest payoff.

I have watched as they struggle for one, two, even three years to think beyond the structure, method, scope, theoretical scaffolding, and presumed argument of the dissertation to conceptualize a related but different project that will eventuate in a book contract. Some have to shed parts that pleased their advisors; some have to pare away the overelaborate apparatus through which they perform their bona fides by citing theorists in an exercise of stringing theory. Some have to eliminate chapters that only limply advance the argument, included for the best of reasons but executed with an often-plodding momentum. Some have to hone a scholarly voice that achieves its own intellectual idioms and rhythms and no longer echoes an intimate conversation carried on with two or three theorists whom they would extend or refute. Some have yet to find their larger argument, and discover they have only a set of brilliant close readings or deft theoretical riffs, not enough to carry the weight of a book. Germano observed this as well from his long experience as an editor, and it takes him a book to "map" the process of moving "from dissertation to book." He sagely quips in his introduction, "Taking that dissertation and making it 'more' isn't a straight path. It's a curving route with loops and off-ramps."[3]

In other contexts, I have observed a concerning pattern in postdoctoral trajectories. In reading applications for various fellowships and for entry-level tenure-track positions, I have observed too often the CV of a humanities scholar with nine to 13 years dedicated to one project: the three to seven years of the dissertation writing; one to three years of a postdoc. They enter a tenure-track position in which they will spend another three to four years finding a book contract, and continually revising. While it's imaginable that a senior scholar could spend 10 to 13 years on a magisterial work, it is hard to imagine that 10 to 13 years spent on the idea of the dissertation doesn't take its toll. Ideas that have become stale. An argument that is outdated, and "so five-years-ago." A research design or methodology that is not adequate to the scope of the project. Writing that is overwrought and lifeless. Now, I'm aware of the trap of arguing from an N of four or five. But I suspect that others have observed this saga of the book too long incubated. There are those occasions when the long incubation eventuates in a stunning first book; but they are rare.

And here's another problem for humanists in the insistence on the long-form dissertation as proto-book. Graduate students are encouraged, professionalized, to break out a piece of the dissertation—most likely, a chapter—and turn it into an essay. But the essay is a different kind of intellectual project; it is not the chapter. The essay has to have its own arc, its own bold argument; it cannot be merely a brilliant deep reading. It has to make its argument from the get-go, enable the reader to glimpse the stakes, and tell a compelling story, either explicitly or implicitly. There can be no long windup that keeps delaying the payoff. Many students make this transition successfully, publishing one, two, or three pieces while in graduate school. Only the long-arc criterion for the dissertation prevents them from having satisfied the requirement for a dissertation. What kind of logic pertains in an argument that a student who has placed three or four essays in peer-reviewed journals (whether published or in press) still has to produce a 300-page work to get the degree? Better to acknowledge that such a student might find intellectual mentors in distinguished scholars who are brilliant in the short form and replete with the agility to move from idea to idea rather than remain constrained by the long form.

Further, I would argue that there is no necessary correlation between writing a long-form dissertation and writing good "books" or a good long form of bookishness. There is a case to be made that it is often the short-form essay that generates the idea for a book, that books often come into shape through forays in several essays that try out arguments, expand the scope. And it is often the short-form essay, now online or in print, that brings attention to a work and gains a readership for it. It is through interlocutors responding to short forms of essay or conference talk that the horizon of a project expands, its methodology deepens, its theoretical framework becomes more precise.

Guinea Pigness?

A second argument asks whether doctoral students opting for alternative forms of the dissertation will be the "guinea pigs" of this experiment in radical change. I may quibble with the idea that this is radical change, but not with the concerns of graduate students who do not want to be disadvantaged in any job search for scarce positions, and not with advisors anxious that their students succeed.

In response to this concern, let me introduce another anecdotal observation from my experience of hiring tenure-track faculty at a large research university. Something like 100 to 300 applications come in, depending upon how the search is organized and what the field in play is. Members of search committees read the short forms: the letter, the research and teaching statements (if requested), and the writing sample. Successful candidates are successful because they write well in the short forms that are formulaic and the short form of the dissertation chapter that either convinces and excites or doesn't. This reading practice is also the case for committees charged with deciding on awards of predoctoral and postdoctoral fellowships.

I know I am overplaying here the idea that most of the information search committees get in the job search involves short forms. I was reminded by a respondent in one audience that letters of recommendation—which are very important in the job search process—are based on the advisor's knowledge and evaluation of the long-form proto-monograph. I should have remembered this, since oftentimes the advisor does a better job than the candidate of presenting the stakes and arguments of the monograph dissertation. Even with this caveat, I remain convinced that promise and quality of mind and passion will just as likely come through to a search committee when students have opted for an alternative form of the dissertation. If a finalist for the position submits a set of discrete or interlocking essays, or a portfolio of several discrete forms directed at different audiences, search committees can get a fuller take on that candidate's scope of interests, maturity of scholarly voice, and flexibility of imagination. And it could be the case that such a candidate takes on the job market a list of publications already out or in press or under review. As noted in the last section, candidates with evidence of publications tended to fare better than others in the analysis of data gathered for *Educating Scholars*.[4]

A more concerning problem is that search committees may be reluctant to hire someone who does not have the proto-monograph not because they doubt the quality of mind or demonstration of promise but because they worry that there is not enough of a book project to ensure success at tenure time. Committees fear that a candidate who has not produced a monograph dissertation cannot assemble the publication record currently required for a successful tenure case. My rejoinder to this concern is several-fold. There is, of course, my observation above that the dissertation monograph is not a book, and that a long-form dissertation can become as much a burden as an unproblematic foundation for a mature and coherent intellectual project.

But to go further. This programmatic response assumes the book as the "gold standard" for tenure. A bolder approach is to advocate more flexible tenure criteria and take action to challenge the singular model of success for hiring and tenure. Pressing for flexibility, as the 2006 MLA task force report on criteria for tenure and promotion argues, will in turn change the concept of the alternative dissertation into an advantage for those with experience in multiple modes of producing scholarship, with a more elastic sense of the scholarly, and with expertise in the shorter-form argument.[5]

There have long been precedents for this flexibility in criteria within humanities disciplines. There are humanities disciplines, among them philosophy and linguistics, for which the short form is the conventional mode of scholarly communication. Some English language and literature programs already offer students the option of a creative dissertation. Doctoral students in rhetoric and composition programs use a variety of methodologies, including human subjects research, statistical methods, and ethnography to compose dissertations differently. The particular pressures of interdisciplinary doctoral programs lead students to different kinds of dissertations, even when in proto-monograph form. Collectively, multiple forms of the dissertation are already an aspect of doctoral education in the humanities.[6] But, for

the most part, humanities programs have neither rethought graduate education tout court nor articulated a clear and purposeful vision of the dissertation as capstone.

There is also evidence emerging across North America that criteria for
tenure and promotion are slowly becoming more capacious, that successful
tenure cases are being built around portfolios of scholarly work in forms and
modes other than the book form, that committees are adopting guidelines for
evaluating born-digital scholarship, that work in the public humanities, despite the formidable difficulties in gaining recognition for it, is beginning to
find a place in tenure and promotion portfolios. Guidelines at the University
of North Carolina–Charlotte, for instance, stipulate a coherent set of research
questions, an ongoing research program of high quality, national recognition, a substantive body of work equivalent to the monograph-plus-article
standard.[7] Finally, there are departments that might welcome candidates with
a broader range of scholarly experiences and facility in adapting multiple
modes of communication, as became clear to me at an ADE Summer Seminar
East when the chair of Iowa State University suggested to me that technology
schools such as Iowa State and Georgia State could take the lead in innovation
and that she was confident her department would be open to hiring people
presenting an alternative dissertation. Granted, these are a limited number of
exemplary cases; and they do not come out of elite universities; but they evidence the slow erosion of a singular gold standard.

And to return to the desirability and hire-ability of candidates demonstrating capacious thoughtfulness, experimentation, and flexibility across
the board, let's remember that candidacies often go awry when applicants
evince little excitement, limited inventiveness, and lackluster interest in teaching. That was my experience when chair. In that room, day after day, with one
candidate after another. Candidates with good résumés hesitated when asked
how they would design such and such a course and could barely get beyond
the platitudes of pedagogical practice in talking about students in the classroom. Imagine how interesting a candidate would be who had written a scholarly essay on some aspect of classroom practice or who had developed as part
of the ensemble dissertation a website at once scholarly and teacherly.

Where's the Graduate School in All This?

Some skeptics suggest to me that graduate schools are the problem; that
programs can't make such a major change to dissertation requirements because the bureaucratic machinery just cannot accommodate such change; that
graduate directors and faculty are hemmed in by forms and guidelines. In responding to this concern, it's important to ask: "Where is it written?"

It isn't very often that humanities departments provide students with a written description of their concept of the dissertation and its scholarly excellence. Oh yes, graduate schools commonly publish guidelines that govern requirements for the dissertation and its submission. Departmental guidelines often include requirements for the dissertation proposal, stipulations regarding the constitution of the dissertation committee, and the dissertator's responsibilities. These are matters of process, regulations. When explicit about the expectations for a dissertation, graduate schools invoke the discourse normative for the academy: it must demonstrate evidence of originality, broad knowledge of the field, and mastery of scholarly habits; make a significant impact on the field; and be of publishable quality. Sometimes departmental guidelines include substantive rather than solely procedural details of the dissertating process. Like statements from graduate schools, statements from departments, when they give a description beyond outlining a process, emphasize the normative discourse encompassing originality, breadth of scope, argumentation, voice, expertise, and contribution to the field.

Most often written descriptions of the dissertation are silent on much that is important at this crossroads in the humanities and the academy. They do not address issues related to the diversity of forms of scholarly communication, the diversity of audiences to which one's discussion of scholarship might be directed, or the importance for future careers in the academy of telling good stories about how scholarly and teaching interests intersect and inform each other. There is little information apparent in material provided about new modes of digital scholarship—archives and archive building, database research, new methodologies, new options for argumentation and display, and the emergent logics of scholarly presentation. In other words, there is no evidence that the discourse of scholarly communication rather than publication has begun to penetrate into the presentation made to students of the work of the humanities scholar. In addition, information about the maximum page length of proto-monograph dissertations is offered without discussion of the current state of scholarly publishing and the new business models being piloted by academic presses.

Ultimately, most graduate schools don't say anything about lengths of humanities dissertations. They would get in a heap of trouble with many humanities graduate directors if they did. In linguistics and philosophy, for instance. And in some disciplines outside the humanities, there has been a shift in the concept of the dissertation, as there has been in economics, which moved from the concept of the monograph dissertation to the concept of the ensemble of three publishable essays.[8] The conceptualization of the dissertation is an issue for departments to decide, not graduate schools.

What if faculty tried to think the dissertation through but also beyond the

terms cited in department meetings and along office corridors? Does the definition of the dissertation capture the new ecology of scholarly and pedagogical activities? Does it project the pleasure of the scholarly and not just reproduce the conformity of the exercise? Does it allude to the distinctiveness of
the dissertation as a performance and not seek recourse in some obligatory
terms yoked together in guidelines? Does it capture the riskiness of intellectual adventures? Does it deepen the concept of "originality" by recognizing
the dialogic nature of scholarly inquiry and the synergy of people working collaboratively? Does it speak to the different kinds of expertise a dissertation
project demands and hones?

Students and faculty benefit from a description of the dissertation that
is worth reading. That asks its interlocutors to become different kinds of
readers and writers. That's not about details of submission. That's not pro
forma. That's not an expression of "It goes without saying." That is, itself,
a teaching document, and a microform essay, signaling so much about doctoral education that is so often treated as if it is transparent. Such a description would tell a story about what doctoral study is about; and about what
the life of the academic humanist is about. It would breathe life into the intellectual project of the humanities, and recognize how diverse are the passions, experiences, visions, and learning modes of the students who seek to
become academic humanists.

The Cart and the Horse?

As all the reports and white papers and interpretation of data so dramatically
capture, the times are roiling in the academy, in the humanities, and in doctoral education. Transitions are by definition hard to negotiate. They throw
into dispute what is the horse, what the cart. Where is the optimal place to
make change first, in the disciplines, in graduate education?

Some faculty will argue that changes in the concept of the dissertation
cannot be introduced before new attitudes toward bookishness and the new
modes of doing and communicating scholarly work take hold in the disciplines, and in the practices of senior faculty. Not before those changes are
factored into tenure and promotion guidelines and criteria. Not before search
committees begin to value different profiles as they read candidate files. Not
before posted job descriptions project new ways of describing needs, professional expertise, and fields. And not before the elite schools take the lead and
authorize the legitimacy of multiple kinds of dissertations.

Oh my. I find this an exhausting list of "not befores."

My argument back is that the change cannot await the checkoffs on this
list of befores, cannot await the imprimatur of the elites. It is time to find

another aphoristic figure and proceed on multiple fronts simultaneously. Changes to the dissertation in particular and graduate education more generally will come on a variety of fronts, indeed, are coming on a variety of fronts, and from a variety of institutions. The directions of change are multiple and intersecting.

Incoming doctoral students are bringing with them practical experiences working in digital environments, commitments to public scholarship, demands for an inclusive climate, willingness to take risks, new kinds of expertise. Responding to the emergent environment of humanities scholarship and teaching, students are pushing faculty beyond their comfort zones and normative terms of evaluation. Faculty at all ranks are beginning new projects in digital archive-building and recognizing the requirements of successful collaborations. Faculty in media studies are building new platforms for scholarly communication. Others are advocating more capacious criteria in evaluating scholarship. Professional organizations are issuing reports and mounting online toolkits. Librarians are putting together workshops for faculty anxious to get training in new skills. Graduate schools are offering symposia on multiple future careers. Enlightened administrators are directing new attention to the humanities, and resources for program development. Elite schools are initiating change, as some humanities departments are doing at Stanford and UC-Irvine with their projects of the five-year doctorate. And programs in flagship state universities have introduced new initiatives, such as the new doctorate in Hispanic studies at the University of Washington that welcomes alternative forms of the dissertation.[9] These changes are not taking place at all institutions, or evenly within institutions. But they are taking place.

Change is not reducible to cart and horse. It's a dynamic system, full of tension and risk and rewards. It is troubling and animating. It is good for you and hard on you, more so for some than for others. I came into my academic career working with feminists at the University of Arizona to start a women's studies program; and I hope to go out of my academic career seeing a 21st-century doctoral education taking hold.

What Is to Be Gained?

Flexibility, expertise in code-switching, the ability to think deeply and across disciplines and networks at once, these are habits of mind that can be cultivated through producing alternative forms of the dissertation. And the academic humanities will need these habits of mind as faculty and students innovate and adjust to the new book, itself performative, multimodal, distributed, interactive, and perhaps even distributed across time, successively updated and revised as needed. These dispositions, these scholarly habits, these intellectual skills, will enhance the attractiveness of students on the job market, as will the demonstration of excellence in whatever form of dissertation they produce, discrete article-length pieces or interlocking essays, born digital online environment or print based book, or however it might be configured or communicated.

Thinking beyond the proto-monograph does not mean proposing a PhD Lite. On the contrary, it just could be that perpetuating the singular mode of the proto-monograph dissertation in the next decades may end up reproducing a PhD Lite inadequate to an environment of higher learning that has changed radically, in ways that excite, in ways that distress, and in ways that remain unpredictable. And failing to redefine the intellectual mission of the doctorate to encompass how academic humanists research, write, and teach now might make doctoral students on the market different kinds of guinea pigs. The operative values should be originality, excellence, impact, and promise in whatever form or mode is appropriate to the topic and the project—not the quantification of 250–500 pages, or 85,000 to 140,000 words.

A 21st-Century Doctoral Education

In the words of Dwight McDonald, the goal of graduate education in the liberal arts is "to train future thought leaders" in humanities fields, in the academy, and beyond.[1] To that end, faculty need to design doctoral programs that are generative experiences for all students rather than experiences in bending toward conformity to a singular model of professionalization and success. Such programs would strive to enable students to stay true to their passions and affiliative commitments, enable them to follow secret desires, be playful and experimental, be irreverent.

Expanding options for the dissertation is one step in that transformation. But there is much to be done in terms of rethinking coursework, pedagogical training, professionalization, mentorship, and preparation for the job market. Just think of the kinds of preparation doctoral students will need for careers in the academic humanities alone, given the everyday life of academic humanists that is explored in Part II. Absolutely, the primary purpose is gaining broad and deep knowledge of one's field and recognizing and producing excellent, lively, and impactful scholarship out of that knowledge. But there is more.

Where to start? Well, at many points of entry. Here I telescope the kinds of responses that might go a ways to meeting heterogeneous preparatory needs, and addressing conditions on the ground.

But let me add a prefatory note before starting. Neither comprehensive nor detailed, my list of further changes incorporates many of the recommendations made in the SSHRC white paper and the MLA task force report, and adds to them. For me, it is an aspirational, overstuffed wish list. I don't imagine for a moment that these suggestions will be taken up by large numbers of faculty. But across North America many individuals and programs are taking on change, modeling new components of doctoral education in the humanities, while others are exploring how to incorporate one or two or a few of these changes into their courses and programs, some through foundation support. The times are good enough, and enough talk of change is in the air.

So let me plow forward.

Changes All Around

Graduate faculty are continually tweaking the introduction to graduate studies course offered to incoming cohorts. Obviously, there is no one model. Some introduce students to faculty in the program and their projects and methodology. Some focus on writing the seminar paper as a prerequisite to success. Some offer a history of the profession. Another iteration might productively offer an introduction to the history and emerging ecology of scholarly inquiry and communication.

Or programs might offer a collaborative minicourse on the model of what Catharine R. Stimpson terms "general education for graduate education."[2] A general education course, suggests Stimpson, might bring graduate students together across disciplines to explore disciplinary differences and cultures, methods and everyday practices; or to discover together the history of the university or the history of disciplines; or to explore the new scholarly ecology of higher education.

Beyond the introduction to graduate study, programs might approach the curriculum as unfolding in multiple kinds of formats and packages. Instead of the uniformity of the three-credit course, perhaps programs could experiment with one- and two- and three-credit courses; or project-based courses running across an academic year or two. They might conceptualize the broad scope of graduate coursework, moving from the intensity of deep reading in the seminar environment to the challenges of unpredictable experiences in projects of engaged scholarship. Programs might join with others to offer interdisciplinary, project-based courses whose goal is to build collaborative experience, provide skills training, explore issues of methodology in the humanities, and bring to fruition some kind of product, whether website or article or teaching resource. Such courses would go a ways to ensuring that students are trained in the skills needed to carry out multimodal digital projects, that they develop skills in visualization, digital design, and perhaps even coding and tool building.

A capstone seminar late in the student's education might focus on writing for publication. A minicourse later in their studies might encourage students to conceptualize and articulate a long-term research agenda or explore alternative careers or hone a transferable skill such as grant writing. A minicourse on self-curation might cover such topics as curating the dissertation and embargoes; cultivating a public persona for different audiences; fund-raising to secure subventions necessary to get one's work in print; blogging to get information about forthcoming work into the open; and establishing a culture of mutual citation.[3]

Within individual graduate courses, faculty might expand the kinds of projects/papers they assign in seminars. Yes, seminar papers are central over the one or two or three years of classes. Seminar papers are where students perfect their writing styles, their understanding of the arc of an argument, where they begin to hone their generative questions, define their areas of specialization, and imagine a dissertation project. But, as Peter H. Klost, Debra Rudder Lohe, and Chuck Sweetman argue in an essay on the "uncoverage" model for seminars, few seminar requirements focus students on "cultivating the awareness of being writers" and learning from others the different objects, methods, and processes of scholarly inquiry and communication.[4] Theirs is a call for writing pedagogy as central to graduate seminars. Others call for more emphasis to be placed in all coursework on scholarly voice, offering opportunities for students to write in multiple genres for experts, peers in other disciplines, an online community, and an educated public.

Across the curriculum as a whole and across particular courses, alternatives to the seminar paper could be introduced. These alternatives include collaborative essays; series of collaborative essays; collectively produced glossaries of terms and concepts; a cohort essay project; a grant application addressed to a real grant program; a deep reading journal; a creative portfolio; a lecture for an undergraduate survey course. Given the emergent ecology of scholarly communication in the humanities, seminars might be organized around a double format analytical project, with submission of scholarly objects in traditional print form and in a multimedia environments such as Wordpress or Scalar; a visualization or mapping project; a curation; a term-long blog; and other options.

Programs might adapt models for graduate training that build on initiatives of participants in the Praxis Network. A consortium of eight institutions, the Praxis Network partners are "engaged in rethinking pedagogy and campus partnerships in relation to the digital. Among other elements, the initiatives emphasize new models of methodological training and collaborative research."[5] Through their activities, students produce e-portfolios or develop software prototypes, such as the Prism tool, developed out of the Praxis program at the University of Virginia, which crowdsources interpretations.

Coursework in pedagogy might incorporate up-to-date research on how students learn now; or on teaching in and through digital environments, or in hybrid formats; or on purposefully encompassing multiple kinds of reading in everyday assignments and discussion. Doctoral students might be asked to write a publishable essay on teaching, or blog on classroom practice, or partake in a simulation game on building a new undergraduate curriculum. Or programs might work with graduate schools and institutional centers to develop non-course-based certificates in teaching, such as the GTC+ certificate offered through the Center for Research on Learning and Teaching at the University of Michigan.[6] The GTC+ asks students to fulfill a set of activities through which they gain experiential knowledge of digital pedagogies and teaching methods, hybrid learning environments, and supportive online teaching networks.

There may be opportunities to develop and offer courses with real work, to invoke the term from Part II's discussion of new concept coursework in undergraduate majors. This argument is advanced by John Wittman and Mariana Abuan in their piece "Socializing Future Professionals: Exploring the Matrix of Assessment." They propose that graduate students benefit from being socialized into the kinds of activities that they will be asked to do in tenure-track positions and in administrative positions they might take up in the future. "For students to develop adequate knowledge about the practices of academia (in this case assessment)," Wittman and Abuan argue, "they need to have opportunities to do so in their graduate education where thoughtful mentors can both encourage and work alongside them."[7]

Alternatively, or at the same time, programs might make funds available for interested students to attend summer institutes and workshops, such as the one at the University of Victoria, to gain expertise in methods of born-digital scholarship. Various funding agencies are currently supporting such institutes and workshops, as the Mellon Foundation is doing through the Humanities Without Walls initiative in the Midwest. In the coming decade there will be more and more opportunities for humanities doctoral students to gain digital literacies necessary for the projects they seek to undertake.

There are also opportunities for programs to develop and pilot new kinds of doctoral programs. The SSHRC white paper mentions two such innovative programs, noted above. And there are other innovative interdisciplinary doctorates waiting to be launched in such areas as narrative and medicine; archives, curation and humanities databases; literatures, languages, and public policy; and humanities and publics. One such new kind of humanities doctoral program is now offered at USC in "Media Arts and Practice," which has as its goal "support[ing] a new generation of scholar-practitioners who are able to combine historical and theoretical knowledge with creative and critical design skills."[8] There are also possibilities for new certificate programs targeted at humanities doctoral students, such as the certificate in public scholarship offered by the Simpson Center for the Humanities at the University of Washington.[9]

Graduate schools and humanities doctoral programs might pursue opportunities for internships, internally with professional staff in libraries or presses, or museums or public relations offices; and externally with cultural institutions or public policy centers or the for-profit sector. They might expand the network of the people critical to successful doctoral education by identifying humanities professionals and others across the academy as mentors, tutors, teachers, and collaborators: humanists in libraries, in digital humanities centers and labs, in university publishing units, in tech labs. The MLA report describes this deployment of an expansive set of educators as "utiliz[ing] the whole university community."[10] The SSHRC white paper talks of internship tutelage by people in arts and cultural institutions outside the academy.[11]

Programs might fund a student-run, open-access journal.

I am fully aware of the pressures such changes put on all parties involved, staff, administrators, faculty, and doctoral students themselves. With a long history of administrative appointments, I know only too well that academics operate within administrative practices with their constraints and inelasticity, even at the unit of the course itself. Yet I know there are small shifts to be made on a pilot basis. I try to make my own changes. I have been teaching the graduate course the English department offers called Writing for Publication for over a half decade now. And students well past their coursework take it and submit their essays to journals at the end of the term. In that course I offer an overview of the changing ecology of scholarly communication. Inevitably, I learn from my students new aspects of that ecology.

Institutional change often moves at a glacial pace. Faculty find themselves enervated by the intensity of their multiple obligations. Many just cannot take on a new kind of course, or introduce new kinds of course requirements. But some do. And some chairs or heads find ways to work with or around obstacles. A more challenging situation obtains when faculty are asked or expected to advise and mentor students on alternative academic positions and alternative careers outside the academy. I know I'm not qualified to successfully provide such mentoring. But there are networks that can be put together—networks of graduates who have gone on to careers outside the academy; networks of people in the university who have humanities doctorates, especially in the library. Mentoring can play out across a distributed network. The same difficulty pertains when programs seek ways to train doctoral students in new skills required for digitally environed scholarship. Humanities faculty, except for those identifying as digital humanists, rarely have the expertise to teach such things as concept design, coding, visualization. Nonetheless, there are often professionals across the campus to enlist in alternative modes of training; graduate students who come in with considerable skills; and tech-savvy undergraduates who can be collaborators in the classroom.

Faculty are making incremental change in the graduate classroom. Some are engaging graduate students in collaborative projects in digital environments. Some are advocating for new kinds of job descriptions. Many programs are introducing elements mentioned in the list above. Some are making paradigm-shifting changes, as are the institutions involved in the Praxis Program. The "mights" listed above have shifted to "done thats." I am buoyed by all the initiatives springing up across North America and elsewhere.

And What about Students?

I've been exploring how graduate schools, doctoral programs, and faculty in and out of the classroom can be agents of change. What about students themselves? Programs are changing, but at different rates and with different effects. And they are changing slowly. Graduate students, on the other hand, have a limited time to prepare themselves for academic positions and for alternative futures. And while on campus, "they are caught up," as Damrosch observes so incisively, "in a process of training and acculturation whose outcome they don't yet know."[12]

So what are they to do?

Doctoral programs appear to be unified in a simple template of successive stages. The people who move through these successive stages, however, move in many other directions as well. They are excited to start, periodically exhausted at the workload, anxious about performance, cynical about outcome. Some feel stuck; some regularly inadequate. I've worked with students who have switched faculty advisors, and then switched again. I've worked with students who have discovered they don't like teaching all that much; that the anxiety of going in front of a classroom regularly is just too excruciating for them. I've worked with students who discover that they just don't like the loneliness of the scholarly life; that it's too much like the loneliness of a long-distance runner, without the endorphins. I've worked with students who found the cloistered sense of graduate study too removed from their political and social commitments, who want to get out in the community to make change happen. I've worked with students for whom the stress has eventuated in a breakdown. I've worked with students who have drifted in and out of their studies. I've worked with students who have followed a partner and then struggled to stay on track. I've worked with one student who returned to complete a dissertation after 15 years out.

So much life is happening. So much struggle, so much euphoria, and so much despondency. And ahead, so much that is unpredictable. How to find ways to work toward the goal with the pressures—intellectual, personal, economic, political—that come at them. How to balance the call of doctoral study with the knowledge that there is always more to life than reading the next book, writing the next paper, preparing for the next exam, keeping the demons at bay. How to claim a space of agency when everything seems so intense, when pressures don't abate, when reserve energy flags, when stress wracks the body.

But there are spaces of agency to claim. Yes, graduate students are constrained by the requirements of their programs and the interests and energy and commitment of the faculty with whom they work. They are concerned about the woeful job market. But they can and do take charge of their own learning, stewarding their intellectual passions, gaining knowledge about the academy now, and, however their formal program is configured, preparing themselves, with whatever help and guidance they can find, for the future ahead.

Here are brief observations on two major arenas of potential agency through which doctoral students can prepare themselves.

Professionalization has become a central feature of doctoral education in the humanities. In the humanities and humanistic social sciences, "professionalization" is commonly understood as gaining experience in giving papers and revising seminar papers and dissertation chapters for submission to journals. Yes, that is a central and critical part of doctoral training, acts of becoming and performing scholarliness. But given the changes in higher education that I have explored here, and given the profile of future faculty I have been projecting, there are many more aspects of the new everyday in the academy that will be beneficial for doctoral students to know about as they prepare for the next stage of their career. Recognizing, gaining, and honing a range of skills should also be part of everyday life in graduate school.

In some cases they will only need to name the skills that they already have. A person speaks three languages fluently. Discovers interesting archives. Organizes a conference or symposium. Works collaboratively to start an online journal. Teaches an innovative, hybrid course. Experiments with new platforms for scholarly communication. Runs a listserv. Takes advantage of seminars on how students learn now, and thus is prepared to motivate people by drawing on that knowledge. Once the list is begun, it can accrue a remarkable number of items, becoming itemization as academic profile.

In other cases, there is agency in determining where to gain knowledge and additional skills, which, by the by, can be understood not as pedestrian but as forms of knowledge in themselves. Perhaps the target is the basic information of how university life is organized and how it works. Perhaps knowledge of the current and projected shifts in institutions and institutional practices in higher education nationally and globally. Perhaps in reading and preparing budgets. Perhaps in coding. Perhaps in project management. Perhaps in social media outreach. Perhaps in advocacy for the humanities. Perhaps in an internship. Or in a public fellows program. In these circumstances, there are institutional resources to find and use. There are summer workshops to locate, initiatives to research, institutes to apply to, fellowships to seek. There are networks to join, through which to deepen one's knowledge of the field, seek career advice, exchange information, swap stories, build audiences for one's work. There are mentors to identify. There are links to be made, steps to be taken, change to be seeded.

Professionalization in the scholarly life is an aspect of career planning. But there is more to thinking about career planning than publishing, presenting papers, gaining skills.

Doctoral students will go on to teach in small liberal arts colleges and in the expanding system of community colleges and in large urban universities. They will go on to teach in Research 1 institutions and regional state universities, in traditionally black colleges and Indian colleges. On the tenure track or tenured, they will pursue scholarship that gains them recognition in their field, or brings new audiences across disciplines, or changes the way colleagues think about their teaching, or develops a community-based humanities project. Some will become public intellectuals. Some will become academic leaders—graduate directors, chairs, deans, presidents. Many will spend their careers changing the academy to meet the Grand Challenges facing higher education. The purposefulness they exercise in gaining breadth and depth in their field, developing their scholarly voice(s), honing their writing and presentational style, and building their repertoire of prodigious skills and competencies will prepare them well for the trajectory of careers in the academy.

Another percentage of students will take up alternative careers in the academy: in the libraries of the future, in academic presses, in administrative positions, in development, in programs reaching across academic and non-academic communities. In these positions they will continue their scholarly work, often in partnership with faculty and students; they will communicate that work in various forms; they will establish collaborative relationships; they will be increasingly central to the work of the humanities and its communication. Some of them will become academic "stars" with national and international reputations as thought leaders. This is true of Bethany Nowviskie, now a CLIR (Council on Library and Information Resources) Distinguished Presidential Fellow and also a special advisor to the provost at the University of Virginia, for the advancement of digital humanities research. She is one of the go-to people for thinking on the future of the humanities in the academy; and she coined the term #alt-ac. [13]

A percentage will take up positions outside the academy in the larger humanities workforce. Some will be drawn to K-12 education; some to the new fields at the intersection of library studies and information science; some to the nonprofit world of the humanities workforce; some to the world of government and public policy; some to research positions in the corporate world; some to heritage institutions—museums, public history projects, in the NEH, the ACLS, in NPR and PBS, in Words Without Borders and human rights venues. Contributions to and leadership in this expanded field of venues also advances the work of humanities in the world. As Paula Krebs argued back in 2010, "placing thoughtful, well-trained humanists in government, nonprofit associations, and even business or the military" is invaluable.[14]

Graduate students who proactively imagine multiple possible futures, define the story they want to tell about the transferability of skills they have already mastered, and create opportunities to gain additional skills become especially attractive and competitive candidates for the positions they pursue. But a cautionary note needs to be added. Students are often cautious about, if not even dissuaded from, talking with faculty advisors about seeking information on alternative careers. There can be repercussions in their departments. There can be repercussions in their relationship with faculty advisors. So if doctoral programs have not reoriented their criteria and culture of success, if they haven't organized opportunities for students to explore alternative careers, students will have to find other resources for support.

Fortunately, there are online resources and networks to tap for information and advice. Students can identify summer institutes on planning for multiple futures. They can look to the *Versatile Ph.D.* website, owned by Paula Chambers, which promises "to help . . . humanities and social science grad students prepare for nonacademic careers."[15] Or they can stayed tuned to "#alt-academy, a mediacommons project," a grassroots gathering place for people "working or seeking employment—generally off the tenure track, but within the academic orbit—in universities and colleges, or allied knowledge and cultural heritage institutions such as museums, libraries, academic presses, historical societies, and governmental humanities organizations."[16] Nowviskie writes of the site:

> The #Alt-Academy site is for them, for their academic partners and institutional leaders, and for the next generation of hybrid humanities scholars—people who are building skills and experience in precisely those areas of the academy that are most in flux, and most in need of guidance and attention by sensitive, capable, imaginative, and well-informed scholar-practitioners.

On the site, students and their mentors can find an open-access e-book entitled *#Alt-Academy*; the SCI Survey Report from August 2013 entitled *Humanities Unbound: Supporting Careers and Scholarship beyond the Tenure Track* written by

Katrina Rogers and reporting on the survey of humanists working in multiple careers; and a call for papers for the online journal *Graduate Training in the 21st Century*.[17]

Final Thoughts

There are dramatic changes to be made to doctoral programs. There are small changes. The challenge, as one of the reviewers of this book observed, is to "strike a reasonable balance between being responsible to current expectations, introducing innovation, and stressing new forms of professionalization." Through these changes, doctoral education must maintain its commitment to the scholarly and pedagogical values of the humanities. It must advance what produces and enhances value in the work of the humanities— nuanced and provocative readings, sophisticated interpretations, pleasure in language, in images and sound, the rhythms of sentences, the arcs of paragraphs, and in narrative; commitment to large and yet-to-be found archives; engagement with consequential issues of this time and of times past; and excitement in the interpretations, theoretical insights, analytical methods, and arguments faculty communicate to diverse individuals and audiences. And there is more that needs to be done—because there are profound changes in the institutions in which academic humanists work, the ecology of knowledge in those institutions, the way humanists will go about their work, the kind of work they will do, the way they will communicate their knowledge, the way they will teach about their fields and meet their obligations to students, and the ways they will advocate for the humanities in the academy and in public life.

It may be that these reorientations, changes both large and bold and small and circumspect, contribute to addressing the attrition rate, the completion rate, the average time to degree, and constrained job prospects for humanities PhDs. But it certainly will be the case that the intellectual and affective life of doctoral students and academic humanists will be enhanced by programs that bend to and with the receiver toward an as-yet-discovered ensemble of achievements. And it will be the case that moving away from the normativizing imperative of the one model of success as implicit ethos of doctoral study professionalization will, as David M. Ball, William Gleason, and Nancy J. Peterson, argue, "make [those students] better scholars and teachers, better advocates for the value of the humanities in the twenty-first century, and better candidates for careers in the range of other fields in which our graduates continue to excel."[18]

The Upside of Change

As a conclusion to this section on posttraditional doctoral education in the humanities, I want to circle around to the troubles with higher education explored in Part I. I do so by foregrounding two potential benefits to transformation that will contribute to the future vitality of humanities programs and the validation of humanities faculty, and humanistic inquiry, more generally. These are the potential upsides of more fully diversifying the professoriate and shrinking the pool of ABDs and PhDs available for exploitation in nontenure-track positions.

Diversifying the Humanities

As noted earlier, the overriding goal for faculty entrusted with educating future humanists is ensuring and sustaining excellence in doctoral education, and passion about its pleasures, commitments, and efficacies. That excellence is an effect of how doctoral education promotes and values intellectual excitement, analytical heft, depth of scholarly habits, imaginative elasticity, reach of influence, the flexible mobilization of scholarly voices crafted for multiple interlocutors. It is an effect of the prodigious set of skills doctoral students take with them onto the job market.

That excellence is necessarily an effect of diversity of questions and approaches. It is about attracting students with diverse lived experiences to the programs and breaking apart a social and intellectual milieu that reproduces procrustean models of professionalization. It is about valuing the potential diversity of the futures toward which it drives. It exists as a critique of the market value of utility by insisting that humanities have utility unaccounted for in the utility of the corporate imaginary, that the framework of utility begs the question about what professions are understood to have what kind of utility and for whom and for what. Doctoral education is key to addressing the higher education accessibility deficit here and abroad, and the key to ensuring a culture of intellectual curiosity, scholarly boldness, and pedagogical innovation as cornerstone to evolving and building 21st-century knowledge institutions.

As Evan Watkins eloquently argued at a symposium at Michigan State University titled "Futures of the English PhD," humanities graduate programs need to attract applicants not solely for the prestige they represent (that is, the universities they turn down) but for the diverse lived experiences, heritages, and knowledges they bring with them.[1] The former value overprivileges those who have learned the rudiments of doing research and thinking like a professor. It is deployed in admissions committees to make less risky calls. It reinforces, as Julie R. Posselt argues, the normativizing application of the concept of "fit" to candidate profiles.[2] The latter value impels admissions committees to seriously consider those candidates who may think outside the box, take risks, try different ways of approaching a research question, demand different theoretical frameworks; candidates who come from less elite universities and colleges, or whose route has taken them from community colleges to regional universities or small colleges; candidates with interesting work histories. The future of the humanities lies in the diverse range of faculty interests, angles of analysis, theoretical investments, and imaginative disruptions of fields; it lies in the diversity of the professoriate.

Doctoral programs in the humanities have long been challenged to attract and admit a diverse cohort of students. There is, of course, the issue of the pipeline for underrepresented minorities: not enough students of color imagine themselves as future professors of literatures and languages, philosophy, history. That is true, as well, for first-generation students. Academic leaders have been tackling the problem of pipeline with special summer programs designed to excite potential candidates about graduate study in the humanities and to model for them the kinds of historical, theoretical, and textual work that humanities scholars do. Valerie Lee at Ohio State University and Paula Krebs, formerly of Wheaton College, have been inspirational advocates for summer immersion opportunities. But pipeline initiatives can be only one strategy in a time when educational inequality is widening at the primary and secondary level; and the cost of higher education continues to impact accessibility and the high opportunity cost to students and their families in a years-long doctoral program that may also bring with it significant debt.

Another strategy for tackling this challenge is to open up the kinds of work students might pursue in their doctoral studies. Certainly, the robustness of ethnic and feminist studies, disability and queer studies, indigenous, global and postcolonial studies, and other emerging fields such as computational studies and the study of algorithmic cultures attracts students with diverse commitments and scholarly passions to doctoral study. That robustness signals openness to studies of marginalized subjects and communities, to new theoretical approaches to historical fields, and to histories of knowledge production itself. To this end, being flexible about how students configure their dissertation project signals that faculty aren't interested in exercises in only one kind of knowledge paradigm, in only one way of demonstrating readiness for the professoriate.

Observations by students responding to an earlier draft of this manifesto stressed how critical the sense of flexible openness can be to doctoral students from underserved and marginalized communities. They spoke eloquently of how some students work hard to gain admission to elite schools, only to discover that many on campus don't believe they belong, only to experience the microaggressions of daily encounters. They commented that there are students who don't want the academy to alienate them from their families and communities, and the humanities to alienate them from certain community values and local knowledges. Savvy in the ways in which higher education is part of "the system" through which inequities are reproduced, they know that doctoral study doesn't just have to do with the kind of job one might get in the future but also with being disciplined into normative values.[3] While introducing greater flexibility and more opportunity for innovation in a doctoral program may not address all the complex issues captured in this description of aspiration and everyday reality, it will shift values away from a one-model-fits-all ethic.

And there are more strategies. Designing programs that can be completed in five or six years, a recommendation of the MLA Task Force on Doctoral Study, encourages students concerned about opportunity costs to imagine a degree that won't require large loans and incur high debt. Offering more robust funding packages with significant fellowship support to offset the attraction of other disciplines would make the commitment to humanities doctoral education more feasible. Further diversifying the curriculum within humanities departments would signal commitment to attracting diverse faculty to the professoriate. Conceptualizing job descriptions that don't reproduce rigid notions of period and field and approach would signal openness to a diverse range of candidate profiles. And offering competitive salaries with start-up packages would seal commitment.

More variety of scholarly activities, products, and venues; more flexible program models, funding and curricular offerings; more collaborative sociality; and a more inclusive environment of commitment to a diverse future—the effects of these shifts would radically transform the climate and systems of support in humanities doctoral education, positioning programs to attract a more heterogeneous range of students. Expanding the diversity of experiential histories that students bring to programs would multiply and complicate the intellectual, affective, and social perspectives that energize the classroom, the seminar table, the student lounge, the student interest group, and the offices of faculty. Doing so, graduate education contributes, however incrementally, to the project of educational justice.

There is another demographic challenge confronting the academic humanities; and it has to do with the demographics of those in the field of digital humanities. Many academic activists have been pressing to "transform DH," by advancing queer, critical race, ethnic studies, and feminist theories, ethics, praxis, and projects within DH fields and DH communities; and by producing scholarship on the history of computational logics. As Alexis Lothian and Amanda Phillips note, activist scholars have illuminated the "less marketable histories of engagement with technology that have emerged from standpoints that critique the privileging of certain gendered, racialized, classed, able-bodied, Western-centric productions of knowledge."[4] They have "unpack[ed] the politics inherent in the force of the digital, the powers that shape the hardware and software that shape our scholarly work."[5] And increasingly, they are addressing the gendered and racialized makeup of the digital humanities community, calling for the advancement of white women and men and women of color in academic DH positions.

According to the Survey of Earned Doctorates for 2012, women are now earning just over 50% of humanities doctorates, though percentages are distributed asymmetrically across humanities disciplines.[6] The balance here is to be desired, as is the gradually increasing number of women in the humanities who are reaching the rank of full professor. Women, however, remain disturbingly underrepresented in the field of the digital humanities, where the signature of belonging is facility in coding and easy familiarity with the languages and discourses of humanities computing. Indeed, in disciplines where the number of women exceeds the number of men, some might see the process of feminization taking hold, coinciding with the public discourse about the "softness" and "inutility" of humanities degrees. The digital humanities, it seems, is the masculine redoubt of the humanities, networked to those in mathematics and computer science, in computer architecture and software design.

Further, the digital humanities, as Tara McPherson has argued, is "so white"; and to understand why that is so, she explores how

certain modes of racial visibility and knowing coincide or dovetail with specific ways of organizing data: if digital computing underwrites today's information economy and is the central technology of post–World War II America, these technologized ways of seeing and knowing took shape in a world also struggling with shifting knowledges about and representations of race.[7]

McPherson elaborates how racialized logics of the post-civil rights era and logics of computational technologies were imbricated in one another. In addition, knowledge systems projected through coding—hidden data, granularity, filters; modularization, standardization, and the simplification of complexity—paralleled the increasing specialization of humanistic scholarship since the 1960s—the compartmentalization of disciplines and subdisciplines, the routinization of critical projects, and the "patterned isolation" of "bureaucratic standardization."[8] Her call is for more work at the intersection of critical code and critical race studies, and for more familiarity with "code languages, operating systems, algorithmic thinking, and systems design"; in other words, for computational literacy, expanded ensembles of inquiry, and new kinds of graduate programs.

More flexible, hybrid, innovative options for pursuing a capstone project, more opportunities for collaboration, more attention to building competencies—such changes in doctoral programs would contribute to unsettling the digital humanities, by, for example, decolonizing the database and archive and expanding the demographic range of its communities of practice. Further, decolonizing the database and archive and expanding the demographic diversity of its community of practice would have an impact on another troubling feature of work in digital humanities fields. In "Toward a New Deal," Bethany Nowviskie observes that "imbalances in gender, race, class, and ethnicity among people working in tech-oriented humanities fields have arguably reinforced a digital archival focus on canonical texts and reified homogenous perspectives."[9] Again, this is a matter of consequence because it concerns diversity of the professoriate, of intellectual projects, and of the climate in which work gains validation.

Intervening in the Economics of Contingency

As noted earlier, the trend to shift teaching load from tenured and tenure-track faculty to contingent faculty is decades old, and by now a prominent feature of the restructuring of the professoriate as costs have skyrocketed, public funding diminished, and facilities expanded. To reprise: the American Association of University Professors reports that "non-tenure-track positions of all types now account for 76 percent of all instructional staff appointments in American higher education"; and across institutions of higher education in the United States "more than 50% of all faculty hold part-time appointments."[10] Across higher education institutions there are large numbers of adjunct and non-tenure-track faculty in humanities units, especially in English and other language departments, where people off the tenure track, and often in contingent positions, provide service courses for the general education curriculum. A large percentage is employed in part-time positions without adequate compensation, benefits, and working conditions. This dramatic imbalance in the distribution of teaching across tenure-track faculty and non-tenure-track faculty is an effect of the intensification of the research mandate across large universities and even small liberal arts colleges starting in the 1970s; the economic constraints on institutions increasing the number of students they serve as state support diminishes; and the increasingly corporate strategies for gaining budget savings and efficiencies. It depends on the available pool of MAs and PhDs for whom the prospect for tenure-track positions remains grim, and, as Marc Bousquet argues, the opportunistic exploitation of graduate student and lecturer labor by universities and colleges looking to find faculty for service courses.[11]

The data on graduate education tell a haunting story of the link between the continuing casualization of the academic workforce and the extended time-to-degree of eight and more years for many. There is the radically differential funding support for students across different institutions; there is the growth in debt levels, especially for students of color; and there is the diminished prospects for a tenure-track position upon completion. The best-funded doctoral students in the elite schools often move through programs in a timely manner because of funding packages made up of fellowships rather than teaching assistantships. They take up a disproportionately high share of the tenure-track positions at elite schools and the flagship state universities.[12]

The large number of students whose support requires teaching face the daunting task of preparing themselves to be successful in the classroom and meeting the high demands of classroom teaching. Yes, teaching experience is a critical component of doctoral education; and these students gain invaluable experience in the classroom. But without fellowship support along the way, the time to completion can stretch out six or seven or eight or more years. Moreover, the institutional reliance on teaching assistants in the classroom contributes to the casualization of the academic labor force: administrators maintain their reliance on non-tenure-track positions, and the rise in the ratio of non-tenure-track faculty adversely impacts the job situation doctoral students enter.

Addressing the significant cascading effects of this situation requires a multipronged set of strategies. One strategy for improving the conditions of non-tenure-track faculty has been the route of unionization. At Michigan, lecturers voted to unionize in 2003. Union contracts here have eventuated in better working conditions, a clear pathway to multiple-year contracts, an improved set of procedures for evaluating and rewarding excellence in the lecturer ranks, and a minimum per course threshold. Other strategies are locally organized—the gradual shift of some non-tenure-track positions to tenure-track ones; or demands by non-tenure-track faculty for improved working conditions, adequate office space and access, institutional support for professional development, multiple-year contracts, and living wages.

As noted in Part I, adjunct organizations, the New Faculty Majority, the Coalition for Contingent Academic Labor, the Adjunct Action Network, and other activists have joined in a national campaign to bring the conditions of contingent faculty to the broader public and to press for more fairness in academic compensation. Adjuncts testified before Congress on the exploitative conditions under which this growing sector of university faculty work; they are unionizing; and they are producing scholarship on the effects of the insecure conditions that characterize the everyday life of non-tenure-track faculty in the academy.[13] And professional organizations in the humanities have joined together in the Coalition on the Academic Workforce to advocate for change in the balance of non-tenure-track and tenured/tenure-track faculty and produced invaluable studies on the makeup of the faculty and on part-time faculty members.[14]

Another strategy for addressing the exploitation of contingent faculty is presented in this manifesto and its plan for envisioning a 21st century graduate education. A percentage, though not the majority, of non-tenure-track faculty are ABDs, and PhDs seeking tenure-track appointment. Expanding forms of the dissertation and opportunities for exploring alternative career paths will impact the current imbalance in the academic workforce. Introducing alternative forms of the dissertation and weaning programs off the proto-monograph as the only indicator of promise, readiness, and dedication to scholarly work will be one contributor to decreasing time-to-degree and eliminating time-to-attrition. Arguably, enabling alternative dissertation options may eventuate in a shorter time-to-degree, say five to six years, which could mean that doctoral students would not be forced by financial exigency to seek part-time teaching as they linger on to complete a monograph dissertation beyond the fifth or sixth year.

In sum, looking forward to a 21st century doctoral education, programs are likely to attract more diverse cohorts. Incorporating opportunities for doctoral students to think more broadly about career paths ahead, and to gain a broad repertoire of skills and experiences, programs prepare doctoral students to imagine and pursue positions outside as well as inside the academy. Those who advance to alternative positions in the academy and careers outside the academy thus become unavailable for recruitment into low-wage positions in higher education. Those who advance to tenure-track positions benefit from what David M. Ball, William Gleason, and Nancy J. Peterson term an "expanded conception of professionalization." Through such opportunities, they opine, graduates will become "cognizant of the changing face of the profession, the threats to it, and the skills they possess both within and beyond higher education" and thus will become "more forceful critics of the systemic structures they inherit."[15] In other words, future faculty will be better prepared to advocate within the academy for greater diversity, more capacious portfolios of scholarly work and pedagogical impact, and higher wages and better benefits for non-tenure-track faculty.

Coda

What gains for the labors of transformation!

A 21st-century doctoral education will prepare the next generation of passionate, dedicated scholars willing to engage what has been thought and created and done, in violence and radical renunciation, in the rapture of belief and the cool of disbelief, amid the frenzy of the crowd and the quiet of solitude, in the name of the past and the aspiration of tomorrow. Willing to reanimate the past, observe the present, and project possible futures, by means of profligate curiosity, ardent receptivity, and incisive critique. Willing to reflect on systems of value, in politics and the academy, in aesthetics and material cultures. Willing to upend thought, reflect on thinking, and think, in Elizabeth Grosz's words, "before, beyond, and after the human."[1]

Their scale of inquiry will reach from the singular image to the cloud of Big Data, from the person to the crowd, from the pulsing contemporary, momentous and ephemeral, to the deep time of the Anthropocene. Their curiosity will embrace embodied, psychic, emotional, affective, intellectual, and ideological attachments, of individuals to objects and others, to language and ideas, to other species and the earth. Their fascinations will turn to the capaciousness of storytelling, epic and episodic, raw and highly stylized, fictive and documentary, historical and ethnographic, syncretic and disruptive. They will open themselves for the stories given up in communities or encased in architectural remnants of past civilizations. They will record and analyze stories others tell of themselves, utopian and dystopian, traumatic and ecstatic. They will pause in slow time to register the impact of a word, a metaphor, a phrase, a photograph, a sound; linger in sustained moments of deep reading or listening or viewing; draw pleasure from an abundance of languages and symbolic systems; relish discoveries in archival serendipity. They will poach ideas and theoretical frameworks from across disciplinary boundaries to better understand material worlds and worldviews, their own and those of others across time and geographical expanse. They will forge critiques of fundamental assumptions about the meaning attached to the "the human" and "the humanities."

They will do, that is, the work of the humanities and humanistic social sciences. But they will have come from programs that did not require them to conform to a one-model-fits-all academic program; that encouraged thinking outside the box; that broadened the concept of professionalization away from the one-model-of-success narrative. Some will be adept at navigating digital environments of data, information, content, platform, and code and at communicating their scholarship in multimodal and multimedia forms. Many will be prepared to assess the options of open access. More and more will be adept at working collaboratively and valuing cultures of participatory inquiry, and thus enacting a new ethos of academic sociality. Others will have expanded their range of scholarly voices and idioms of communication. Many will not see teaching as an obstruction to their careers defined solely in terms of publication rate and record; they will have gained sophistication in a range of pedagogical practices. They will be able to explain for diverse audiences that it is not easy to teach humanities courses; that to do so well, faculty must remain active scholars and researchers.

By the time they graduate, they will have been prepared for careers that unfold through diverse trajectories. Some will find exciting careers outside the academy, some careers in the academy as librarians and program administrators. Those who go on to the professoriate will be prepared to pressure colleagues and administrators to adopt more expansive criteria for earning tenure and promotion, and will themselves contribute heterogeneous portfolios for advancement. They will think more capaciously about the venues of humanistic inquiry, and extend scholarly tracks to public footprints and public partnerships. They will recognize that their formidable skills have prepared them for leadership positions of all kinds in the university. They will recognize themselves as part of a larger network of humanists, those in alternative academic careers and doctorally trained professionals outside the academy. They will be prepared to contribute to the long project of changing higher education through critique, innovative initiative, advocacy, and activism, including activism directed at making the climate more inclusive, intervening in the economics of contingency, and diversifying the demographics of the professoriate.

This has been my manifesto, this my vision for the future of the humanities in the academy and the world.

The times, indeed, are good enough.

Notes

Realities on the Ground

1. Sean Coughlan, "Italian University Switches to English," *BBC News*, May 16, 2012, http://www.bbc.co.uk/news/business-17958520. Jonathan Cole considers increased global competition a global good in itself. See "Can Graduate Education Survive as We Know It?" (presentation, Rackham Graduate School, University of Michigan, April 5, 2012).

2. See John Aubrey Douglass, "The Cold War, Technology and the American University" (Research and Occasional Paper Series CSHE.2.99, Center for Studies in Higher Education, University of California, Berkeley, July 1999), accessed June 16, 2015, http://www.cshe.berkeley.edu/sites/default/files/shared/publications/docs/PP.JD.Sputnik_Tech.2.99.pdf.

3. University of Michigan Public Relations Office, "Understanding Tuition," accessed December 26, 2014, http://www.vpcomm.umich.edu/pa/key/understandingtuition.html.

4. As Seth Godin observed: "College has gotten expensive far faster than wages have gone up." Seth Godin, "The Coming Meltdown in Higher Education (as Seen by a Marketer)," *Chronicle of Higher Education*, May 3, 2010, https://chronicle.com/article/The-Coming-Meltdown-in-Higher/65398/.

5. Sara Goldrick-Rab, "The Proposed New Badger Partnership: Implications for Equity and Diversity," *Sifting and Winnowing* (blog), March 14, 2011, http://siftingandwinnowing.org/2011/03/14/the-proposed-new-badger-partnership-implications-for-equity-and-diversity/. Goldrick-Rab parses the upward trend in income in this way: "This will stem from sticker shock . . . , decreases in the purchasing power of financial aid, and the perception of an elitist culture that would feel a 'poor fit' for children from working-class families."

6. Halah Touryalai, "$1 Trillion Student Loan Problem Keeps Getting Worse," *Forbes*, February 21, 2014, http://www.forbes.com/sites/halahtouryalai/2014/02/21/1-trillion-student-loan-problem-keeps-getting-worse/.

7. In 2012 Janet Lorin of *Bloomberg News* wrote of "indentured students" in a series on the history, politics, lived experiences, and legacies of high student loans. "Indentured Students Rise as Loans Corrode College Ticket," *Bloomberg*, July 9, 2012, http://www.bloomberg.com/news/2012-07-09/indentured-students-rise-as-loans-corrode-college-ticket.html.

8. William H. Frey, "New Projections Point to a Majority Minority Nation in 2044," December 12, 2014, *The Avenue: Rethinking Metropolitan America* (blog), Brookings Institution, http://www.brookings.edu/blogs/the-avenue/posts/2014/12/12-majority-minority-nation-2044-frey.

9. Kathleen Woodward, "We Are All Non-traditional Learners Now: Community Colleges, Long-Life Learning, and Problem-Solving Humanities for the Public Good," in *A New Deal for the Humanities: Liberal Arts and the Future of Public Higher Education*, ed. Gordon Hutner and Feisal Mohamed (New Brunswick, NJ: Rutgers University Press, forthcoming).

10. National Research Council, *Research Universities and the Future of America: Ten Breakthrough Actions Vital to Our Nation's Prosperity and Security* (Washington, DC: National Academies Press, 2012), 3, http://sites.nationalacademies.org/pga/cs/groups/pgasite/documents/webpage/pga_070193.pdf.

11. Ibid.

12. "Background Facts on Contingent Faculty," American Association of University Professors, accessed August 12, 2015, http://www.aaup.org/issues/contingency/background-facts.

13. Paul Basken and Paul Voosen, "Strapped Scientists Abandon Research and Students," *Chronicle of Higher Education*, February 24, 2014, http://chronicle.com/article/Strapped-Scientists-Abandon/144921/.

14. Gary Carnivale, "Making the Case for the Humanities" (paper presented at the National Humanities Alliance Conference, George Washington University, Washington, DC, March 10, 2009).

15. Florida's governor, Rick Scott, observed of anthropology majors in a radio interview in 2011: "It's a great degree if people want to get it. But we don't need them here." Michael C. Bender, "Scott: Florida Doesn't Need More Anthropology Majors," *The Buzz* (blog), *Tampa Bay Times*, October 10, 2011, http://www.tampabay.com/blogs/the-buzz-florida-politics/content/scott-florida-doesnt-need-more-anthropology-majors. For McCrory's statement, see Tyler Kingkade, "Pat McCrory Lashes Out Against 'Educational Elite' and Liberal Arts College Courses." *The Huffington Post*, February 2, 2013, updated February 3, 2013.

16. Lance Lambert, "States Are Eager to Collect Graduates' Job Data: Here's Where That Effort Stands," *Chronicle of Higher Education*, March 25, 2015, http://chronicle.com/article/States-Are-Eager-to-Collect/228745/?cid=at&utm_source=at&utm_medium=en.

17. This situation prompted the Association of Departments of Foreign Languages of the Modern Language Association to develop its "Tool Kit for Department Advocacy," which provides links to documents and rhetoric for arguments in support of robust language programs and units. See "Resources for Departments," Association of Departments of Foreign Languages, accessed August 12, 2015, http://www.adfl.org/resources/index.htm.

18. Coalition on the Academic Workforce, *A Portrait of Part-Time Faculty Members*, June 2012, http://www.academicworkforce.org/CAW_portrait_2012.pdf.

19. "Trends in the Demographics of Humanities Faculty: Key Indicators from the 2012–2013 Humanities Departmental Survey," Humanities Indicators, accessed May 25, 2015, http://www.humanitiesindicators.org/content/indicatordoc.aspx?i=461.

20. See Kay Steiger, "The Pink Collar Workforce of Academia," *Nation*, July 11, 2013, http://www.thenation.com/article/175214/academias-pink-collar-workforce.

21. Lynn Hunt, "Democratization and Decline? The Consequences of Demographic Change in the Humanities," in *What's Happened to the Humanities?*, ed. Alvin B. Kernan (Princeton, NJ: Princeton University Press, 2014), 28. See also the other essays in *What's Happened to the Humanities?*

22. Derek Bok, *Universities in the Marketplace: The Commercialization of Higher Education* (Princeton, NJ: Princeton University Press, 2004); Jennifer Washburn, *University, Inc.: The Corporate Corruption of Higher Education* (New York: Basic Books, 2006); Ellen Schrecker, *The Lost Soul of Higher Education: Corporatization, the Assault on Academic Freedom, and the End of the American University* (New York: New Press, 2010); Cary Nelson, *No University Is an Island: Saving Academic Freedom* (New York: New York University Press, 2010); Gayle Tuchman, *Wannabe U: Inside the Corporate University* (Chicago: University of Chicago Press, 2011); Christopher Newfield, *Unmaking the Public University: The Forty-Year Assault on the Middle Class* (Cambridge, MA: Harvard University Press, 2011); Benjamin Ginsberg, *The Fall of the Faculty: The Rise of the All-Administrative University and Why It Matters* (New York: Oxford University Press, 2011). For books on the humanities, see Frank Donoghue, *The Last Professors: The Corporate University and the Fate of the Humanities* (New York: Fordham University Press, 2008), Martha Nussbaum, *Not for Profit: Why Democracy Needs the Humanities* (Princeton, NJ: Princeton University Press, 2010), and Louis Menand, *The Marketplace of Ideas: Reform and Reaction in the American University* (New York: Norton, 2010).

What Is to Be Done?

1. Jacques Barzun, *The American University: How It Runs, Where It Is Going* (New York: HarperCollins, 1968), 240–41.

2. Ibid., 235.

3. I am indebted to Cass Adair, Tiffany Ball, and Jina Kim for their generous conversation about the ways in which humanities departments are alienating environments.

4. Marc Bousquet, "Condemned to Repeat: On the Racism and Sexism of Failing to Address Structure," *Pedagogy* 15, no. 1 (2015): 162.

5. See Mary Ann Mason, "What You Need to Know If You're an Academic and Want to Be a Mom," *Room for Debate* (blog), *New York Times*, July 16, 2013, http://www.nytimes.com/roomfordebate/2013/07/08/should-women-delay-motherhood/what-you-need-to-know-if-youre-an-academic-and-want-to-be-a-mom. Previewing the book she cowrote with Marc Goulden and Nicolas H. Wolfinger entitled *Do Babies Matter? Gender and Family in the Ivory Tower*, Mason writes: "For men, having children is a career advantage; and for women it is a career killer. And women who do advance through the faculty ranks do so at a high price. They are far less likely to be married with children." See *Do Babies Matter? Gender and Family in the Ivory Tower* (New Brunswick, NJ: Rutgers University Press, 2013).

6. Paul Courant, "Demographics of Faculty in Tenure Track Appointments," June 24, 2015.

7. Lee Siegel, "Who Ruined the Humanities?" *Wall Street Journal*, July 12, 2013, C1, http://online.wsj.com/news/articles/SB10001424127887323823004578459580329679 8048.

8. Mark Bauerlein, "What Dido Did, Satan Saw & O'Keeffe Painted," *New Criterion*, November 2013, 3.

9. And yes, this is a purposeful, jarring nod to the impact of what the Chicago Lab Text at the University of Chicago describes as "computational approaches to the study of culture." Hoyt Long, "Announcing 'Cultural Analytics'—a Major Conference on Computational Approaches to the Study of Culture," *Chicago Text Lab* (blog), November 13, 2014, https://lucian.uchicago.edu/blogs/literarynetworks/.

10. Paul Jay, *The Humanities "Crisis" and the Future of Literary Studies* (New York: Palgrave Macmillan, 2014).

11. Michael Bérubé, "The Humanities, Declining? Not According to the Numbers," *Chronicle of Higher Education*, July 1, 2013, http://chronicle.com/article/The-Humanities-Declining-Not/140093/.

12. Russell A. Berman, "Response to New York Times," n.d., unpublished.

13. "Humanities Indicators: A Project of the American Academy of Arts and Sciences," Humanities Indicators, accessed June 30, 2014, http://www.humanitiesindicators.org/.

14. Linguistics Society of America, *The State of Linguistics in Higher Education: Annual Report 2014*, 2nd ed. (March 2015), http://www.linguisticsociety.org/files/Lx_Annual_Report_2014.pdf, 5.

15. "Humanities Indicators: A Project of the American Academy of Arts and Sciences," Humanities Indicators, accessed June 30, 2014, http://www.humanitiesindicators.org/.

16. "The State of the Humanities: Higher Education 2015," Humanities Indicators, accessed April 22, 2015, http://www.humanitiesindicators.org/.

17. Ibid., 17.

18. Christopher Newfield, "The Future of the Public University" (presented at "Humanities, Publics, and the State," Annual Meeting of the Consortium for Humanities Centers and Institutes, University of Kansas, Lawrence, 2013), http://chcinetwork.org/2013-annual-meeting/.

19. Robert N. Watson, "The Humanities Really Do Produce a Profit," *Chronicle of Higher Education*, March 21, 2010, http://chronicle.com/article/The-Humanities-Really-Do-Pr/64740/.

20. "One-Third of College-Educated Workers Do Not Work in Occupations Related to Their College Major," *Careerbuilder*, November 14, 2013, http://www.careerbuilder.com/share/aboutus/pressreleasesdetail.aspx?sd=11%2f14%2f2013&siteid=cbpr&sc_cmp1=cb_pr790_&id=pr790&ed=12%2f31%2f2013.

21. Jaison R. Abel and Richard Deitz, "Do Big Cities Help College Graduates Find Better Jobs?" *Liberty Street Economics*, May 20, 2013, accessed October 13, 2015, http://libertystreeteconomics.newyorkfed.org/2013/05/do-big-cities-help-college-graduates-find-better-jobs.html#.VhotvstBIpI.

22. Alan Liu, "The Meaning of Digital Humanities," *PMLA* 128, no. 2 (2013): 420.

23. "Academic Workforce Advocacy Kit," Modern Language Association, accessed August 12, 2015, http://www.mla.org/advocacy_kit.

24. House Committee on Education and the Workforce Democratic Staff, *The Just-In-Time Professor: A Staff Report Summarizing eForum Responses on the Working Conditions of Contingent Faculty in Higher Education*, January 2014, http://democrats.edworkforce.house.gov/sites/democrats.edworkforce.house.gov/files/documents/1.24.14-AdjunctEforumReport.pdf.

25. "The Delphi Project on the Changing Faculty and Student Success," Pullias Center for Higher Education, University of Southern California, accessed August 12, 2015, www.thechangingfaculty.org.

26. "The Adjunct Project," accessed April 23, 2015, http://cunyadjunctproject.org/.

27. "Humanities Indicators: A Project of the American Academy of Arts and Sciences," Humanities Indicators, accessed June 30, 2014, http://www.humanitiesindicators.org/.

28. "American Alliance of Museums," accessed May 26, 2015, http://www.aam-us.org/about-museums/museum-facts.

29. Funded by the Mellon Foundation, Connected Academics expands "mentoring and networking activities at the MLA Annual Convention and at regional MLA meetings, where job seekers can meet with mentors in a variety of occupations." "Connected Academics," Modern Language Association of America, accessed June 23, 2015, https://www.mla.org/connected_academics.

30. Bousquet, "Condemned to Repeat," 161.

31. David Colander and Daisy Zhuo, "Where Do PhDs in English Get Jobs? An Economist's View of the English PhD Market," *Pedagogy* 15, no. 1 (2015): 143.

The Distributed University

1. Michael M. Crow and William B. Dabars, *Designing the New American University* (Baltimore: Johns Hopkins University Press, 2015).

2. University of the People, accessed June 18, 2013, http://uopeople.edu/.

3. "Our Students," University of the People, accessed June 18, 2013, http://uopeople.edu.

4. "Catalog: University of the People: September 1, 2013–August 31, 2014," University of the People, accessed June 18, 2013, http://www.uopeople.org/files/Pdf/university_catalog.pdf.

5. William Lawton and Alex Katsomitros, *International Branch Campuses: Data and Developments*, Observatory on Borderless Higher Education, December 1, 2012, http://www.obhe.ac.uk/documents/view_details?id=894; Tamar Lewin, "Colleges Slower to Branch Out Abroad," *New York Times*, January 12, 2012, sec. Education, http://www.nytimes.com/2012/01/12/education/colleges-slower-to-branch-out-abroad.html.

6. Lewin, "Colleges Slower," A6.

7. Nigel Thrift, "The World Needs Global Research Cooperation Urgently, and Now," *Chronicle of Higher Education*, February 19, 2010, http://chronicle.com/article/Urgently-Needed-Global-Coo/64130/.

8. "What Is the Bologna Process?," European University Association, accessed August 6, 2014, http://www.eua.be/eua-work-and-policy-area/building-the-european-higher-education-area/bologna-basics.aspx.

9. *Salzburg II Recommendations: European Universities' Achievements since 2005 in Implementing the Salzburg Principles* (European University Association, 2010), http://www.eua.be/Libraries/Publications_homepage_list/Salzburg_II_Recommendations.sflb.ashx.

10. With the increase in the number of cross-border institutions, programs, and initiatives, the ACE (American Council on Education), AUCC (Association of Universities and Colleges in Canada), and CHEA (Council for Higher Education Accreditation), issued a joint statement of principles and good practices in cross-border education. See ACE, AUCC, and CHEA, "Sharing Higher Education across Borders: A Statement on Behalf of Higher Education Institutions Worldwide," January 2005, http://www.chea.org/pdf/StatementFinal0105.pdf.

11. National Research Council, *Research Universities*.

12. James J. Duderstadt, "A Master Plan for Higher Education in the Midwest: A Roadmap to the Future of the Nation's Heartland" (Heartland Papers No. 3, Heartland Papers by the Chicago Council of Global Affairs, 2011), 47, http://www.thechicagocouncil.org/Userfiles/File/Globalmidwest/A_Master_Plan_for_Higher_Education_FINAL.pdf. Duderstadt directs his call, most particularly, to enhancing work in STEM fields; for the most part his call for collaboration is not encompassing of cultural institutions and humanities fields.

13. Consortium of Humanities Centers and Institutes, accessed August 7, 2014, http://chcinetwork.org/.

14. "CHCI Receives Second Major A. W. Mellon Foundation Grant," Consortium of Humanities Centers and Institutes, accessed August 7, 2014, http://chcinetwork.org/chci-receives-second-major-a-w-foundation-grant/.

15. Ibid.

16. "About CenterNet," CenterNet, accessed August 12, 2015, http://digitalhumanities.org/centernet/centers/.

17. HASTAC, accessed August 8, 2014, http://www.hastac.org/.

18. Humanities Without Walls, accessed July 25, 2012, http://www.humanitieswithoutwalls.illinois.edu/.

19. "The First Public-Private Joint Venture in German Graduate Education in the Nation," Graduate Program in German Studies, University of North Carolina and Duke University, accessed August 12, 2015, http://carolina-duke-grad.german.duke.edu/about.

20. CHCI, "CHCI Receives Second Major."

21. See chapters 5 and 7 of Cathy N. Davidson and David Theo Goldberg, *The Future of Thinking: Learning Institutions in a Digital Age* (Cambridge, MA: MIT Press, 2010), https://mitpress.mit.edu/sites/default/files/titles/free_download/978026251374,6_Future_of_Thinking.pdf.

22. Rosi Braidotti, *The Posthuman* (Malden, MA: Polity Press, 2013), 179.

23. Daniel E. Atkins, "Cyberinfrastructure: Technical+Social=Transformation If You Help" (presented at the Humanities, Arts, Science, and Technology Advanced Collaboratory, University of Michigan, Ann Arbor, December 2, 2011), presentation slides available at http://www.hastac.org/documents/cyberinfrastructure.

Knowledge Environments

1. HathiTrust's content is predominantly Google Books derivatives.

2. Carolyn Fox, "Review of the New Digital Public Library of America," OpenSource.com, May 21, 2013, http://opensource.com/education/13/5/review-dpla. According to its website, the Digital Library of America serves as "a non-commercial alternative to Google's proposed digital library."

3. Margaret Hedstrom and John Leslie King, "Epistemic Infrastructure in the Rise of the Knowledge Economy," in *Advancing Knowledge and the Knowledge Economy*, ed. Brian Kahin and Foray Dominique (Cambridge: MIT Press, 2006), 113–34, http://jlking.people.si.umich.edu/EpistemicInfrast-MITPress.pdf.

4. Lisbet Rausing, "Toward a New Alexandria," *New Republic*, March 12, 2010, http://www.newrepublic.com/article/books-and-arts/toward-new-alexandria#; Duderstadt, "Master Plan," 89.

5. Hedstrom and King, "Epistemic Infrastructure," 13–15.

6. Ibid., 10–11.

7. Jerome McGann, "A Note on the Current State of Humanities Scholarship," *Critical Inquiry* 30, no. 2 (2004): 410.

8. Bethany Nowviskie, "Toward a New Deal," *Bethany Nowviskie* (blog), September 25, 2013, http://nowviskie.org/2013/new-deal/.

9. See Daniel H. Pink, *A Whole New Mind: Moving from the Information Age to the Conceptual Age* (New York: Riverhead Books, 2005). See also "How 21st Century Thinking Is

Different . . . and What That Means for Kids and Creativity," *iPad Art Room*, accessed August 28, 2014, http://www.ipadartroom.com/how-21st-century-thinking-is-different/.

10. Liu, "Meaning of Digital Humanities," 416.

11. Paul Conway, "Re-making Books in the Digital Archive." Paper delivered at "Books/Texts/Fonts/Archives in a Brave New Digital World." Institute for the Humanities, University of Michigan, April 9, 2013.

12. Franco Moretti, *Distant Reading* (New York: Verso, 2013).

13. Donald J. Waters, "An Overview of the Digital Humanities," *Research Library Issues: A Report from ARL, CNI, and SPARC*, RLI no. 284 (2013), 5–6. http://publications.arl.org/rli284/.

14. Ibid., 8.

15. William G. Thomas III, "Trends in Digital Humanities: Remarks at the CIC Humanities Summit ('The Keynote in the Dark')," William G. Thomas III (blog), April 28, 2012, http://railroads.unl.edu/blog/?p=794.

16. Christa Williford and Charles Henry, *One Culture. Computationally Intensive Research in the Humanities and Social Sciences: A Report on the Experiences of First Respondents to the Digging into Data Challenge* (Washington, DC: Council on Library and Information Resources, June 2012), 8.

17. McGann, "Note on Current State," 412.

18. Josh Greenberg, "Data, Code, and Research at Scale" (presented at the Humanities, Arts, Science, and Technology Advanced Collaboratory 2011, University of Michigan, Ann Arbor, December 3, 2011), http://www.hastac.org/documents/data-code-and-research-scale.

19. Sydney J. Shep, "Digital Lives: Digital History/Biography" (presented at the International Auto/Biography Association Biennial Meeting, Canberra, Australia, July 18, 2012).

20. Trevor Owens, "Defining Data for Humanists: Text, Artifact, Information or Evidence?," *Journal of Digital Humanities*, March 16, 2012, http://journalofdigitalhumanities.org/1-1/defining-data-for-humanists-by-trevor-owens/.

21. Franco Moretti, *"Operationalizing": Or the Function of Measurement in Modern Literary Theory*, Stanford Literary Lab Pamphlet 6 (December 2013), 2, http://litlab.stanford.edu/LiteraryLabPamphlet6.pdf.

22. Stephen Ramsay, "The Hermeneutics of Screwing Around; or, What You Do with a Million Books," in *Pastplay: Teaching and Learning History with Technology*, ed. Kevin Kee (Ann Arbor: University of Michigan Press, 2014), 118.

23. Seth Denbo, "Diggable Data, Scalable Reading, and New Humanities Scholarship," Maryland Institute for Technology in the Humanities Blog, October 18, 2011, http://mith.umd.edu/diggable-data-scalable-reading-and-new-humanities-scholarship/.

24. Liu, "Meaning of Digital Humanities," 411.

25. Ibid., 416.

26. Ibid., 411.

27. Christian Sandvig, Kevin Hamilton, Karrie Karahalios, and Cedric Langbort. "Auditing Algorithms: Research Methods for Detecting Discrimination on Internet Platforms" (presented at "Data and Discrimination: Converting Critical Concerns into Productive Inquiry," preconference at the 64th Annual Meeting of the International Communication Association, Seattle, May 24, 2014).

28. Kevin Ashton, "That 'Internet of Things' Thing," *RFID Journal*, June 22, 2009, 4.

29. Harbor Research, "The Internet of Things Meets the Internet of People," accessed August 12, 2015, http://www.slideshare.net/harborresearch/harbor-research-internet-of-things-meets-internet-of-people, 3–4.

30. Ibid., 7.

31. Jentery Sayers, "On Data Representations and the Humanities" (presented at "Data, Social Justice, and the Humanities," University of Michigan Institute for the Humanities, October 3, 2014).

32. "Linked Data," W3C, accessed August 12, 2015, http://www.w3.org/standards/semanticweb/data.

33. Tim Berners-Lee, *Weaving the Web: The Original Design and Ultimate Destiny of the World Wide Web by Its Inventor* (New York: HarperCollins, 1999), 169–70.

34. Pochoda, "The Big One: The Epistemic System Break in Scholarly Monograph Publishing," *New Media & Society* 15, no. 3 (May 1, 2013): 359–78, 368.

35. It will also tax the academy to respond adequately to new kinds of humanities projects. In the words of the executive summary of the *One Culture* report:

> To realize the benefits of data-intensive social sciences and humanities, institutions and scholarly societies must expand their notions of what kinds of activities constitute research and reconsider how these activities are supported, assessed, and rewarded. Computationally intensive research projects rely upon four diverse kinds of expertise, each described in detail in section two of this report: **domain (or subject) expertise, analytical expertise, data expertise,** and **project management expertise.** The active engagement of each of these kinds of experts in the research enterprise is essential. A re-evaluation of hiring practices, job requirements, and tenets of promotion is requisite. (Williford and Henry, *One Culture*, 2)

36. Ibid., 2.

37. "About—Critical Commons," Critical Commons, accessed August 11, 2014, http://www.criticalcommons.org/about-us.

38. Tara McPherson, "After the Archive: Scholarship in the Digital Era" (presented at the Digital Humanities Brown Bag Lecture, University of Michigan, Ann Arbor, November 29, 2011).

39. Johanna Drucker, "Blind Spots: Humanists Must Plan Their Digital Future," *Chronicle Review*, April 3, 2009, B6–B8, http://chronicle.com/article/Blind-Spots/9348.

40. Liu, "Meaning of Digital Humanities," 412.

41. See Bethany Nowviskie's blog on acknowledging power differentials in parties to collaboration related to their status in the institution. She writes:

> "Consciously ignoring disparities in the institutional status of your collaborators is just as bad as being unthinkingly complicit in the problems these disparities create. This is because of the careless way your disregard reads to the people it damages. These people are: your junior colleagues; your graduate students; academics on the "general," "administrative," or "research faculty;" the lost souls euphemistically referred to as academic "contingent labor;" and the least privileged among us, members of your institution's staff: those of your collaborators who are classified as service personnel. This latter group includes programmers, sysadmins, instructional technologists, and credentialed librarians and cultural heritage workers."

"Monopolies of Invention," *Bethany Nowviskie* (blog), December 30, 2009, http://nowviskie.org/2009/monopolies-of-invention/.

42. Davidson and Goldberg, *The Future of Thinking*, 138.

43. Nowviskie, "Toward a New Deal."

The New Media and Modes of Scholarly Communication

1. Philip Pochoda, "Digital, Scholarly Publishing: A Systems View" (University of Michigan Institute for the Humanities Brown Bag Lecture, October 25, 2011), abstract at http://lecb.physics.lsa.umich.edu/CWIS/browser.php?ResourceId=4116.

2. Ibid. See also Pochoda, "The Big One."

3. For an important discussion of the move of libraries into publishing, see Monica McCormick, "Are You a Press or Are You a Library? An Interview with NYU's Monica McCormick," interview by Adeline Koh, *Chronicle of Higher Education Blogs: ProfHacker*, March 27, 2012, http://chronicle.com/blogs/profhacker/press-or-library/39216.

4. Jennifer Howard, "Humanities Journals Confront Identity Crisis," *Chronicle of Higher Education*, March 27, 2009, http://chronicle.com/article/Humanities-Journals-Confront/28342.

5. Tara McPherson, "Scaling Vectors: Thoughts on the Future of Scholarly Communication," *Journal of Electronic Publishing* 13, no. 2 (Fall 2010), 3, http://quod.lib.umich.edu/j/jep/3336451.0013.208?view=text;rgn=main.

6. The SCI8 report provides an illuminating visual schema for thinking about process—authoring, publishing, stewardship, and use—and the actors involved—producers, disseminators, stewards, and audiences. Abby Smith Rumsey, *SCI8: Emerging Genres in Scholarly Communication* (University of Virginia Library: Scholarly Communication Institute, n.d.), 5.

7. Claire Bond Potter, "Is Digital Publishing Killing Books?" *Perspectives on History* 153, no. 4 (2015): 22–23.

8. Andrew Pettegree, *The Book in the Renaissance* (New Haven: Yale University Press, 2010).

9. Alan Liu, *This Is Not a Book: Long Forms of Shared Attention in the Digital Age*, Vimeo, 2011, http://vimeo.com/24306792; see also Alan Liu, "The End of the End of the Book: Dead Books, Lively Margins, and Social Computing," *Michigan Quarterly Review* 48 (2009): 499–520.

10. Ibid.

11. Craig Mod, "The Digital Physical," @craigMod, March 2012, http://craigmod.com/journal/digital_physical/.

12. Ibid.

13. Ibid.

14. Paul Conway, "The Fetishization of the Long Form Book," October 2, 2014.

15. McPherson, "Scaling Vectors," 3.

16. DIRT: Digital Research Tools, accessed August 13, 2014, http://dirtdirectory.org/.

17. Zotero, accessed August 8, 205, https://www.zotero.org/; Scribd, accessed August 13, 2014, http://www.scribd.com/.

18. PressForward, accessed August 13, 2014, http://pressforward.org/.

19. "Introducing PressForward," Roy Rosenzweig Center for History and New Media, June 24, 2011, http://chnm.gmu.edu/news/introducing-pressforward/.

20. Scalar's beta version was launched in spring 2013. Writing for *PC World*, William Fenton announces of Scalar that "despite its embryonic status (open beta), Scalar delivers an exciting new Web-publishing platform that will scale to and perhaps expand the boundaries of your book, chapter, or online project." William Fenton, "Scalar," *PC*, accessed August 13, 2014, http://www.pcmag.com/article2/0,2817,2419697,00.asp. http://www.pcmag.com/article2/0,2817,2419697,00.asp.

21. "WVU Receives $1 Million Grant from Mellon Foundation for First-of-Its-Kind Digital Publishing System," *WVUtoday*, February 3, 2015.

22. Pochoda, "The Big One," 367.

23. "TRIOS," University of Chicago Press," accessed March 2, 2015, http://press.uchicago.edu/ucp/books/series/TRIOS.html.

24. "Palgrave Pivot Breaking Boundaries," Palgrave Macmillan, accessed June 26, 2015, http://www.palgrave.com/page/about-us-palgrave-pivot/.

25. Paul Conway, "Fixing the Long Form," October 2, 2014.

26. Dan Cohen, remarks made on the panel "The Future of Digital Publishing" (presented at the Humanities, Arts, Science, and Technology Advanced Collaboratory, University of Michigan, Ann Arbor, December 2, 2011), http://www.hastac.org/content/hastac-2011-digital-scholarly-communication.

27. Cohen also asked, "Can you 'almost' publish your scholarly work?" In other words, can there be "partial" communication, "sort of" publishing of bits of work? Ibid.

28. As theorists of graphic narratives emphasize, in graphic narrative the visual is textualized and the textual is visualized; and the words may narrate one story and the visuals tell another; while the syncopation of frames and gutters projects yet other stories and meanings.

29. McPherson, "Scaling Vectors," 5.

30. Matthew G. Kirschenbaum, "Done: Finishing Projects in the Digital Humanities." *Digital Humanities Quarterly* 3, no. 2 (2009), par. 6, http://digitalhumanities.org:8080/dhq/vol/3/2/000037/000037.html.

31. Rumsey, *SCI8*, 9.

32. Ibid., 12.

33. Jentery Sayers, "Writing with Sound: Composing Multimodal, Long-Form Scholarship" (presented at the Digital Humanities 2012 conference, University of Hamburg, July 16, 2012), https://lecture2go.uni-hamburg.de/konferenzen/-/k/13920.

34. Kathleen Fitzpatrick, *Planned Obsolescence: Publishing, Technology, and the Future of the Academy* (New York: New York University Press, 2011), Part 1.

35. See "Open Review: A Study of Contexts and Practices," MediaCommons Press, accessed July 10, 2015, http://mcpress.media-commons.org/open-review/.

36. Jennifer Howard, "Hot Type: No Reviews of Digital Scholarship = No Respect," *Chronicle of Higher Education*, May 23, 2010, http://chronicle.com/article/Hot-Type-No-Reviews-of/65644/.

37. Howard quotes an e-mail she received from Brett Bobley. "Hot Type."

38. Ibid.

39. Howard quotes from a phone conversation between Julia Flanders and herself; ibid., 3.

40. "Guidelines for Evaluating Work in Digital Humanities and Digital Media," Modern Language Association, n.d., http://www.mla.org/guidelines_evaluation_digital.

41. "The New Rigor," Five College Digital Humanities, accessed June 26, 2015, http://thenewrigor.5colldh.org/.

42. In the words of the SCI8 report, scholars, technicians, and librarians will collaborate in an environment in which scholarship is "born archival" (Rumsey, *SCI8*, 9).

43. Pochoda, "The Big One," 370-71.

44. Dan Cohen, "Open Access Publishing and Scholarly Values," *Dan Cohen* (blog),

May 27, 2010, http://www.dancohen.org/2010/05/27/open-access-publishing-and-scholarly-values/, 2.

Going Open

1. Definitions of the two modes diverge, and understandings remain imprecise and confusing; but I am not taking this imprecision and confusion up here. See Simon Huggard, "Green v Gold Open Access Publishing SlideShare" (presented at the International Open Access Week: Library Research Forum, La Trobe University, October 25, 2013), http://www.slideshare.net/healthsciences/green-versus-gold-open-access. On confusion about the distinctions between green and gold open access, see Dan Cohen, "A Conversation with Richard Stallman about Open Access," *Dan Cohen* (blog), November 23, 2010, http://www.dancohen.org/2010/11/23/a-conversation-with-richard-stallman-about-open-access/.

2. See Siva Vaidhyanathan, "The Technocultural Imagination" (presented to the Humanities, Arts, Science, and Technology Advanced Collaboratory, University of Michigan, Ann Arbor, December 3, 2011), http://lecb.physics.lsa.umich.edu/CWIS/browser.php?ResourceId=4179.

3. Tom Cochrane, "Open Access," interview by Radio National and Robyn Williams, *Ockham's Razor*, June 15, 2014, http://www.abc.net.au/radionational/programs/ockhamsrazor/open-access/5519196.

4. Term used by Michel Bauwens in Richard Poynder, "Open and Shut? Working for a Phase Transition to an Open Commons-Based Knowledge Society: Interview with Michel Bauwens," *Open and Shut?* (blog), May 27, 2014, http://poynder.blogspot.com/2014/05/working-for-phase-transition-to-open.html.

5. Paul Conway, "History of OA and Scholarly Publishing," October 2, 2014.

6. Ibid.

7. For an overview of the history, documents, and initiatives in open access, see Open Access Directory, accessed August 12, 2015, http://oad.simmons.edu/oadwiki/Main_Page.

8. Leslie Chan et al., "Read the Budapest Open Access Initiative," Budapest Open Access Initiative, February 14, 2002, http://www.budapestopenaccessinitiative.org/read.

9. Ibid.

10. Conway, "History of OA and Scholarly Publishing."

11. "Public Access Policy: When and How to Comply," U.S. Department of Health and Human Services, accessed August 17, 2014, http://publicaccess.nih.gov/.

12. 11 Research University Provosts, "Values and Scholarship," *Inside Higher Ed*, February 23, 2012, https://www.insidehighered.com/views/2012/02/23/essay-open-access-scholarship.

13. Ibid.

14. "UCSF Implements Open Access Policy Office of Scholarly Communication," University of California Office of Scholarly Communication, May 24, 2012, http://osc.universityofcalifornia.edu/2012/05/ucsf-implements-open-access-policy/.

15. John P. Holdren, director, Office of Science and Technology Policy, Executive Office of the President, "Increasing Access to the Results of Federally Funded Scientific Research," Memorandum for the Heads of Departments and Agencies, February 22,

2013, http://www.whitehouse.gov/sites/default/files/microsites/ostp/ostp_public_access_memo_2013.pdf.

16. Scott Aaronson et al., "The Cost of Knowledge," February 2012, http://gowers.files.wordpress.com/2012/02/elsevierstatementfinal.pdf, 1. For a review of the boycott after its first year, see the mathematics blog Gowers's Weblog: Doug Arnold et al., "The Elsevier Boycott One Year On," January 28, 2013, http://gowers.wordpress.com/2013/01/28/the-elsevier-boycott-one-year-on/. The comment section is particularly interesting for a take on how researchers in mathematics fields debate issues of open access.

17. *The Guardian*, editorial "Academic Journals: An Open and Shut Case," April 10, 2012, accessed July 31,2012. http://www.theguardian.com/commentisfree/2012/apr/11/academic-journals-access-wellcome-trust.

18. In Arnold et al., "Elsevier Boycott," a group of mathematicians recommitted to sustaining the boycott, calling on libraries to cancel subscriptions, bundled by Elsevier into "Big Deals," recognizing that "this continues to do real damage, such as forcing [libraries] to cancel subscriptions to more independent journals and to reduce their spending on books."

19. Peter Suber, "Promoting Open Access in the Humanities," *Syllecta Classica* 16 (2005): 231–46.

20. Ibid., 232.

21. Dan Cohen, "Open Access Publishing and Scholarly Values," Dan Cohen blog, May 27, 2010, accessed June 20, 2014, http://www.dancohen,org/2010/05/27/open-access-publishing-and-scholarly-values/.

22. Martin Paul Eve, *Open Access and the Humanities: Contexts, Controversies and the Future* (Cambridge: Cambridge University Press, 2014), http://ebooks.cambridge.org/ebook.jsf?bid=CBO9781316161012.

23. MLA Commons, accessed June 22, 2014, http://commons.mla.org/.

24. Digital Humanities Now, accessed March 3, 2015, http://digitalhumanitiesnow.org/about/.

25. PressForward, accessed August 13, 2014, http://pressforward.org/.

26. See Directory of Open Access Journals, accessed August 12, 2015, http://doaj.org/. The work of the education scholar John Willinsky and his Public Knowledge Project is particularly important to the rise of the number of open-access journals worldwide. He developed and makes available free the widely used online journal-publishing software; see also Peter Schmidt, "New Journals, Free Online, Let Scholars Speak Out," *Chronicle of Higher Education*, February 14, 2010.

27. I am indebted here to Rebecca Welzenbach, journals coordinator at MPublishing, for her seminar: Rebecca Welzenbach, "Publishing Practice Series: Starting and Sustaining a Journal" (University of Michigan, October 22, 2013), http://www.lib.umich.edu/michigan-publishing/events/starting-and-sustaining-a-journal.

28. *Medieval Review*, accessed June 30, 2014, https://scholarworks.iu.edu/dspace/handle/2022/3631; *Southern Spaces*, accessed August 12, 2015, http://www.southernspaces.org/; *Networks and Neighbours*, accessed August 12, 2015, http://networksandneighbours.org/index.php/n.

29. *Postmedieval Forum*, accessed June 30, 2014, http://postmedieval-forum.com/.

30. In the sciences, it is important to note, issues have arisen about bogus journals run by companies or individuals eager to make profit off the APCs exacted for publication in open-access journals in STEM and medicine and public health. In October

2013, *Science* ran an article by John Bohannon in which he reports on sending a bogus science paper on a potential anticancer substance out to 304 open-access journals. Bohannon reports the results:

> By the time *Science* went to press, 157 of the journals had accepted the paper and 98 had rejected it. Of the remaining 49 journals, 29 seem to be derelict: websites abandoned by their creators. Editors from the other 20 had e-mailed the fictitious corresponding authors stating that the paper was still under review; those, too, are excluded from this analysis. Acceptance took 40 days on average, compared to 24 days to elicit a rejection.

For his analysis, and for letters challenging his methodology and conclusions, see John Bohannon, "Who's Afraid of Peer Review?," *Science* 342, no. 6154 (October 4, 2013): 60–65, doi:10.1126/science.342.6154.60; Elizabeth Marincola, "Science Communication: Power of Community," *Science* 342, no. 6163 (December 6, 2013): 1168–69, doi:10.1126/science.342.6163.1168-b.

While issues of the integrity of peer review processes are equally of concern to humanities faculty, the paucity of grant funding in the humanities means there is little expectation of profit from fraudulent humanities open-access journals.

31. Chris Wickham, "Open Access in the Humanities and Social Sciences: An Interview with Chris Wickham," interview by David Crotty, *Scholarly Kitchen*, accessed June 18, 2014, http://scholarlykitchen.sspnet.org/2014/04/17/open-access-in-the-humanities-and-social-sciences-an-interview-with-chris-wickham/. The second pressure Wickham cites is "usage half-life," that is, the length of time it takes for reads of scholarly work to drop off substantially. She observes:

> Usage half-life is a different issue: it is the analysis of when it is that half of the downloads of each article, averaged across each journal and then each discipline, have been made. So one is a political/moral/financial battleground; the other is simply an observed set of data. They are not fully commensurable, and you can't read one off into the other without considerable nuancing. Half-lives are about double these embargo figures, in fact, but that doesn't necessarily mean that embargoes should be longer; that depends on many other factors.

32. See Medieval Academy of America, "Statement on Online Dissertation Embargoes," accessed June 20, 2014, http://c.ymcdn.com/sites/www.medievalacademy.org/resource/resmgr/pdfs/13d._Dissertation_embargoes.pdf.

33. Wickham.

34. "Can't Find It, Can't Sign It: On Dissertation Embargoes," Harvard University Press Blog, July 26, 2013, http://harvardpress.typepad.com/hup_publicity/2013/07/cant-find-it-cant-sign-it-on-dissertation-embargoes.html.

35. "Open Humanities Press Principles and Goals," Open Humanities Press, accessed June 22, 2014, http://openhumanitiespress.org/principles-and-goals.html.

36. Gary Hall, "Radical Open Access in the Humanities" (presented at the Scholarly Communication Program, Columbia University, October 18, 2010), http://scholcomm.columbia.edu/2011/01/18/radical-open-access-in-the-humanities/.

37. "Spontaneous Acts of Scholarly Combustion," Punctum Books, accessed August 18, 2014, http://punctumbooks.com/.

38. "About," Punctum Books, accessed August 18, 2014, http://punctumbooks.com/about/.

39. danah boyd, *It's Complicated: The Social Lives of Networked Teens* (New Haven: Yale University Press, 2014), http://www.danah.org/books/ItsComplicated.pdf.

40. "MediaCommons Press Welcome," MediaCommons Press, accessed August 18, 2014, http://mcpress.media-commons.org/.

41. "The Piracy Crusade," MediaCommons Press, accessed June 18, 2014, http://mcpress.media-commons.org/piracycrusade/.

42. Ibid.

43. Ibid.

44. "About Debates in the Digital Humanities," Debates in the Digital Humanities, accessed June 20, 2014, http://dhdebates.gc.cuny.edu/about#2012-a.

45. Ibid.

46. Ibid.

47. Suber, "Promoting Open Access."

48. "How It Works—Knowledge Unlatched," Knowledge Unlatched, accessed July 2, 2014, http://www.knowledgeunlatched.org/about/how-it-works/.

49. Lucy Montgomery et al., *Pilot Proof of Concept Progress Summary* (Knowledge Unlatched, May 2014), http://collections.knowledgeunlatched.org/wp-content/uploads/2013/09/KU_Pilot_Progress_Summary_Report4.pdf.

50. "Code of Best Practices in Fair Use for Online Video," Center for Media & Social Impact, February 22, 2010, http://www.cmsimpact.org/fair-use/best-practices/code-best-practices-fair-use-online-video.

51. Pamela Samuelson and David R. Hansen, "Brief of Amicus Curiae Authors Alliance in Support of Defendant-Appellees and Affirmance (The Authors Guild, Inc., et Al. v. Google, Inc., et Al.) (Second Circuit)," SSRN Scholarly Paper, Social Science Research Network, Rochester, NY, July 10, 2014, http://papers.ssrn.com/abstract=2470549.

52. *The Authors Guild* (blog), accessed August 12, 2015, http://www.authorsguild.org/.

53. Truth in advertising. I serve on the Author's Alliance Advisory Board; "About Us," Authors Alliance, accessed June 27, 2014, http://www.authorsalliance.org/about/.

54. Denny Chin, "Opinion of the United States District Court Southern District of New York, The Authors Guild, Inc., and Betty Miles, Joseph Goulden, and Jim Bouton, on Behalf of Themselves and Other Similarly Situated, Plaintiffs, against GOOGLE INC., Defendant," November 14, 2013. Here is Judge Denny Chin's finding:

> In my view, Google Books provides significant public benefits. It advances the progress of the arts and sciences, while maintaining respectful consideration for the rights of authors and other creative individuals, and without adversely impacting the rights of copyright holders. It has become an invaluable research tool that permits students, teachers, librarians, and others to more efficiently identify and locate books. It has given scholars the ability, for the first time, to conduct full-text searches of tens of millions of books. It preserves books, in particular out-of-print and old books that have been forgotten in the bowels of libraries, and it gives them new life. It facilitates access to books for print-disabled and remote or underserved populations. It generates new audiences and creates new sources of income for authors and publishers. Indeed, all society benefits. (26)

55. See "About the Licenses," Creative Commons, accessed August 12, 2015, http://creativecommons.org/licenses/.

Here is the description of creative commons licensing on this website.

All Creative Commons licenses have many important features in common. Every license helps creators—we call them licensors if they use our tools—retain copyright while allowing others to copy, distribute, and make some uses of their work—at least non-commercially. Every Creative Commons license also ensures licensors get the credit for their work they deserve. Every Creative Commons license works around the world and lasts as long as applicable copyright lasts (because they are built on copyright).

56. A constantly updated list of OAJs and information about their review policies are available at the Simmons website, under the tab for the directory of open-access journals (Directory of Open Access Journals, accessed August 12, 2015, http://doaj.org/).

57. Daniel Atkins made the point that "one of the big challenges we face regarding sharing data, has to get people past the idea that if I share my data I give up my value to the institution." Atkins, "Cyberinfrastructure."

58. Cohen, "Open Access Publishing and Scholarly Values," Dan Cohen blog, May 27, 2010. Cohen, Ramsay, and Fitzpatrick, "Open Access Publishing."

Learning, Pedagogy, and Curricular Environments; or, How We Teach Now

1. *The Condition of Education 2010*, U.S. Department of Education, Institute of Education Sciences, National Center for Education Statistics (2010); qtd in Louis Soares, "Post-traditional Learners and the Transformation of Postsecondary Education: A Manifesto for College Leaders," American Council on Education (January 2013), http://louissoares.com/publications/?pblctn=360. Accessed August 26, 2015.

2. Brian Rotman, *Becoming Beside Ourselves: The Alphabet, Ghosts, and Distributed Human Being* (Durham, NC: Duke University Press, 2008).

3. N. Katherine Hayles, "What Are New Media and Why Are They in English Departments?" (presented at the 2010 ADE Summer Seminar East, University of Maryland, June 5, 2010), http://www.ade.org/seminars/index.htm.

4. N. Katherine Hayles, "Hyper and Deep Attention: The Generational Divide in Cognitive Modes," *Profession* 2007: 187–99.

5. Ibid., 197.

6. Naomi S. Baron, "How E-Reading Threatens Learning in the Humanities," *Chronicle of Higher Education*, July 14, 2014, http://chronicle.com/article/How-E-Reading-Threatens/147661/?cid=at&utm_source=at&utm_medium=en.

7. Neil Butcher, *A Guide to Quality in Post-traditional Online Higher Education* (Dallas, TX: Academic Partnerships, n.d.), http://www.icde.org/filestore/News/2014_March-April/Guide2.pdf.

8. Peter K. Bol, Benjamin G. Lewis, and Weihe Wendy Guan, "Extending World-Map to Make It Easier for Humanists and Others to Find, Use, and Publish Geospatial Information" (presented at the Second International Conference on DuberGIS and Geodesign, Redlands, California, August 19, 2014), http://cybergis.illinois.edu/events/cybergis14/assets/pdf/day3_plenaryinsights_guan.pdf.

9. 2012 World Open Educational Resources (OER) Congress, "2012 Paris OER Declaration," June 22, 2012, UNESCO.

10. James J. Duderstadt, "The Impact of Technology on Discovery and Learning in Research Universities" (presented at the Ninth Glion Colloquium, June 5–9, 2013), 10,

http://milproj.dc.umich.edu/pdfs/2013/2013%20Glion%20MOOCs%20JJD%20FI-NAL.pdf.

11. "About," Coursera, accessed July 25, 2012, https://www.coursera.org/about/.

12. edX, accessed July 3, 2014, https://www.edx.org/.

13. "About," Coursera.

14. Tamar Lewin, "'Mechanical MOOC' to Rely on Free Learning Sites," *New York Times*, August 21, 2012, sec. Education, http://www.nytimes.com/2012/08/21/education/mechanical-mooc-to-rely-on-free-learning-sites.html.

15. Thomas L. Friedman, "Revolution Hits the Universities," *New York Times*, January 26, 2013, sec. Opinion / Sunday Review, http://www.nytimes.com/2013/01/27/opinion/sunday/friedman-revolution-hits-the-universities.html.

16. Jonah Newman and Soo Oh, "8 Things You Should Know about MOOCs," *Chronicle of Higher Education*, June 13, 2014, http://chronicle.com/article/8-Things-You-Should-Know-About/146901/; Davidson and Goldberg, *The Future of Thinking*; Steve Kolowich, "5 Things Researchers Have Discovered about MOOCs," *Chronicle of Higher Education Blogs: Wired Campus*, June 27, 2014, http://chronicle.com/blogs/wiredcampus/5-things-researchers-have-discovered-about-moocs/53585?cid=at&utm_source=at&utm_medium=en.

17. Steve Kolowich, "MIT Will Offer MOOC Curricula, Not Just Single Courses, on edX," *Chronicle of Higher Education Blogs: Wired Campus*, September 18, 2013, http://chronicle.com/blogs/wiredcampus/mit-will-offer-mooc-curricula-not-just-single-courses-on-edx/46715?cid=at&utm_source=at&utm_medium=en.

18. Nina Augustsson, "Massive Open Online Courses (MOOCS): Challenging Traditional Learning," *Agenda: Suramérica* (Foro Nacional Internacional) 10 (2014): 5.

19. Leland Carver and Laura M. Harrison, "MOOCs and Democratic Education," *Liberal Education* 99, no. 4 (Fall 2013), https://www.aacu.org/liberaleducation/2013/fall/carver-harrison.

20. Augustsson, "Massive Open Online Courses," 5.

21. Laura Perna et al., "The Life Cycle of a Million MOOC Users" (presented at the MOOC Research Initiative Conference, December 5, 2013), http://www.gse.upenn.edu/pressroom/press-releases/2013/12/penn-gse-study-shows-moocs-have-relatively-few-active-users-only-few-persisti.

22. Newman and Oh, "8 Things."

23. Butcher, *Guide to Quality*, 9.

24. Steve Kolowich, "The Professors behind the MOOC Hype," *Chronicle of Higher Education*, March 18, 2013, http://chronicle.com/article/The%20Professors-Behind-the%20MOOC/137905/?cid=at&utm_source=at&utm_medium+en#id=overview.

25. Newman and Oh, "8 Things."

26. Augustsson, "Massive Open Online Courses," 5.

27. In fall 2012, for instance, the following humanities courses were offered through Coursera: Jeremy Adelman's A History of the World since 1300, an Introduction to Philosophy offered by seven faculty at the University of Edinburgh, Peter Struck's Greek and Roman Mythology, and Philip Zelikow's The Modern World: Global History since 1760. In spring 2014, edX offered a modest range of humanities-based courses, among them Laura Thatcher Ulrich's Tangible Things: Discovering History Through Artworks, Artifacts, Scientific Specimens, and the Stuff around You; Robert Pinsky's The Art of Poetry; and Maggie Sokolik's Principles of Written English, Part 3.

28. *The Innovative University: What College Presidents Think about Change in American Higher Education* (research report for the *Chronicle of Higher Education*, 2014), http://strategicplanning.fairfield.edu/sites/default/files/innovative_university_140516.pdf.

29. Aaron Bady, "The MOOC Moment and the End of Reform," *Liberal Education* 99, no. 4 (Fall 2013), http://thenewinquiry.com/blogs/zunguzungu/the-mooc-moment-and-the-end-of-reform/.

30. Butcher, *Guide to Quality*, 9; L. Johnson et al., *NMC Horizon Report: 2013 Higher Education Edition* (Austin, TX: New Media Consortium, 2013), http://www.nmc.org/pdf/2013-horizon-report-HE.pdf.

31. Bady, "MOOC Moment."

32. Jonathan Haber, *MOOC* (Cambridge, MA: MIT Press, 2014).

33. Cathy N. Davidson, "History and Future of (Mostly) Higher Education," Coursera, https://www.coursera.org/course/highered; Cathy N. Davidson, "Clearing Up Some Myths about MOOCs," HASTAC blog, June 11, 2013, http://www.hastac.org/blogs/cathy-davidson/2013/06/11/clearing-some-myths-about-moocs.

34. FemTechNet Commons, accessed August 30, 2014, http://femtechnet.newschool.edu/.

35. "DOCC 2013 Video Dialogues | Forum | Feminism, Technology, and Wiki Storming | FemTechNet," FemTechNet Commons, 2013, http://femtechnet.newschool.edu/groups/docc-2013-video-dialogs/forum/topic/feminism-technology-and-wiki-storming/#post.

36. See the Ithaka S+R report entitled Interactive Online Learning on Campus: Testing MOOCS and Other Platforms in Hybrid Formats in the University System of Maryland. The report presents its findings that "online learning technologies show promise for educating more people in innovative ways that can lower costs for universities and colleges." The report also reveals issues related to time of adaptation, incompatible platforms, and prohibitive licensing fees for MOOCS. But it did register that students could succeed in courses that were in hybrid form. Rebecca Griffiths, Matthew Chingos, Christine Mulhern, and Richard Spies, *Interactive Online Learning on Campus: Testing MOOCS and Other Platforms in Hybrid Formats in the University System of Maryland* (Ithaka S+R, July 11, 2014), http://www.sr.ithaka.org/research-publications/Interactive-Online-Learning-on-Campus.

37. "Online Courses," *LAS Online*, accessed August 13, 2015, http://www.lasonline.illinois.edu/courses/.

38. Kolowich, "Professors behind the MOOC."

39. Derek Curtis Bok, *Our Underachieving Colleges: A Candid Look at How Much Students Learn and Why They Should Be Learning More* (Princeton, NJ: Princeton University Press, 2008), 318.

40. Nancy Cantor, Tri-Campus Provosts' Seminar Keynote Address. October 22, 2013, University of Michigan. Seminar Title: Engaged Learning, Community Based Research and the Community Engagement Corridor Presented by University of Michigan, Michigan State University, and Wayne State University.

41. Randy Bass, "Disrupting Ourselves: The Problem of Learning in Higher Education," *Educause Review*, April 2012, 32.

42. Ibid., 24. See also Davidson and Goldberg, *Future*, 21–48.

43. John Seely Brown and Richard P. Adler, "Minds on Fire: Open Education, the Long Tail, and Learning 2.0," *Educause Review* 43, no. 1 (February 2008): 16–32; Bass, "Disrupting Ourselves."

44. Eric Rabkin, "Real Work Is Better Than Homework," presented at University of Michigan, November 19, 2008.

45. David Damrosch, "National Literatures in an Age of Globalization," presented at the ADE Seminar West, Flamingo, Las Vegas, June 22, 2009.

46. "William Pannapacker to Direct GLCA Digital Liberal Arts Initiative," *Hope College: Hope Today News*, October 1, 2013, http://www.hope.edu/2013/10/01/william-pannapacker-direct-glca-digital-liberal-arts-initiative.

47. Richard E. Miller, "Reading in Slow Motion," presented at the session "The New Dissertation: Thinking Outside the (Proto)-Book," Annual Convention of the Modern Language Association, Seattle, January 5, 2012.

48. Scott L. Newstok, "A Plea for 'Close Learning,'" *Liberal Education* 99, no. 4 (Fall 2013), http://www.aacu.org/liberaleducation/le-fa13/newstok.cfm; *The Innovative University*, 18.

49. Butcher, *Guide to Quality*, 12.

50. Davidson and Goldberg, *The Future of Thinking*, 7.

The Possibly Posthuman Humanities Scholar

1. This discussion of Mitchell is adapted from my essay entitled "Reading the Posthuman Backward: Mary Rowlandson's Doubled Witnessing," *Biography* 35, no. 1 (Winter 2012): 137–52.

2. William J. Mitchell, *Me++: The Cyborg Self and the Networked City* (Cambridge, MA: MIT Press, 2003), 62. The double plus here evokes the double plus in the coding language C++

3. Ibid.

4. The quantified self is constituted of people who digitally self-monitor their bodily processes. One might think of the self in this context as a site of time-stamped data. But the thing that interests me about the quantified self is the capacity of people to become contributors to Big Data, databases that will be the source of research in the biomedical sciences. In her piece on the quantified self, Emily Singer observes that "the most interesting consequences of the self-tracking movement will come when its adherents merge their findings into databases. The Zeo, for example, gives its users the option of making anonymized data available for research; the result is a database orders of magnitude larger than any other repository of information on sleep stages" (41). She also notes that "patient groups formed around specific diseases have been among the first to recognize the benefits to be derived from aggregating such information and sharing it" (43). Emily Singer, "The Measured Life," *MIT Technology Review*, August 2011, http://m.technologyreview.com/biomedicine/37784/.

5. Siva Vaidhyanathan, "Apple Demystified," *Chronicle Review*, October 11, 2011, http://chronicle.com/article/Apple-Demystified/129347/.

6. David Weinberger, *Too Big to Know: Rethinking Knowledge Now That the Facts Aren't the Facts, Experts Are Everywhere, and the Smartest Person in the Room Is the Room* (New York: Basic Books, 2011).

7. Jane Bennett, *Vibrant Matter: A Political Ecology of Things* (Durham, NC: Duke University Press, 2009), viii.

8. Ibid., 37, ix.

9. Cited in Williford and Henry, *One Culture*, 18.

10. Donna Jeanne Haraway, *How Like a Leaf: An Interview with Thyrza Nichols Goodeve* (New York: Routledge, 2000), 160.

11. Rosi Braidotti, "Posthuman, All Too Human: Towards a New Process Ontology," *Theory Culture Society* 23, nos. 7–8 (2006): 206.

12. Leela Fernandes, *Transnational Feminism in the United States: Knowledge, Ethics, and Power* (New York: New York University Press, 2013), 122.

Manifesto for a Sustainable Humanities

1. In "Vectors of Change," in Envisioning the Future of Doctoral Education: Preparing Stewards of the Discipline, ed. Chris M. Golde and George E. Walker (San Francisco: Jossey-Bass, 2006), 34–45, a piece written for the Carnegie Foundation for the Advancement of Teaching, David Damrosch eloquently insists that all university communities have their contribution to make in changing higher education in the humanities.

A Time of Troubles, a Time of Opportunity

1. I am indebted to the analyses regularly provided by David Laurence, director of research and ADE (Association of Departments of English), and Doug Steward, associate director of programs and ADE for the MLA.

2. Mark Fiegener, *Survey of Earned Doctorates* (National Science Foundation, last updated June 17, 2015), http://www.nsf.gov/statistics/srvydoctorates/.

3. Doug Steward, *Report on the Survey of Earned Doctorates, 2010–11 and 2011–12* (Modern Language Association, June 2014), 23.

4. "Advanced Degrees in the Humanities," Humanities Indicators, January 2015, http://www.humanitiesindicators.org/content/indicatorDoc.aspx?i=44.

5. Ibid.

6. Fiegener, *Survey of Earned Doctorates*; Steward, *Report on Survey*.

7. "Attrition in Humanities Doctorate Programs," Humanities Indicators, accessed July 8, 2015, http://www.humanitiesindicators.org/content/indicatordoc. aspx?i=51#fig237.

8. "Quantitative Data," Ph.D. Completion Project, Council of Graduate Schools, accessed July 26, 2012, http://www.phdcompletion.org/quantitative/quant_list. asp#hum. A cautionary note on statistics is needed. David Laurence, director of research for the MLA, clarified for me that "the finding that the humanities have a 49% completion rate, and that the completion rate in the humanities is the lowest of all disciplinary branches, are in part artifacts of this 10-year wall" (personal correspondence). David Laurence, "Humanities Completion Rate," n.d.

9. This quote comes from "How to Help Graduate Students Reach Their Destination," by Ronald G. Ehrenberg, Harriet Zuckerman, Jeffrey A. Groen, and Sharon M. Brucker. It is a teaser piece by the authors of *Educating Scholars* to present summary findings to a large audience. Ronald G. Ehrenberg et al., "How to Help Graduate Students Reach Their Destination," *Chronicle of Higher Education*, October 12, 2009, http:// chronicle.com/article/How-to-Help-Graduate-Students/48752/.

10. Ibid.

11. Carlos J. Alonso et al., *Report of the MLA Task Force on Doctoral Study in Modern Lan-*

guage and Literature (Modern Language Association, May 2014), 4, http://www.mla.org/pdf/taskforcedocstudy2014.pdf.

12. Cited by David Laurence, "From the Editor: What's Next for Graduate Education," *ADE Bulletin* 149 (2010): 3–7; David Orr, "The Job Market in English and Foreign Languages," *PMLA* 85, no. 6 (1970): 1185–98.

13. Colleen Flaherty, "Report Reveals Divergent Trends in Modern Language Job Market," *Inside Higher Ed*, December 21, 2012, http://www.inside highered.com.

14. MLA Office of Research, *Report on the MLA Job Information List*, 2013–14 (Fall 2014), http://www.mla.org/pdf/rpt_jil_1314web.pdf, 1.

15. Laurence, "From the Editor: What's Next for Graduate Education," 3.

16. Ibid.

17. Steward, *Report on Survey*.

18. "Paying for Graduate School," Humanities Indicators, accessed June 28, 2014, http://www.humanitiesIndicators.org/content/indicatorDoc.aspx?i=50.

19. Steward, *Report on Survey*.

20. "Paying for Graduate School," Humanities Indicators, accessed June 28, 2014, http://www.humanitiesIndicators.org/content/indicatorDoc.aspx?i=50.

21. Katherine Kidd, "Chapter 1 Notes," May 29, 2014.

22. Fiegener, *Survey of Earned Doctorates*.

23. Ronald G. Ehrenberg et al., *Educating Scholars: Doctoral Education in the Humanities* (Princeton, NJ: Princeton University Press, 2010), 250–52. For a summary of the findings of the report on GEI, see David Laurence, "From the Editor: The Job Market and Graduate Education," *ADE Bulletin* 149 (2010): 3–7.

24. Delay of personal life has always been an issue for women in the academy. Yet job satisfaction and career development in the profession, as the MLA report on the associate professor rank observes, is related to the satisfactory balancing of work/life desires and obligations. Sara S. Poor, Rosemarie Scullion, and Kathleen Woodward, *Standing Still: The Associate Professor Survey* (MLA Committee on the Status of Women in the Profession, April 27, 2009), http://www.mla.org/pdf/cswp_final042909.pdf.

25. Robert Barsky et al., *White Paper on the Future of the PhD in the Humanities* (Social Sciences and Humanities Research Council of Canada, December 2013), 7, http://www.mcgill.ca/iplai/sites/mcgill.ca.iplai/files/white_paper_on_the_future_of_the_phd_in_the_humanities_dec_2013_0.pdf.

26. "Mellon Mays Graduate Initiatives Programs," SSRC, accessed August 13, 2015, http://www.ssrc.org/programs/mellon-mays-graduate-initiatives-program/; "Carnegie Initiative on the Doctorate," Carnegie Foundation for the Advancement of Teaching, accessed August 13, 2015, http://www.carnegiefoundation.org/previous-work/professional-graduate-education; Ph.D. Completion Project, Council of Graduate Schools, accessed August 13, 2015, http://www.phdcompletion.org/.

27. Russell A. Berman et al., "The Future of the Humanities PhD at Stanford," Humanities Education Focal Group, 2012, 24. In his Presidential Address at the 2012 MLA Convention, Berman challenged his colleagues to reconceptualize doctoral programs so that they can be completed in five years. See Berman, "2012 Presidential Address."

28. "Mellon Foundation Grants $2.7 Million to School of the Humanities Graduate Programs," *UCI News*, June 23, 2015, http://news.uci.edu/press-releases/mellon-foundation-grants-2-7-million-to-school-of-humanities-graduate-programs/.

29. Cathy Wendler et al., *The Path Forward: The Future of Graduate Education in the United*

States (Princeton, NJ: Council of Graduate Schools and Educational Testing Services, 2010), 29, http://www.fgereport.org/rsc/pdf/CFGE_report.pdf.

30. Anthony T. Grafton and James Grossman, "No More Plan B: A Very Modest Proposal for Graduate Programs in History," *Perspectives on History*, October 2011, http://www.historians.org/publications-and-directories/perspectives-on-history/october-2011/no-more-plan-b.

31. Ibid.

32. Woodrow Wilson National Fellowship Foundation, "The Responsive PhD: Innovations in U.S. Doctoral Education," accessed July 18, 2014, http://www.woodrow.org/wp/wp-content/uploads/2013/06/WW_RespPhD_execsum_w_caselist.pdf.

33. "About ACLS," American Council of Learned Societies, accessed August 13, 2015, http://www.acls.org/about/.

34. Imagining America, accessed March 6, 2015, http://imaginingamerica.org/.

35. Walter Chapin Simpson Center for the Humanities, accessed March 6, 2015, https://simpsoncenter.org/.

36. Barsky et al., *Future of the PhD*.

37. See ibid.

38. Alonso et al., *Report on Doctoral Study*.

39. Leonard Cassuto, *The Graduate School Mess: What Caused It and How We Can Fix It* (Cambridge, MA: Harvard University Press, 2015); Julie R. Posselt, *Inside Graduate Admissions: Merit, Diversity, and Faculty Gatekeeping* (Cambridge, MA: Harvard University Press, 2015), http://www.hup.harvard.edu/catalog.php?isbn=9780674088696. I am indebted to Leonard Cassuto for making the page proofs of his book available to me.

40. Barsky et al., *Future of the PhD*, 1. National reports on the state of doctoral education also make the case. In 2012 the National Academy of Sciences, National Academy of Engineering, Institute of Medicine, and National Research Council published a white paper, *Research Universities and the Future of America: Ten Breakthrough Actions Vital to Our Nation's Prosperity and Security*. The report makes the case for robust doctoral programs in the humanities "because of the increasing breadth of academic and professional disciplines necessary to address the challenges facing our changing world" (15). And in 2013 the Commission on Humanities and the Social Sciences, American Academy of Arts & Sciences report *The Heart of the Matter: The Humanities and Social Sciences for a Vibrant, Competitive, and Secure Nation*, made the case eloquently: "Advanced training is essential to the renewal of the professoriate"; and it "can also develop skills of enormous potential value to government agencies, nonprofit organizations, museums and other cultural institutions, libraries and archives, and diverse segments of the public sector" (43).

41. Scott Jaschik, "Top Ph.D. Programs, Shrinking," *Inside Higher Ed*, May 13, 2009, https://www.insidehighered.com/news/2009/05/13/doctoral; Robin Wilson, "Cutbacks in Enrollment Redefine Graduate Education and Faculty Jobs," *Chronicle of Higher Education*, May 11, 2012, http://chronicle.com/article/Graduate-Programs-in/131123/.

42. Russell A. Berman, "Essay Defending the MLA Report on Doctoral Education," *Inside Higher Ed*, July 21, 2014, http://www.insidehighered.com/views/2014/07/21/essay-defending-mla-report-doctoral-education#sthash.29bQpSzp.PF9S4z3r.dpbs.

43. Dolan Hubbard, "Education without Representation," *Black Issues in Higher Education* 19, no. 17 (2002): 97.

Breathing Life into the Dissertation

1. Alonso et al., *Report on Doctoral Study*; Barsky et al., *Future of the PhD*.

2. Council of Graduate Schools, *Ph.D. Completion and Attrition: Policies and Practices to Promote Student Success* (Washington, DC: Council of Graduate Schools, March 2010).

3. David Damrosch, *We Scholars: Changing the Culture of the University* (Cambridge, MA: Harvard University Press, 1995); William James, "The Ph.D. Octopus," *Education Review* 55 (1918): 149–57. Reprint of original edition published in *The Harvard Monthly* in March 1903.

4. Domna Stanton et al., *Report of the MLA Task Force on Evaluating Scholarship for Tenure and Promotion* (New York: Modern Language Association, December 2006), 12.

5. "The practice of credit sharing," writes Chang, "applied to all fields of knowledge taught at the university" (349). Ku-ming (Kevin) Chang, "Collaborative Production and Experimental Labor: Two Models of Dissertation Authorship in the Eighteenth Century," *Studies in History and Philosophy of Biological and Biomedical Sciences* 41 (2010): 349.

6. Ibid.

7. Barbara Crossouard, "The Doctoral Viva Voce as a Cultural Practice: The Gendered Production of Academic Subjects," *Gender and Education* 23, no. 3 (May 2011): 314.

8. Chang, "Collaborative Production," 348.

9. See Cecile M. Jagodzinski, "The University Press in North America: A Brief History," *Journal of Scholarly Publishing* 40, no. 1 (October 2008): 3.

10. Cassuto, *The Graduate School Mess*, 29.

11. Ibid., 4.

12. Gary A. Olson and Julie Drew, "(Re)Reenvisioning the Dissertation in English Studies," *College English* 61, no. 1 (September 1998): 57.

13. Ibid., 59.

14. Pochoda, "The Big One," 362.

15. Pochoda observes that "the idea of applying scholarly standards to monographs was not an innovation of course: many press editors and many post-publication reviewers had long invoked them on a somewhat haphazard basis. What changed were the uniformity, rigor, and consistency of the application of such standards—and the immediate and significant negative consequences of failure to conform (the negative feedback loop). Post-publication administration *accreditation*, when layered upon the pre-publication peer review, *authorization*, provided strong likelihood that monographs published within the university press system could be relied upon to meet at least a minimum scholarly standard. Manuscripts that failed to achieve such authorization would (in principle, at least) not be published; faculty who produced insufficient vetted publications would (again, in principle) not be retained or promoted (*accredited*)." Ibid., 363.

16. Stanton et al., *Report on Evaluating Scholarship*.

17. Ibid., 30–31.

18. Ibid., 31.

19. Olson and Drew, "(Re)envisioning the Dissertation," 59.

20. Lindsay Waters, "The Tyranny of the Monograph and the Plight of the Publisher," *Publishing Research Quarterly* 17, no. 3 (Fall 2001): 19–25.

21. Leslie Monkman, "Confronting Change," *ESC: English Studies in Canada* 32, no. 2 (2006): 22.

22. Stanton et al., *Report on Evaluating Scholarship*, 11.

23. Ibid., 60.

24. Damrosch, *We Scholars*, 148. Damrosch writes: "Rather than varying our program requirements to suit different emerging scholarly personalities, we present a single norm, forcing the students either to adapt or to fall away" (151).

25. Cassuto, *The Graduate School Mess*, 29.

26. Bulbul Tiwari, "Shift(s)in(g) the Humanities: Hanging Roots, Hyperlinks, and Other Networks of Schizoanalysis in Maha Multipedia" (presented at the CIC Summit on Digital Humanities, Institute for the Humanities, University of Michigan, December 8, 2009). To view Tiwari's revised digital dissertation, see Bulbul Tiwari, "MahaMultipedia Welcome," *MahaMultipedia*, accessed August 26, 2014, http://www.mahamultipedia.com/.

27. William Germano, "Do We Dare Write for Readers?," *Chronicle of Higher Education*, April 26, 2013, B7.

28. Ibid.

29. Ibid., B8.

30. Rebecca A. Bryant and Megan Pincus Kajitani, "A Ph.D. and a Failure," *Chronicle of Higher Education*, March 24, 2005, http://chronicle.com/article/A-PhDa-Failure/44884/.

31. Grafton and Grossman, "No More Plan B."

32. Damrosch, *We Scholars*, 162.

33. Some data reported in Ehrenberg et al., *Educating Scholars*, suggest that job applicants with publications fare somewhat better on the job market for tenure-track positions than those without publications.

34. Thanks to Jesse Lander, Director of Graduate Studies in English at Notre Dame, for this clarification offered me at the Michigan State University Symposium "Futures of the English PhD."

35. Julie Ellison and Timothy K. Eatman, *Scholarship in Public: Knowledge Creation and the Tenure Policy in the Engaged University* (Artists and Scholars in Public Life Tenure Team Initiative on Public Scholarship, Imagining America, 2008), 1, http://ccrec.ucsc.edu/sites/default/files/tti_final.pdf.

36. Kathleen Woodward, "The Future of the Humanities in the Present and in Public," *Daedalus* 138, no. 1 (Winter 2009): 120, http://csid.unt.edu/files/Daedalus%20Winter%202009/10.Woodward.pdf.

37. Ibid.

38. For excerpts from Nick Sousanis's dissertation, see Nick Sousanis, "Nick Sousanis Dissertation Excerpts," Academia, accessed August 13, 2015, https://tc.academia.edu/NickSousanis/Dissertation-Excerpts.

39. Visconti's three-minute video can be viewed to get a sense of the project's dynamic dissertation mode. Amanda Visconti. *Infinite Ulysses*, accessed July 8, 2015, http://mith.umd.edu/infinite-ulysses-designing-public-humanities-conversation/.

40. "HASTAC 2015 Schedule," HASTAC 2015, accessed August 13, 2015, http://www.hastac2015.org/schedule/.

41. Futures Initiative: Advancing Equity and Innovation in Higher Education, accessed July 8, 2015, http://futures.gc.cuny.edu/.

42. For a chronicle of the current difficulties students face in realizing an alternative dissertation vision, see Melanie Lee, "The Melancholy Odyssey of a Dissertation with Pictures," *Pedagogy: Critical Approaches to Teaching Literature, Language, Composition, and Culture* 15, no. 1 (2015): 93–101.

43. Andrea Abernethy Lunsford, "Rethinking the Ph.D. in English," in *Envisioning the Future of Doctoral Education: Preparing Stewards of the Discipline*, ed. Chris M. Golde and George E. Walker (San Francisco: Jossey-Bass, 2006), 357–69.

44. Barsky et al., *Future of the PhD*, 11–12.

45. Ibid., 14.

46. Ibid., 19.

47. I am indebted to Nancy Linthicum, 2014–2015 graduate student fellow at the Institute for the Humanities, University of Michigan, for her observation about the prospectus. "Sorry We Couldn't Talk Yesterday," e-mail to the author, March 27, 2015.

48. Damrosch, *We Scholars*, 163.

Responding to Counterarguments

1. Grafton and Grossman, "No More Plan B," 2.

2. William Germano, *From Dissertation to Book*, 2nd ed. (Chicago: University of Chicago Press, 2013).

3. Ibid., 1.

4. Ehrenberg et al., *Educating Scholars*.

5. Stanton et al., *Report on Evaluating Scholarship*.

6. Indeed, doctoral programs at universities not considered among the elite (whether private or public flagship) may already have made changes in dissertation options that make sense for their mission and for the kinds of institutions that hire their graduates.

7. "University Policy 102.12, Tenure Policies, Regulations, and Procedures of the University of North Carolina and Charlotte," UNC Charlotte Office of Legal Affairs, accessed August 13, 2015, http://legal.uncc.edu/policies/up-102.13.

8. Former Economics department chair Linda Tesar informed me that economics as a discipline shifted to an essay-based dissertation format from the monograph form some years ago. Her observation was that students benefited in their job search from having a very tight and polished essay off of which to give their job talk.

9. "Academic Requirements for Hispanic Studies," Spanish and Portuguese Studies, University of Washington," accessed August 13, 2015, https://spanport.washington.edu/phd-degree-requirements.

A 21st-Century Doctoral Education

1. Dwight MacDonald, "Real Talk about Graduate Education in the Liberal Arts and Sciences" (presented at "Liberal Arts and Sciences in the Research University Today: Histories, Challenges, Futures," University of Michigan, March 22, 2013).

2. Catharine R. Stimpson, "General Education for Graduate Education: A Theory Waiting for Practitioners," *Peer Review: Emerging Trends and Key Debates in Undergraduate Education* 6, no. 3 (Spring 2004): 13–15.

3. Rumsey, *SCI8*; Lisa Quinn, "Some Observations," presented at the International Association for Biography and Autobiography Graduate Student and New Scholar Workshop, Banff, Canada, May 29, 2014.

4. Peter H. Klost, Debra Rudder Lohe, and Chuck Sweetman, "Rethinking and Unthinking the Graduate Seminar," *Pedagogy* 15, no. 1 (2015): 23, 26.

5. Praxis Network, accessed August 2, 2014, http://praxis-network.org/index.html#mission.

6. "GTC+: Digital Currents at the University of Michigan," Center for Research on Learning and Teaching, University of Michigan, accessed August 13, 2015, http://www.crlt.umich.edu/category/tags/no-parent/gtc.

7. John Wittman and Mariana Abuan, "Socializing Future Professionals: Exploring the Matrix of Assessment," *Pedagogy* 15, no. 1 (2015): 63.

8. "Interdivisional Media Arts + Practice (iMAP)," School of Cinematic Arts, University of Southern California, accessed August 13, 2015, http://www.gradschools.com/program-details/university-of-southern-california/interdivisional-media-arts-practice-imap-256008_1.

9. "Certificate in Public Scholarship," Walter Chapin Simpson Center for the Humanities, University of Washington, accessed August 28, 2014, http://depts.washington.edu/uwch/programs/curriculum/certificate-in-public-scholarship.

10. Alonso et al., *Report on Doctoral Study*, 2, 17.

11. Barsky et al., *Future of the PhD*.

12. Damrosch, "Vectors of Change," 43.

13. Bethany Nowviskie, "The #alt-Ac Track: Negotiating Your 'Alternative Academic' Appointment," *Chronicle of Higher Education Blogs: ProfHacker*, August 31, 2010, http://chronicle.com/blogs/profhacker/the-alt-ac-track-negotiating-your-alternative-academic-appointment-2/26539.

14. Paula Krebs, "A New Humanities Ph.D.," *Inside Higher Ed*, May 24, 2010, https://www.insidehighered.com/views/2010/05/24/krebs.

15. The Versatile PhD, accessed July 30, 2012, http://versatilephd.com/.

16. Bethany Nowviskie, *#Alt-Academy: Alternative Academic Careers for Humanities Scholars*, http://mediacommons.futureofthebook.org/alt-ac/sites/mediacommons.futureofthebook.org.alt-ac/files/alt-academy01.pdf.

17. Katina Rogers, *Humanities Unbound: Supporting Careers and Scholarship Beyond the Tenure Track* (Scholarly Communication Institute, University of Virginia Library, August 2013), http://katinarogers.com/wp-content/uploads/2013/08/Rogers_SCI_Survey_Report_09AUG13.pdf.

18. David M. Ball, William Gleason, and Nancy J. Peterson, "From All Sides: Rethinking Professionalization in a Changing Job Market," *Pedagogy* 15, no. 1 (2015): 104.

The Upside of Change

1. Evan Watkins, "Recruiting Prestige" (keynote presentation to "Futures of the English PhD," Michigan State University, May 15, 2010), http://futuresoftheenglishphd.weebly.com/.

2. Posselt, *Inside Graduate Admissions*.

3. I am indebted to Cass Adair, Tiffany Ball, and Jina Kim for bringing to life this portrait of humanities graduate students.

4. Alexis Lothian and Amanda Phillips, "Can Digital Humanities Mean Transformative Critique?," *Journal of E-Media Studies* 3, no. 1 (2013), http://journals.dartmouth.edu/cgibin/WebObjects/Journals.woa/1/xmlpage/4/article/425.

5. Ibid.

6. National Science Foundation and National Center for Science and Engineering Statistics, *Doctorate Recipients from U.S. Universities 2012* (National Science Foundation, January 2014), http://www.nsf.gov/statistics/sed/digest/2012/nsf14305.pdf.

7. Tara McPherson, "Why Are the Digital Humanities So White? Or Thinking the Histories of Race and Computation," in *Debates in the Digital Humanities*, ed. Matthew K. Gold (Minneapolis: University of Minnesota Press, 2012), 143.

8. Ibid., 150. McPherson is adapting Gerald Graff's discussion of the new criticism and its Cold War logics. See Gerald Graff, *Professing Literature: An Institutional History* (Chicago: University of Chicago Press, 1989).

9. Nowviskie, "Toward a New Deal."

10. "Background Facts on Contingent Faculty," American Association of University Professors, accessed August 5, 2014, http://www.aaup.org/issues/contingency/background-facts.

11. Bousquet, "Condemned to Repeat."

12. Colander, and Zhuo, "PhDs in English," 143.

13. New Faculty Majority, "The New Faculty Majority," *Salsa Labs*, August 5, 2014, https://salsa4.salsalabs.com/o/50833/t/0/blastContent.jsp?email_blast_KEY=1244411; "New Faculty Majority," New Faculty Majority, accessed August 28, 2014, http://www.newfacultymajority.info/.

14. Coalition on the Academic Workforce, *Portrait of Part-Time Faculty*, 104. The MLA, a member of CAW, offers on its website the "Academic Workforce Advocacy Kit," a collection of briefs, reports, and information, including the "Professional Employment Practices for Non-Tenure-Track Faculty Members: Recommendations and Evaluative Questions (2011) and the "MLA Issue Brief: The Academic Workforce" (2009). "Academic Workforce Advocacy Kit," Modern Language Association, accessed August 12, 2015, http://www.mla.org/advocacy_kit. The theme of the 2013 MLA convention, organized by 2012 president Michael Bérubé, was "Avenues of Access," a rubric under which were gathered many sessions exploring issues of access to tenure-track careers and issues of alternative careers.

15. Ball, Gleason, and Peterson, "From All Sides," 104.

Coda

1. Elizabeth Grosz, *Becoming Undone: Darwinian Reflections on Life, Politics, and Art* (Durham, NC: Duke University Press, 2011), 11.

Bibliography

11 Research University Provosts. "Values and Scholarship." *Inside Higher Ed*, February 23, 2012. https://www.insidehighered.com/views/2012/02/23/essay-open-access-scholarship.

Abel, Jaison R., and Richard Deitz. "Do Big Cities Help College Graduates Find Better Jobs?" *Liberty Street Economics*, May 20, 2013. http://libertystreeteconomics.newyorkfed.org/2013/05/do-big-cities-help-college-graduates-find-better-jobs.html#.VhotvstBIpI.

Alonso, Carlos J., Russell A. Berman, Sylvie Debevec Henning, Lanisa Kitchener, Bethany Nowviskie, Elizabeth Schwartz Crane, Sidonie Smith, and Kathleen Woodward. *Report of the MLA Task Force on Doctoral Study in Modern Language and Literature.* Modern Language Association, May 2014. http://www.mla.org/pdf/taskforcedocstudy2014.pdf.

Altbach, Philip G., and Roberta Malee Bassett. "Nix the BRICS—at Least for Higher Education Scholarship." *Change: The Magazine of Higher Learning*, October 2014, 30–32.

American Council on Education, Association of Universities and Colleges in Canada, and Council for Higher Education Accreditation. "Sharing Higher Education across Borders: A Statement on Behalf of Higher Education Institutions Worldwide." January 2005. http://www.chea.org/pdf/StatementFinal0105.pdf.

American Council on Education and National Commission on Higher Education. "An Open Letter to College and University Leaders: College Completion Must Be Our Priority." Washington, DC, January 2013.

Ashton, Kevin. "That 'Internet of Things' Thing." *RFID Journal*, June 22, 2009, 4.

Atkins, Daniel E. "Cyberinfrastructure: Technical+Social=Transformation If You Help." Presented at the Humanities, Arts, Science, and Technology Advanced Collaboratory, University of Michigan, December 2, 2011. Presentation slides available at http://www.hastac.org/documents/cyberinfrastructure.

Augustsson, Nina. "Massive Open Online Courses (MOOCS): Challenging Traditional Learning." *Agenda: Suramérica* (Foro Nacional Internacional) 10 (2014): 4–5.

Bady, Aaron. "The MOOC Moment and the End of Reform." *Liberal Education* 99, no. 4 (Fall 2013). http://thenewinquiry.com/blogs/zunguzungu/the-mooc-moment-and-the-end-of-reform/.

Ball, David M., William Gleason, and Nancy J. Peterson. "From All Sides: Rethinking Professionalization in a Changing Job Market." *Pedagogy* 15, no. 1 (2015): 103–18.

Baron, Naomi S. "How E-Reading Threatens Learning in the Humanities." *Chronicle of Higher Education*, July 14, 2014. http://chronicle.com/article/How-E-Reading-Threatens/147661/.

Barsky, Robert, Jay Clayton, Lesley Cormack, Rebecca Duclos, Geoffrey Harpham, Michael Jemtrud, Martin Kreiswirth, et al. *White Paper on the Future of the PhD in the Humanities*. Social Sciences and Humanities Research Council of Canada, December 2013. http://www.mcgill.ca/iplai/sites/mcgill.ca.iplai/files/white_paper_on_the_future_of_the_phd_in_the_humanities_dec_2013_0.pdf.

Barzun, Jacques. *The American University: How It Runs, Where It Is Going*. New York: HarperCollins, 1968.

Basken, Paul, and Paul Voosen. "Strapped Scientists Abandon Research and Students." *Chronicle of Higher Education*, February 24, 2014. http://chronicle.com/article/Strapped-Scientists-Abandon/144921/.

Bass, Randy. "Disrupting Ourselves: The Problem of Learning in Higher Education." *Educause Review*, April 2012, 23–33.

Bauerlein, Mark. "What Dido Did, Satan Saw & O'Keeffe Painted." *New Criterion*, November 2013, 4–9.

Bennett, Jane. "The Agency of Assemblages and the North American Blackout." *Public Culture* 17, no. 3 (Fall 2005): 445–66.

Bennett, Jane. *Vibrant Matter: A Political Ecology of Things*. Durham, NC: Duke University Press, 2009.

Berman, Russell A. "Essay Defending the MLA Report on Doctoral Education." *Inside Higher Ed*, July 21, 2014. http://www.insidehighered.com/views/2014/07/21/essay-defending-mla-report-doctoral-education#sthash.29bQpSzp.PF9S4z3r.dpbs.

Berners-Lee, Tim. *Weaving the Web: The Original Design and Ultimate Destiny of the World Wide Web by Its Inventor*. New York: HarperCollins, 1999.

Bérubé, Michael. "The Humanities, Declining? Not According to the Numbers." *Chronicle of Higher Education*, July 1, 2013. http://chronicle.com/article/The-Humanities-Declining-Not/140093/.

Bohannon, John. "Who's Afraid of Peer Review?" *Science* 342, no. 6154 (October 4, 2013): 60–65. doi:10.1126/science.342.6154.60.

Bok, Derek. *Our Underachieving Colleges: A Candid Look at How Much Students Learn and Why They Should Be Learning More*. Princeton, NJ: Princeton University Press, 2008.

Bok, Derek. *Universities in the Marketplace: The Commercialization of Higher Education*. Princeton, NJ: Princeton University Press, 2004.

Bol, Pater K., Benjamin G. Lewis, and Weihe Wendy Guan. "Extending WorldMap to Make It Easier for Humanists and Others to Find, Use, and Publish Geospatial Information." Presented at the Second International Conference on DuberGIS and Geodesign, Redlands, California, August 19, 2014. http://cybergis.illinois.edu/events/cybergis14/assets/pdf/day3_plenaryinsights_guan.pdf.

Bousquet, Marc. "Condemned to Repeat: On the Racism and Sexism of Failing to Address Structure." *Pedagogy* 15, no. 1 (2015): 157–68.

Bousquet, Marc. *How the University Works: Higher Education and the Low Wage Nation*. New York: New York University Press, 2008.

boyd, danah. *It's Complicated: The Social Lives of Networked Teens*. New Haven: Yale University Press, 2014. http://www.danah.org/books/ItsComplicated.pdf.

Braidotti, Rosi. *The Posthuman*. Malden, MA: Polity Press, 2013.

Braidotti, Rosi. "Posthuman, All Too Human: Towards a New Process Ontology." *Theory Culture Society* 23, nos. 7–8 (2006): 197–208.

Brown, John Seely, and Richard P. Adler. "Minds on Fire: Open Education, The Long Tail, and Learning 2.0." *Educause Review* 43, no. 1 (February 2008): 16–32.

Bryant, Rebecca A., and Megan Pincus Kajitani. "A Ph.D. and a Failure." *Chronicle of Higher Education*, March 24, 2005. http://chronicle.com/article/A-PhDa-Failure/44884/.

Butcher, Neil. *A Guide to Quality in Post-traditional Online Higher Education*. Dallas, TX: Academic Partnerships, n.d. http://www.icde.org/filestore/News/2014_March-April/Guide2.pdf.

Cantor, Nancy. Tri-Campus Provosts' Seminar Keynote Address. October 22, 2013, University of Michigan. Seminar Title: Engaged Learning, Community Based Research and the Community Engagement Corridor Presented by University of Michigan, Michigan State University, and Wayne State University.

Carnivale, Gary. "Making the Case for the Humanities." Presented at the National Humanities Alliance Conference, George Washington University, Washington, DC, March 10, 2009.

Carver, Leland, and Laura M. Harrison. "MOOCs and Democratic Education." *Liberal Education* 99, no. 4 (Fall 2013). https://www.aacu.org/liberaleducation/2013/fall/carver-harrison.

Cassuto, Leonard. *The Graduate School Mess: What Caused It and How We Can Fix It*. Cambridge, MA: Harvard University Press, 2015.

Center for Social Media. *Code of Best Practices in Fair Use for Online Video*. February 22, 2010. http://www.cmsimpact.org/fair-use/best-practices/code-best-practices-fair-use-online-video.

Century Foundation Task Force on Preventing Community Colleges from Becoming Separate and Unequal. *Bridging the Higher Education Divide: Strengthening Community Colleges and Restoring the American Dream*. Century Foundation Press, May 23, 2013. http://tcf.org/bookstore/detail/bridging-the-higher-education-divide.

Chang, Ku-ming (Kevin). "Collaborative Production and Experimental Labor: Two Models of Dissertation Authorship in the Eighteenth Century." *Studies in History and Philosophy of Biological and Biomedical Sciences* 41 (2010): 347–55.

Claire Bond Potter. "Is Digital Publishing Killing Books?" *Perspectives on History* 153, no. 4 (2015): 22–23.

Coalition on the Academic Workforce. *A Portrait of Part-Time Faculty Members*. June 2012. http://www.academicworkforce.org/CAW_portrait_2012.pdf.

Cochrane, Tom. "Open Access." *Ockham's Razor*. Interview by Radio National and Robyn Williams, June 15, 2014. http://www.abc.net.au/radionational/programs/ockhamsrazor/open-access/5519196.

Cohan, Peter. "To Boost Post-college Prospects, Cut Humanities Departments." *Forbes*. Accessed August 27, 2014. http://www.forbes.com/sites/petercohan/2012/05/29/to-boost-post-college-prospects-cut-humanities-departments/.

Cohen, Dan. Remarks on the panel "The Future of Digital Publishing." Humanities, Arts, Science, and Technology Advanced Collaboratory, University of Michigan, Ann Arbor, December 2, 2011. http://www.hastac.org/content/hastac-2011-digital-scholarly-communication.

Cohen, Dan, Stephen Ramsay, and Kathleen Fitzpatrick. "Open Access Publishing and Scholarly Values." *Dan Cohen*, May 27, 2010. http://www.dancohen.org/2010/05/27/open-access-publishing-and-scholarly-values/.

Cohen, Dan, and Tom Scheinfeldt, eds. *Hacking the Academy: New Approaches to Scholarship and Teaching from Digital Humanities*. Ann Arbor: University of Michigan Press, 2013. http://www.digitalculture.org/books/hacking-the-academy-new-approaches-to-scholarship-and-teaching-from-digital-humanities/.

Colander, David, and Daisy Zhuo. "Where Do PhDs in English Get Jobs? An Economist's View of the English PhD Market." *Pedagogy* 15, no. 1 (2015): 139–56.

Cole, Jonathan R. "Can Graduate Education Survive as We Know It?" Presentation to Rackham Graduate School, University of Michigan, April 5, 2012.

Cole, Jonathan R. *The Great American University: Its Rise to Preeminence, Its Indispensable National Role, Why It Must Be Protected.* New York: PublicAffairs, 2012.

Commission on Humanities and the Social Sciences, American Academy of Arts and Sciences. The Heart of the Matter: The Humanities and Social Sciences for a Vibrant, Competitive, and Secure Nation. 2013.

The Condition of Education 2010, U.S. Department of Education, Institute of Education Sciences, National Center for Education Statistics (2010); qtd in Louis Soares, "Post-traditional Learners and the Transformation of Postsecondary Education: A Manifesto for College Leaders," American Council on Education (January 2013), http://louissoares.com/publications/?pblctn=360. Accessed August 26, 2015.Conway, Paul. "The Festishization of the Long Form Book." October 2, 2014.

Conway, Paul. "Fixing the Long Form." October 3, 2014.

Conway, Paul. "History of OA and Scholarly Publishing." October 3, 2014.

Conway, Paul. "Re-making Books in the Digital Archive." Paper presented to "Books/Texts/Fonts/Archives in a Brave New Digital World," Institute for the Humanities, University of Michigan, April 9, 2013.

Coughlan, Sean. "Italian University Switches to English." *BBC News*, May 16, 2012. http://www.bbc.co.uk/news/business-17958520.

Crossouard, Barbara. "The Doctoral Viva Voce as a Cultural Practice: The Gendered Production of Academic Subjects." *Gender and Education* 23, no. 3 (May 2011): 313–29.

Crow, Michael M., and William B. Dabars. *Designing the New American University.* Baltimore: Johns Hopkins University Press, 2015.

Damrosch, David. "National Literatures in an Age of Globalization." Presented at the ADE Seminar West, Flamingo, Las Vegas, June 22, 2009.

Damrosch, David. "Vectors of Change." In *Envisioning the Future of Doctoral Education: Preparing Stewards of the Discipline*, ed. Chris M. Golde and George E. Walker, 34–45. San Francisco: Jossey-Bass, 2006.

Damrosch, David. *We Scholars: Changing the Culture of the University.* Cambridge, MA: Harvard University Press, 1995.

Davidson, Cathy N., and David Theo Goldberg. *The Future of Thinking: Learning Institutions in a Digital Age.* Cambridge, MA: MIT Press, 2010. https://mitpress.mit.edu/sites/default/files/titles/free_download/9780262513746_Future_of_Thinking.pdf.

Donoghue, Frank. *The Last Professors: The Corporate University and the Fate of the Humanities.* New York: Fordham University Press, 2008.

Douglass, John Aubrey. "The Cold War, Technology and the American University." Research and Occasional Paper Series CSHE.2.99, Center for Studies in Higher Education, University of California, Berkeley (July 1999). http://www.cshe.berkeley.edu/sites/default/files/shared/publications/docs/PP.JD.Sputnik_Tech.2.99.pdf.

Drucker, Johanna. "Blind Spots: Humanists Must Plan Their Digital Future." *Chronicle Review*, April 3, 2009, B6–B8. http://chronicle.com/article/Blind-Spots/9348.

Duderstadt, James J. "The Impact of Technology on Discovery and Learning in Research Universities." Presented at the Ninth Glion Colloquium, June 5–9, 2013.

http://milproj.dc.umich.edu/pdfs/2013/2013%20Glion%20MOOCs%20JJD%20
FINAL.pdf.

Duderstadt, James J. "A Master Plan for Higher Education in the Midwest: A Roadmap
to the Future of the Nation's Heartland." Heartland Papers no. 3, Heartland Papers
by the Chicago Council of Global Affairs, 2011. http://www.thechicagocouncil.org/
Userfiles/File/Globalmidwest/A_Master_Plan_for_Higher_Education_FINAL.pdf.

Ehrenberg, Ronald G., Harriet Zuckerman, Jeffery A. Groen, and Sharon M. Brucker.
Educating Scholars: Doctoral Education in the Humanities. Princeton, NJ: Princeton University Press, 2010.

Ehrenberg, Ronald G., Harriet Zuckerman, Jeffery A. Groen, and Sharon M.
Brucker. "How to Help Graduate Students Reach Their Destination." *Chronicle of Higher Education,* October 12, 2009. http://chronicle.com/article/
How-to-Help-Graduate-Students/48752/.

Ellison, Julie, and Timothy K. Eatman. *Scholarship in Public: Knowledge Creation and the
Tenure Policy in the Engaged University.* Artists and Scholars in Public Life Tenure
Team Initiative on Public Scholarship, Imagining America, 2008. http://ccrec.ucsc.
edu/sites/default/files/tti_final.pdf.

Eve, Martin Paul. *Open Access and the Humanities: Contexts, Controversies and the Future.* Cambridge: Cambridge University Press, 2014. http://ebooks.cambridge.org/ebook.
jsf?bid=CBO9781316161012.

Fernandes, Leela. *Transnational Feminism in the United States: Knowledge, Ethics, and Power.*
New York: New York University Press, 2013.

Fitzpatrick, Kathleen. *Planned Obsolescence: Publishing, Technology, and the Future of the
Academy.* New York: New York University Press, 2011.

Flaherty, Colleen. "Pricing Out the Humanities." *Inside Higher Ed,* November 26, 2012.
http://www.insidehighered.com/news/2012/11/26/u-florida-history-professors-
fight-differential-tuition#ixzz2GCYh5e9a.

Flaherty, Colleen. "Report Reveals Divergent Trends in Modern Language Job Market."
Inside Higher Ed, December 21, 2012. http://www.inside highered.com.

Germano, William. "Do We Dare Write for Readers?" *Chronicle of Higher Education,* April
26, 2013.

Germano, William. *From Dissertation to Book.* 2nd ed. Chicago: University of Chicago
Press, 2013.

Ginsberg, Benjamin. *The Fall of the Faculty: The Rise of the All-Administrative University and
Why It Matters.* New York: Oxford University Press, 2011.

Godin, Seth. "The Coming Meltdown in Higher Education (as Seen by a Marketer)." *Chronicle of Higher Education,* May 3, 2010. https://chronicle.com/article/
The-Coming-Meltdown-in-Higher/65398/.

Graff, Gerald. *Professing Literature: An Institutional History.* Chicago: University of Chicago Press, 1989.

Grafton, Anthony T., and James Grossman. "No More Plan B: A Very Modest Proposal for Graduate Programs in History." *Perspectives on History,* October 2011.
http://www.historians.org/publications-and-directories/perspectives-on-history/
october-2011/no-more-plan-b.

Greenberg, Josh. "Data, Code, and Research at Scale." Presented at HASTAC 2011,
University of Michigan, Ann Arbor, December 3, 2011. http://www.hastac.org/
documents/data-code-and-research-scale.

Griffiths, Rebecca, Matthew Chingos, Christine Mulhern, and Richard Spies. Interactive Online Learning on Campus: Testing MOOCS and Other Platforms in Hybrid Formats in the University System of Maryland. Ithaka S+R, July 11, 2014. http://www.sr.ithaka.org/research-publications/Interactive-Online-Learning-on-Campus.

Grosz, Elizabeth. *Becoming Undone: Darwinian Reflections on Life, Politics, and Art.* Durham, NC: Duke University Press, 2011.

The Guardian. Editorial. "Academic Journals: An Open and Shut Case." April 10, 2012. http://www.theguardian.com/commentisfree/2012/apr/11/academic-journals-access-wellcome-trust.

Haber, Jonathan. *MOOC.* Cambridge, MA: MIT Press, 2014.

Hall, Gary. "Radical Open Access in the Humanities." Presented at the Scholarly Communication Program, Columbia University, October 18, 2010. http://scholcomm.columbia.edu/2011/01/18/radical-open-access-in-the-humanities/.

Haraway, Donna Jeanne. *How Like a Leaf: An Interview with Thyrza Nichols Goodeve.* New York: Routledge, 2000.

Haraway, Donna Jeanne. *ModestWitness@SecondMillennium: Female Man Meets OncoMouse: Feminism and Technoscience.* New York: Routledge, 1997.

Hayles, N. Katherine. "Hyper and Deep Attention: The Generational Divide in Cognitive Modes." *Profession* 2007: 187–99.

Hayles, N. Katherine. "What Are New Media and Why Are They in English Departments?" Presented at the 2010 SDE Summer Seminar East, University of Maryland, June 5, 2010. http://www.ade.org/seminars/index.htm.

Hedstrom, Margaret, and John Leslie King. "Epistemic Infrastructure in the Rise of the Knowledge Economy." In *Advancing Knowledge and the Knowledge Economy,* edited by Brian Kahin and Foray Dominique, 113–34. Cambridge, MA: MIT Press, 2006. http://jlking.people.si.umich.edu/EpistemicInfrast-MITPress.pdf.

Holdren, John P., director, Office of Science and Technology Policy, Executive Office of the President. "Increasing Access to the Results of Federally Funded Scientific Research." Memorandum for the Heads of Departments and Agencies, February 22, 2013. http://www.whitehouse.gov/sites/default/files/microsites/ostp/ostp_public_access_memo_2013.pdf.

Hope Today News. "William Pannapacker to Direct GLCA Digital Liberal Arts Initiative." October 1, 2013. http://www.hope.edu/2013/10/01/william-pannapacker-direct-glca-digital-liberal-arts-initiative.

House Committee on Education and the Workforce Democratic Staff. *The Just-In-Time Professor: A Staff Report Summarizing eForum Responses on the Working Conditions of Contingent Faculty in Higher Education.* January 2014. http://democrats.edworkforce.house.gov/sites/democrats.edworkforce.house.gov/files/documents/1.24.14-AdjunctEforumReport.pdf.

Howard, Jennifer. "Hot Type: No Reviews of Digital Scholarship = No Respect." *Chronicle of Higher Education,* May 23, 2010. http://chronicle.com/article/Hot-Type-No-Reviews-of/65644/.

Howard, Jennifer. "Humanities Journals Confront Identity Crisis." *Chronicle of Higher Education,* March 27, 2009. http://chronicle.com/article/Humanities-Journals-Confront/28342.

Hubbard, Dolan. "Education without Representation." *Black Issues in Higher Education* 19, no. 17 (2002): 97.

Huggard, Simon. "Green v Gold Open Access Publishing SlideShare." Presented at the International Open Access Week: Library Research Forum, La Trobe University, October 25, 2013. http://www.slideshare.net/healthsciences/green-versus-gold-open-access.

Humanities Editorial Office. "Acknowledgement to Reviewers of Humanities in 2013." *Humanities* 3, no. 1 (February 27, 2014): 71–72. doi:10.3390/h3010071.

Hunt, Lynn. "Democratization and Decline? The Consequences of Demographic Change in the Humanities." In *What's Happened to the Humanities?*, ed. Alvin B. Kernan, 17–31. Princeton, NJ: Princeton University Press, 2014.

The Innovative University: What College Presidents Think about Change in American Higher Education. Research report for the *Chronicle of Higher Education*, 2014. http://strategic-planning.fairfield.edu/sites/default/files/innovative_university_140516.pdf.

Jagodzinski, Cecile M. "The University Press in North America: A Brief History." *Journal of Scholarly Publishing* 40, no. 1 (October 2008): 1–20.

James, William. "The Ph.D. Octopus." *Education Review* 55 (1918): 149–57.

Jaschik, Scott. "Florida GOP vs. Social Science." *Inside Higher Ed*, October 12, 2011. http://www.insidehighered.com/news/2011/10/12/florida_governor_challenges_idea_of_non_stem_degrees#sthash.StaDWPoI.dpbs.

Jaschik, Scott. "Top Ph.D. Programs, Shrinking." *Inside Higher Ed*, May 13, 2009. https://www.insidehighered.com/news/2009/05/13/doctoral.

Jay, Paul. *The Humanities "Crisis" and the Future of Literary Studies*. New York: Palgrave Macmillan, 2014.

Johnson, L., S. Adams Becker, M. Cummins, V. Estrada, A. Freeman, and H. Ludgate. *NMC Horizon Report: 2013 Higher Education Edition*. Austin, TX: New Media Consortium, 2013. http://www.nmc.org/pdf/2013-horizon-report-HE.pdf.

Joshi, Sam. "Hippo Meets Dissertator on Forked Path in Academic Jungle." *Journal of Scholarly Publishing* 36, no. 1 (2004): 23–26. doi:10.1353/scp.2004.0031.

Kernan, Alvin B., ed. *What's Happened to the Humanities?* Princeton, NJ: Princeton University Press, 2014.

Kiley, Kevin. "North Carolina Governor Joins Chorus of Republicans Critical of Liberal Arts." *Inside Higher Ed*, January 20, 2013. http://www.insidehighered.com/news/2013/01/30/north-carolina-governor-joins-chorus-republicans-critical-liberal-arts#sthash.B2FvTvU1.dpbs.

Kirschenbaum, Matthew G. "Done: Finishing Projects in the Digital Humanities." *Digital Humanities Quarterly* 3, no. 2 (2009), n.p. http://digitalhumanities.org:8080/dhq/vol/3/2/000037/000037.html.

Kingkade, Tyler. "Pat McCrory Lashes Out Against 'Educational Elite' and Liberal Arts College Courses." *The Huffington Post*. February 2, 2013, updated February 3, 2013.

Klost, Peter H., Debra Rudder Lohe, and Chuck Sweetman. "Rethinking and Unthinking the Graduate Seminar." *Pedagogy* 15, no. 1 (2015): 19–30.

Kolowich, Steve. "The MOOC 'Revolution' May Not Be as Disruptive as Some Had Imagined." *Chronicle of Higher Education*, August 8, 2013. http://chronicle.com/article/MOOCs-May-Not-Be-So-Disruptive/140965/?cid=at&utm_source=at&utm_medium=en.

Kolowich, Steve. "New Seal of Approval." *Inside Higher Ed*, February 13, 2012. https://www.insidehighered.com/news/2012/02/13/anvil-academic-aims-provide-platform-digital-scholarship.

Kolowich, Steve. "The Professors behind the MOOC Hype." *Chronicle of Higher Education*, March 18, 2013. http://chronicle.com/article/The%20Professors-Behind-the%20MOOC/137905/?cid=at&utm_source=at&utm_medium+en#id=overview.

Krebs, Paula. "A New Humanities Ph.D." *Inside Higher Ed*, May 24, 2010. https://www.insidehighered.com/views/2010/05/24/krebs.

Lambert, Lance. "States Are Eager to Collect Graduates' Job Data. Here's Where That Effort Stands." *Chronicle of Higher Education*, March 25, 2015. http://chronicle.com/article/States-Are-Eager-to-Collect/228745/?cid=at&utm_source=at&utm_medium=en.

Laurence, David. "From the Editor: The Job Market and Graduate Education." *ADE Bulletin* 149 (2010): 3–7.

Laurence, David. "From the Editor: What's Next for Graduate Education." *ADE Bulletin* 152 (2012): 3–6.

Lee, Melanie. "The Melancholy Odyssey of a Dissertation with Pictures." *Pedagogy* 15, no. 1 (2015): 93–101.

Lepore, Jill. "The New Economy of Letters." *Chronicle of Higher Education*, September 3, 2013. http://chronicle.com/article/The-New-Economy-of-Letters/141291/.

Linguistics Society of America. The State of Linguistics in Higher Education: Annual Report 2014. 2nd ed., March 2015. http://www.linguisticsociety.org/files/Lx_Annual_Report_2014.pdf.

Liu, Alan. "The End of the End of the Book: Dead Books, Lively Margins, and Social Computing." *Michigan Quarterly Review* 48 (2009): 499–520.

Liu, Alan. "The Meaning of Digital Humanities." *PMLA* 128, no. 2 (2013): 409–23.

Liu, Alan. *This Is Not a Book: Long Forms of Shared Attention in the Digital Age.* Vimeo, 2011. http://vimeo.com/24306792.

Lorin, Janet. "Indentured Students Rise as Loans Corrode College Ticket." *Bloomberg*, July 9, 2012. http://www.bloomberg.com/news/2012-07-09/indentured-students-rise-as-loans-corrode-college-ticket.html.

Lothian, Alexis, and Amanda Phillips. "Can Digital Humanities Mean Transformative Critique?" *Journal of E-Media Studies* 3, no. 1 (2013). http://journals.dartmouth.edu/cgi-bin/WebObjects/Journals.woa/1/xmlpage/4/article/425.

Lunsford, Andrea Abernethy. "Rethinking the Ph.D. in English." In *Envisioning the Future of Doctoral Education: Preparing Stewards of the Discipline,* edited by Chris M. Golde and George E. Walker, 357–69. San Francisco: Jossey-Bass, 2006.

MacDonald, Dwight. "Real Talk about Graduate Education in the Liberal Arts and Sciences." Presented at "Liberal Arts & Sciences in the Research University Today: Histories, Challenges, Futures," University of Michigan, March 22, 2013.

Marincola, Elizabeth. "Science Communication: Power of Community." *Science* 342, no. 6163 (December 6, 2013): 1168–69. doi:10.1126/science.342.6163.1168-b.

Mason, Mary Ann. *Do Babies Matter? Gender and Family in the Ivory Tower.* New Brunswick, NJ: Rutgers University Press, 2013.

May, Meredith. "New Authors Alliance Wants to Ease Some Copyright Rules." *SFGate*, May 31, 2014. http://www.sfgate.com/business/article/New-Authors-Alliance-wants-to-ease-some-copyright-5519746.php#src=fb.

McGann, Jerome. "The Future Is Digital." *Journal of Victorian Culture* 13, no. 1 (Spring 2008): 80–88.

McGann, Jerome. "A Note on the Current State of Humanities Scholarship." *Critical Inquiry* 30, no. 2 (2004): 409–13.

McPherson, Tara. "After the Archive: Scholarship in the Digital Era." Presented at the Digital Humanities Brown Bag Lecture, University of Michigan, Ann Arbor, November 29, 2011.

McPherson, Tara. "Scaling Vectors: Thoughts on the Future of Scholarly Communication." *Journal of Electronic Publishing* 13, no. 2 (Fall 2010). http://quod.lib.umich.edu/j/jep/3336451.0013.208?view=text;rgn=main.

McPherson, Tara. "Why Are the Digital Humanities So White? or, Thinking the Histories of Race and Computation." In *Debates in the Digital Humanities*, ed. Matthew K. Gold, 139–60. Minneapolis: University of Minnesota Press, 2012.

Menand, Louis. *The Marketplace of Ideas: Reform and Reaction in the American University*. New York: Norton, 2010.

Miller, Richard E. "The New Dissertation: Thinking Outside the (Proto)-Book Session." Presented at the Annual Convention of the Modern Language Association, Seattle, January 5, 2012.

Mitchell, William J. *Me++: The Cyborg Self and the Networked City*. Cambridge, MA: MIT Press, 2003.

MLA Office of Research. *Report on the MLA Job Information List, 2012–13*. October 2013. http://www.mla.org/pdf/rptjil12_13web.pdf.

Mod, Craig. "The Digital Physical." @craigMod, March 2012. http://craigmod.com/journal/digital_physical/.

MLA Office of Research. *Report on the MLA Job Information List, 2013–14*. Fall 2014. http://www.mla.org/pdf/rpt_jil_1314web.pdf.

Monkman, Leslie. "Confronting Change." *ESC: English Studies in Canada* 32, no. 2 (2006): 19–23. doi:10.1353/esc.2007.0096.

Montgomery, Lucy, Christina Emery, Frances Pinter, and Leon Loberman. *Pilot Proof of Concept Progress Summary*. Knowledge Unlatched, May 2014. http://collections.knowledgeunlatched.org/wp-content/uploads/2013/09/KU_Pilot_Progress_Summary_Report4.pdf.

Moretti, Franco. *Distant Reading*. New York: Verso, 2013.

Moretti, Franco. *"Operationalizing": Or, the Function of Measurement in Modern Literary Theory*. Stanford Literary Lab Pamphlet 6, December 2013. http://litlab.stanford.edu/LiteraryLabPamphlet6.pdf.

National Research Council. *Research Universities and the Future of America: Ten Breakthrough Actions Vital to Our Nation's Prosperity and Security*. Washington, DC: National Academies Press, 2012. http://sites.nationalacademies.org/pga/cs/groups/pgasite/documents/webpage/pga_070193.pdf.

National Science Foundation and National Center for Science and Engineering Statistics. *Doctorate Recipients from U.S. Universities 2012*. National Science Foundation, January 2014. http://www.nsf.gov/statistics/sed/digest/2012/nsf14305.pdf.

Nelson, Cary. *No University Is an Island: Saving Academic Freedom*. New York: New York University Press, 2010.

Newfield, Christopher. "The Future of the Public University." Presented at "Humanities, Publics, and the State," Annual Meeting of the Consortium for Humanities Centers and Institutes, University of Kansas, Lawrence, 2013. http://chcinetwork.org/2013-annual-meeting/.

Newfield, Christopher. *Unmaking the Public University: The Forty-Year Assault on the Middle Class*. Cambridge, MA: Harvard University Press, 2011.

Newman, Jonah, and Soo Oh. "8 Things You Should Know about MOOCs." *Chronicle of Higher Education*, June 13, 2014. http://chronicle.com/article/8-Things-You-Should-Know-About/146901/.

Newstok, Scott L. "A Plea for 'Close Learning.'" *Liberal Education* 99, no. 4 (Fall 2013). http://www.aacu.org/liberaleducation/le-fa13/newstok.cfm.

Nowviskie, Bethany. *#Alt-Academy: Alternative Academic Careers for Humanities Scholars*.

http://mediacommons.futureofthebook.org/alt-ac/sites/mediacommons.future-ofthebook.org.alt-ac/files/alt-academy01.pdf.

Nowviskie, Bethany. "Toward a New Deal." http://nowviskie.org/2013/new-deal/.

Nussbaum, Martha C. *Not for Profit: Why Democracy Needs the Humanities.* Princeton, NJ: Princeton University Press, 2010.

Ochocka, Joanna, and Rich Janzen. "Breathing Life into Theory: Illustrations of Community-Based Research—Hallmarks, Functions and Phases." *Gateways: International Journal of Community Research and Engagement* 7, no. 1 (June 19, 2014): 18–33.

Olson, Gary A., and Julie Drew. "(Re)Reenvisioning the Dissertation in English Studies." *College English* 61, no. 1 (September 1998): 56. doi:10.2307/379058.

Organisation for Economic Co-operation and Development. *OECD Factbook 2011: Economic, Environmental and Social Statistics.* Paris: Organisation for Economic Co-operation and Development, 2011. http://www.credoreference.com/book/oecdfactbook.

Orr, David. "The Job Market in English and Foreign Languages." *PMLA* 85, no. 6 (1970): 1185–98.

Owens, Trevor. "Defining Data for Humanists: Text, Artifact, Information or Evidence?" *Journal of Digital Humanities*, March 16, 2012. http://journalofdigitalhumanities.org/1-1/defining-data-for-humanists-by-trevor-owens/.

Perna, Laura, Alan Ruby, Robert Boruch, Nicole Wang, Janie Scull, Chad Evans, and Seher Ahmad. "The Life Cycle of a Million MOOC Users." Presented at the MOOC Research Initiative Conference, December 5, 2013. http://www.gse.upenn.edu/pdf/ahead/perna_ruby_boruch_moocs_dec2013.pdf.

Pettegree, Andrew. *The Book in the Renaissance.* New Haven: Yale University Press, 2010.

Pink, Daniel H. *A Whole New Mind: Moving from the Information Age to the Conceptual Age.* New York: Riverhead Books, 2005.

Pinker, Steven. "Why Academics Stink at Writing." *Chronicle of Higher Education*, September 26, 2014. http://chronicle.com/article/Why-Academics-Writing-Stinks/148989/.

Pochoda, Phil. "The Big One: The Epistemic System Break in Scholarly Monograph Publishing." *New Media & Society* 15, no. 3 (May 1, 2013): 359–78.

Pochoda, Philip. "Digital, Scholarly Publishing: A Systems View." University of Michigan Institute for the Humanities Brown Bag Lecture, October 25, 2011. Abstract at http://lecb.physics.lsa.umich.edu/CWIS/browser.php?ResourceId=4116.

Poor, Sara S., Rosemarie Scullion, and Kathleen Woodward. *Standing Still: The Associate Professor Survey.* MLA Committee on the Status of Women in the Profession, April 27, 2009. http://www.mla.org/pdf/cswp_final042909.pdf.

Posselt, Julie R. *Inside Graduate Admissions: Merit, Diversity, and Faculty Gatekeeping.* Cambridge, MA: Harvard University Press, 2015.

Quinn, Lisa. "Some Observations." Presented at the International Association for Biography and Autobiography Graduate Student and New Scholar Workshop, Banff, Canada, May 29, 2014.

Rabkin, Eric. "Real Work Is Better Than Homework." University of Michigan, November 19, 2008.

Ramsay, Stephen. "The Hermeneutics of Screwing Around; or, What You Do with a Million Books." In *Pastplay: Teaching and Learning History with Technology*, ed. Kevin Lee, 110–20. Ann Arbor: University of Michigan Press, 2014.

Raughley, Lynne. "Federal Appeals Court Upholds Library Digitization Project." *University Record*, June 11, 2014. http://record.umich.edu/articles/federal-appeals-court-upholds-library-digitization-project.

Rausing, Lisbet. "Toward a New Alexandria." *New Republic*, March 12, 2010. http://www.newrepublic.com/article/books-and-arts/toward-new-alexandria#.

Rogers, Katina. *Humanities Unbound: Supporting Careers and Scholarship beyond the Tenure Track.* Scholarly Communication Institute, University of Virginia Library, August 2013. http://katinarogers.com/wp-content/uploads/2013/08/Rogers_SCI_Survey_Report_09AUG13.pdf.

Rotman, Brian. *Becoming Beside Ourselves: The Alphabet, Ghosts, and Distributed Human Being.* Durham, NC: Duke University Press, 2008.

Rumsey, Abby Smith. *SCI8: Emerging Genres in Scholarly Communication.* University of Virginia Library, Scholarly Communication Institute, n.d.

Samuelson, Pamela, and David R. Hansen. "Brief of Amicus Curiae Authors Alliance in Support of Defendant-Appellees and Affirmance (The Authors Guild, Inc., et Al. v. Google, Inc., et Al.) (Second Circuit)." SSRN Scholarly Paper Social Science Research Network, Rochester, NY, July 10, 2014. http://papers.ssrn.com/abstract=2470549.

Sandvig, Christian, Kevin Hamilton, Karrie Karahalios, and Cedric Langbort. "Auditing Algorithms: Research Methods for Detecting Discrimination on Internet Platforms." Presented at "Data and Discrimination: Converting Critical Concerns into Productive Inquiry," preconference at the 64th Annual Meeting of the International Communication Association, Seattle, May 24, 2014.

Sayers, Jentery. "On Data Representations and the Humanities." Presented at "Data, Social Justice, and the Humanities," University of Michigan Institute for the Humanities, July 20, 2012.

Sayers, Jentery. "Writing with Sound: Composing Multimodal, Long-Form Scholarship." Presented at the Digital Humanities 2012 conference, University of Hamburg, July 16, 2012. https://lecture2go.uni-hamburg.de/konferenzen/-/k/13920.

Schep, Sydney J. "Digital Lives: Digital History/Biography." Paper presented at the International Auto/Biography Association Biennial Conference. Canberra, Australia, July 20, 2012.

Schmidt, Peter. "New Journals, Free Online, Let Scholars Speak Out." *Chronicle of Higher Education*, February 14, 2010. http://chronicle.com/article/Open-Access-Journals-Break/64143/.

Schrecker, Ellen. *The Lost Soul of Higher Education: Corporatization, the Assault on Academic Freedom, and the End of the American University.* New York: New Press, 2010.

Singer, Emily. "The Measured Life." *MIT Technology Review*, August 2011. http://m.technologyreview.com/biomedicine/37784/.

Smith, Sidonie. "Reading the Posthuman Backwards: Mary Rowlandson's Doubled Witnessing." *Biography* 35, no. 1 (2012): 137–52. doi:10.1353/bio.2012.0004.

Stanton, Domna, Michael Bérubé, Leonard Cassuto, Morris Eaves, John Guillory, Donald E. Hall, and Sean Latham. *Report of the MLA Task Force on Evaluating Scholarship for Tenure and Promotion.* New York: Modern Language Association, December 2006.

Steiger, Kay. "The Pink Collar Workforce of Academia." *Nation*, July 11, 2013. http://www.thenation.com/article/175214/academias-pink-collar-workforce.

Steward, Doug. *Report on the Survey of Earned Doctorates, 2010–11 and 2011–12.* Modern Language Association, June 2014.

Stimpson, Catharine R. "General Education for Graduate Education: A Theory Waiting for Practitioners." *Peer Review: Emerging Trends and Key Debates in Undergraduate Education* 6, no. 3 (Spring 2004): 13–15.

Suber, Peter. "Promoting Open Access in the Humanities." *Syllecta Classica* 16 (2005): 231–46.

Thrift, Nigel. "The World Needs Global Research Cooperation Urgently, and Now." *Chronicle of Higher Education*, February 19, 2010. http://chronicle.com/article/ Urgently-Needed-Global-Coo/64130/.

Tiwari, Bulbul. "MahaMultipedia Welcome." Digital dissertation. MahaMultipedia. http://www.mahamultipedia.com/.

Tiwari, Bulbul. "Shift(s)in(g) the Humanities: Hanging Roots, Hyperlinks, and Other Networks of Schizoanalysis in Maha Multipedia." Presented at the CIC Summit on Digital Humanities, Institute for the Humanities, University of Michigan, December 8, 2009.

Toor, Rachel. "Things You Should Know before Publishing a Book." *Chronicle of Higher Education*, July 28, 2014. http://chronicle.com/article/Things-You-Should-Know-Before/147943/?cid=at&utm_source=at&utm_medium=en.

Touryalai, Halah. "$1 Trillion Student Loan Problem Keeps Getting Worse." *Forbes*, February 21, 2014. http://www.forbes.com/sites/halahtouryalai/2014/02/21/1-trillion-student-loan-problem-keeps-getting-worse/.

Tuchman, Gaye. *Wannabe U: Inside the Corporate University*. Chicago: University of Chicago Press, 2011.

UCI News. "Mellon Foundation Grants $2.7 Million to School of the Humanities Graduate Programs." June 23, 2015. http://news.uci.edu/press-releases/mellon-foundation-grants-2–7-million-to-school-of-humanities-graduate-programs/.

Vaidhyanathan, Siva. "Apple Demystified." *Chronicle Review*, October 11, 2011. http:// chronicle.com/article/Apple-Demystified/129347/.

Visconti, Amanda. *Infinite Ulysses*. http://mith.umd.edu/infinite-ulysses-designing-public-humanities-conversation/.

Washburn, Jennifer. *University, Inc.: The Corporate Corruption of Higher Education*. New York: Basic Books, 2006.

Waters, Donald J. "Overview of the Digital Humanities (RLI 284, 2013)." *Research Libraries Issues* 284 (December 18, 2013): 6–7.

Waters, Lindsay. "The Tyranny of the Monograph and the Plight of the Publisher." *Publishing Research Quarterly* 17, no. 3 (Fall 2001): 19–25.

Watkins, Evan. "Recruiting Prestige." Keynote presentation at "Futures of the English PhD," Michigan State University, May 15, 2010. http://futuresoftheenglishphd. weebly.com/.

Watson, Robert N. "The Humanities Really Do Produce a Profit." *Chronicle of Higher Education*, March 21, 2010. http://chronicle.com/article/The-Humanities-Really-Do-Pr/64740/.

Weinberger, David. *Too Big to Know: Rethinking Knowledge Now That the Facts Aren't the Facts, Experts Are Everywhere, and the Smartest Person in the Room Is the Room*. New York: Basic Books, 2011.

Wendler, Cathy, Brent Bridgeman, Fred Cline, Catherine Millett, JoAnn Rock, Nathan Bell, and Patricia McAllister. *The Path Forward: The Future of Graduate Education in the United States*. Princeton, NJ: Council of Graduate Schools and Educational Testing Services, 2010. http://www.fgereport.org/rsc/pdf/CFGE_report.pdf.

Williford, Christa, and Charles Henry. *One Culture. Computationally Intensive Research in the Humanities and Social Sciences: A Report on the Experiences of First Respondents to the Digging Into Data Challenge*. Council on Library and Information Resources, June 2012.

Wilson, Robin. "Cutbacks in Enrollment Redefine Graduate Education and Faculty Jobs." *Chronicle of Higher Education*, May 11, 2012. http://chronicle.com/article/Graduate-Programs-in/131123/.

Wittman, John, and Mariana Abuan. "Socializing Future Professionals: Exploring the Matrix of Assessment." *Pedagogy* 15, no. 1 (2015): 59–70.

Woodward, Kathleen. "The Future of the Humanities in the Present and in Public." *Daedalus* 138, no. 1 (Winter 2009). http://csid.unt.edu/files/Daedalus%20Winter%202009/10.Woodward.pdf.

Woodward, Kathleen. "We Are All Non-traditional Learners Now: Community Colleges, Long-Life Learning, and Problem-Solving Humanities for the Public Good." In *A New Deal for the Humanities: Liberal Arts and the Future of Public Higher Education*, ed. Gordon Hutner and Feisal Mohamed. New Brunswick, NJ: Rutgers University Press, forthcoming.

Index

Rotman, Brian, 89
Rumsey, Abby Smith, 56–57, 62

Sandvig, Christian, 50
Sayers, Jentery, 51, 62
Scalar, 60, 62, 183n20
scaling up of curriculum, 13
scholarly and professional associations
  and dissertations, 133
  and embargo periods, 76
  and evaluative criteria, 64
  faculty advocacy by, 28, 29
  and open access, 73, 75, 76, 81, 90
  reports from on job openings, 116–17
  See also Modern Language Association
    (MLA)
scholarly communication
  and the book, 57–59
  and born-digital scholarship, 61–62
  evaluation of, 63–65
  hidden cost in closed publication
    system, 72
  journal publications, 73–75
  long-form book, 77–81
  modes of open access to, 67–68
  new forms of, 60–61
  and relationships with readers, 62–63
  and review processes, 63
  short-form writing, 73
  STEM journals' publishing system,
    68–71
  terminology of, 55
  tools and platforms for, 59–60
  transitions in, 55–57, 65–66
  See also dissertations
Scholarly Communication Institute,
  56–57, 123
scholarly networks, 136–37, 159
scholars, posthuman, 103–7
scholarship, public, 123–24, 138–39, 141
*Scholarship in Public: Knowledge Creation and
  Tenure Policy in the Engaged University*
  (Ellison and Eatman), 123
sciences, the. *See* STEM (science, technology, engineering, and math) fields
Scott, Rick, 12, 176n15
Scribd.com, 59
search committees, 148–49

Seattle Attic, 51
SED. *See* Survey of Earned Doctorates
  (SED)
Semantic Web, the, 51–52
seminars, 156–57
Shep, Sydney, 48–49
short-form writing
  and dissertations, 140–41, 145–46,
    147–48, 148–49, 151
  open access in, 73
Siegel, Lee, 22
Simpson Center for the Humanities, 123,
  158
Sinnreich, Arem, 78
Slave Biographies project, 47
Small Data, 46–47
"Socializing Future Professionals: Ex-
  ploring the Matrix of Assessment"
  (Wittman and Abuan), 158
social media, 73, 83
Social Science and Humanities Research
  Council of Canada (SSHRC), 41, 121,
  124, 125, 129, 135, 142
Sousanis, Nick, 141–42
Southern Spaces, 74
SSHRC. *See* Social Science and Humani-
  ties Research Council of Canada
  (SSHRC)
Stanford, 25, 92, 122, 153
"Statement on Online Dissertation
  Embargoes" (Medieval Academy of
  America), 76
*State of the Humanities, The: Higher Educa-
  tion 2015* (American Academy of
  Arts and Sciences), 26
STEM (science, technology, engineering,
  and math) fields
  call for open access in, 69–71,
    186–87n31
  costs of programs in, 26
  and faculty pay, 14
  jobs related to majors in, 27
  journals in, 56, 68–71
  MOOCs in, 92–93
  political effects on, 10, 11
  transnational institutes for advances
    in, 37
Stimpson, Catharine R., 156